BIRDS

OF THE

NORTH GULF COAST -

PRINCE WILLIAM SOUND REGION,

ALASKA

by

M. E. "PETE" ISLEIB
Cordova, Alaska

and

BRINA KESSEL
University of Alaska
Fairbanks, Alaska

BIOLOGICAL PAPERS OF THE UNIVERSITY
OF ALASKA

Number 14 November 1973

Reprinted by the University of Alaska Press
April 1989

Editor

JAMES E. MORROW

Department of Biological Sciences
University of Alaska

ISBN 0-912006-39-0

This reprinting supported in part by a grant to the University of Alaska Press from *Alyeska Pipeline Service Company.*

Abstract

The North Gulf Coast-Prince William Sound region of Alaska, phytogeographically, lies at the northern limit of the Sitka Spruce-hemlock coastal/subalpine forests of the Pacific Coast; it includes approximately 178,500 km^2 and a shoreline of approximately 8,500 km. Fourteen habitats are utilized by birds: tundra; shrub thickets; hemlock-Sitka Spruce forests; bogs; mixed deciduous-spruce woodlands; marshes; lacustrine waters; fluviatile waters; cliffs, bluffs, and screes; moraines, alluvia, and barrier islands; beaches and tidal flats; rocky shores and reefs; inshore waters; and offshore waters.

Two hundred nineteen species of birds have been recorded in the region, 111 of which are primarily water-related. Status, abundance, habitat, and seasonal occurrence are discussed in the annotated list of species. The geographic location and restrictive topography of the region make it a spectacular corridor for millions of migrating birds. In spring millions of Pintails, Dunlins, Western Sandpipers, and Northern Phalaropes move through the region, as do tens of thousands of Whistling Swans, Snow Geese, Knots, and Sanderlings. Fall concentrations of White-fronted Geese and Sandhill Cranes may exceed 100,000's. Species with notably large summering populations include Trumpeter Swans (several hundred breeding pairs), Bald Eagles (1,800-2,000 breeding pairs), Aleutian Terns (150-250 breeding pairs on Copper River Delta), Marbled Murrelets (probably millions), and Kittlitz's Murrelets (probably a few 100,000's).

Significant range extensions reported include Yellow-billed Loons (fairly common in winter), Pink-footed and Pale-footed shearwaters, Brandt's Cormorants (breeding), Red-faced Cormorants (breeding), Steller's Eiders (winter), Bristle-thighed Curlews (migrant), Bar-tailed Godwits (migrant), Crested Auklets (winter), and northernmost wintering populations of waterfowl (Canada Geese, Gadwalls, Pintails, Green-winged Teals, American Widgeons) and shorebirds (Surfbirds, Black Turnstones, Dunlins, and Sanderlings). Some unexpected species reported include Skua, Anna's Hummingbird, Purple Martin, Yellowthroat, Common Grackle, and White-throated Sparrow.

TABLE OF CONTENTS

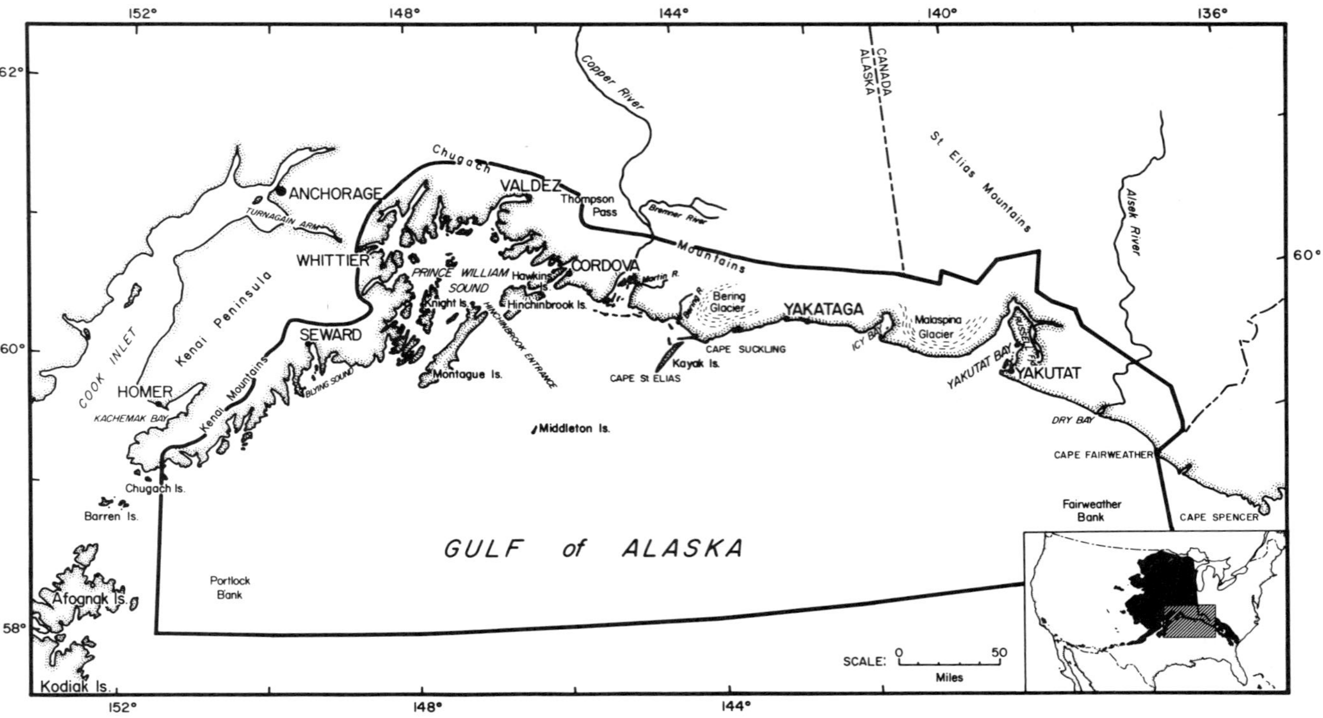

Fig. 1. Map of the North Gulf Coast — Prince William Sound region.

Birds of the North Gulf Coast-Prince William Sound Region, Alaska

by

M. E. "Pete" Isleib and Brina Kessel

One of the poorly-known avifaunas of Alaska is that of the vast North Gulf Coast-Prince William Sound region (Fig. 1). The first naturalist to set foot in Alaska, Georg Wilhelm Steller, did so within this region on Kayak Island on 20 July 1741 (Stejneger, 1936), returning to ship with a specimen of a jay later named in his honor — the Steller's Jay, *Cyanocitta stelleri*. Since that day, a number of naturalists and ornithologists have visited the region (see Gabrielson and Lincoln, 1959), but most have been transients, spending a maximum of a few days while enroute to other areas, and many have been otherwise employed, with their bird observations limited to fortuitous moments.

Only four faunal publications of major significance to the ornithology of the region have been published: 1) Joseph Grinnell (1910a) reported on the extensive investigations of the 1908 Alexander Expedition which visited a cross-section of Prince William Sound habitats between 3 June and 22 September 1908; the paper includes a discussion of the composition of the Prince William Sound avifauna, and several new subspecies have been described from specimens collected by this expedition. 2) T. M. Shortt (1939) reported on the expedition that he and a party from the Royal Ontario Museum of Zoology made to Yakutat Bay area from 13 May to 24 August 1936, a report which provides the only source of record or breeding data for several species within the region. 3) Robert L. Rausch (1958) participated in a biological reconnaissance of Middleton Island during 15 days of June 1956 and reported on the birds observed and the ecological distribution of the breeding species. 4) And, finally, the monumental work, *Birds of Alaska*, by Ira N. Gabrielson and Frederick C. Lincoln (1959) not only compiles almost all of the published and unpublished data prior to 1956 for all of Alaska, including the North Gulf Coast-Prince William Sound region, but also includes original observations by Gabrielson obtained on his brief visits within the region between 1940 and 1950

The sum of information published during the past 232 years remains small and sketchy, however, particularly in relation to migratory and wintering birds; and a review of the entire literature yields a grossly inadequate picture of the utilization of the region by birds.

During the last 20 years, our knowledge of the birds of the North Gulf Coast-Prince William Sound region has increased dramatically, partly because several field ornithologists have taken up residence in the region and partly because of the increasing interests shown by the Alaska Department of Fish and Game and the U. S. Fish and Wildlife Service in understanding and managing the large populations of waterfowl and other birds that frequent the region.

M. E. "Pete" Isleib, the senior author, began visiting the region in 1961 and took up residence in Cordova in 1964. In addition to his life-long active interest in field ornithology, which provides the main foundation for this publication, his vocation of commercial fishing has provided extra opportunities to observe the birds of the inshore and offshore waters.

Boyd Shaffer, artist/naturalist and a resident of Moose Pass on the Kenai Peninsula since 1960, has been a valuable source of information on the birds of the Resurrection Valley-Seward area, an area differing ecologically from much of the rest of the region.

J. D. Solf, Fisheries Biologist for the Alaska Department of Fish and Game, has lived in the Copper River Delta-Prince William Sound area since 1954. An observant naturalist, he has added considerably to our understanding of the complexities of the avian utilization of the region.

The U. S. Fish and Wildlife Service and the Alaska Department of Fish and Game have carried out major programs in recent years on the Copper River Delta and the adjacent Bremner River area, emphasizing waterfowl, especially the Trumpeter Swan (Hansen et al., 1971) and the Canada Goose (Hansen, 1962). In February 1971, the U. S. Fish and Wildlife Service began seasonal waterbird surveys in the Prince William Sound area from low-flying aircraft and from boat to obtain estimates of the various populations and their utilization of the Sound; these studies have been executed by LeRoy W. Sowl and J. Larry Haddock, Special Studies Branch, and Isleib has been an active participant and observer on the surveys.

In view of the substantial increase over the last two decades of knowledge regarding the avifauna of the region and the probability of greatly increased industrial activity in the region in the near future, there is need for a consolidated, up-to-date summary of the known data on the status, abundance, and general distribution of the birds of the region. This publication is an attempt at such a summary, although we realize that our knowledge is still fragmentary and that new knowledge will continue to accumulate at a rapid rate.

We have received considerable assistance from many people in the process of compiling materials for this publication, and we are pleased to acknowledge and express deep appreciation for all this help. We are especially grateful for the extensive contributions from Boyd Shaffer and J. D. Solf, and from personnel of the Alaska Department of Fish and Game and the U. S. Fish and Wildlife Service. We are further indebted to several individuals who have spent time in the region and who have summarized some of their unpublished field notes for us: Daniel D. Gibson, University of Alaska (Thompson Pass to Valdez, 5 and 6 May 1972); L. Jack Lyon, Andrew C. Browne, and Ronald Krash, then on military duty at Whittier (Whittier and vicinity, April-September 1954); Carl W. McIlroy, Alaska Department of Fish and Game (Valdez, Long Bay, Jonah Bay, and vicinity, 11 May-5 September 1969); David G. Roseneau, University of Alaska (East and West Amatuli Islands and Sugarloaf Island of the Barren Islands, 25 May-1 July 1965); and George C. West and Leonard J. Peyton, University of Alaska (Cordova and vicinity, 28 April-9 May 1970). In addition, Loyal J. Johnson, Alaska Department of Fish and Game and a resident of Cordova for several years, and Peter E. K. Shepherd, Alaska Department of Fish and Game, have kindly allowed us to extract data from their personal field notes and have provided other data verbally; and Larry Humberg, seaman aboard the Coast Guard cutter *Sedge* during 1968 and 1969 while it plied the waters of the Gulf of Alaska, told us of his many sightings at sea. We appreciate, too, the significant contributions made by the many individuals whose names are mentioned throughout the Annotated List of Birds in relation to the specific contributions.

Over and above all of the assistance we have received in gathering data, we also have received extensive cooperation from a number of individuals in the preparation of the manuscript. Many of the above-cited individuals have double-checked our written statements. Others have read and criticized specific sections of the text, including Bonita J. Neiland, University of Alaska; L. R. Mayo, U. S. Geological Survey; David F. Murray, University of Alaska; and Robert S. Velikanje, U. S. Corps of Engineers. Daniel D. Gibson, University of Alaska, has reviewed the entire manuscript, making many helpful suggestions. We, the authors, however, remain responsible for the accuracy of all statements. Shirley A. Miers, University of Alaska, cheerfully did yeoman service in translating our original, rough handwritten script into a readable, typed manuscript.

Finally we are deeply obliged to Ruth Isleib, wife of the senior author and a field ornithologist in her own right. Not only did she successfully withstand the periods of extended absence of her husband while he was in the field, but her management of the household during the preparation of this manuscript contributed significantly to its prompt completion.

General Description of the Region

Geographically, this publication covers the area of Prince William Sound, the northern coast of the Gulf of Alaska, and adjacent waters (Fig. 1). The region is separated from the valleys of interior Alaska by the steep slopes of the Chugach and Kenai mountains and is still largely pristine in nature. Its geographic location and restrictive topography make the region a spectacular corridor for millions of migrant birds, especially in the spring as they push through to their northern breeding grounds.

PHYSIOGRAPHY

More specifically, we have delineated the North Gulf Coast-Prince William Sound region as follows: from Cape Fairweather (58°48' N, 137° 57' W) on the east to the Chugach Islands (59°08' N, 151°30' W) on the west; and from an arc in the north formed by the crest of the Kenai and Chugach mountains and extending eastward to include the Alaskan part of the St. Elias Mountains to a line in the south extending from the outer Fairweather Bank (58°00' N, 137°56' W), about 47 miles (76 km) south of Cape Fairweather, west across the Gulf of Alaska along 58°00' N to 151°30' W, 68 miles (109 km) south of the Chugach Islands. The region includes the Alsek River as far as the Alaska-Yukon border (59°27' N, 137°58' W) and the Copper River to and including Baird Canyon (60°50' N, 144°30' W).

The region includes approximately 18,500 sq miles (48,000 km²) of land mass, approximately 50,400 sq miles (130,500 km²) of inshore and offshore waters, and has a shoreline of approximately 5,300 miles (8,500 km) within a general coastal arc of almost 500 miles (800 km).

The main land mass is arcuate, formed by the seaward slopes of three contiguous mountain groups: the Kenai Mountains, the Chugach Mountains, and the St. Elias Mountains. These mountains are progressively higher from west to east, with numerous peaks in the Kenai Mountains ranging in height from 4,000 to 7,000 ft (1,200-2,100 m), in the Chugach Mountains from 7,000 to 13,000 ft (2,100-4,000 m), and in the St. Elias Mountains from 10,000 to 18,000 ft (3,000-5,500 m). They show the sharp ruggedness of geological youth, and, as a result of heavy snow accumulation, they contain the most extensive system of valley glaciers and the largest ice fields of North America.

The coast of the Gulf of Alaska is also arc-shaped, with Prince William Sound forming an extensive northerly embayment near the center of the Gulf coast. Along the outer Kenai Peninsula and through Prince William Sound, the shoreline is intricately incised by numerous long, narrow fiords and by many lesser bays and coves formed by a rugged, drowned coastline, which also results in the mountains rising directly from the shoreline. The mainland shoreline of Prince William Sound is some 1,800 miles (2,900 km) in length, and there is another 1,200 miles (1,900 km) of shoreline around the islands – all within a geographic area only about 80 miles (125 km) in diameter (Fig. 2). Within this area there are some 34 major islands (1 sq mi [2.6 km^2] or larger), 150 lesser islands, and hundreds of islets, sea stacks, rocks and reefs. The Sound is deep, exceeding 475 fathoms (870 m) just off Lone Island. The western portion of the North Gulf Coast, along the outer Kenai Peninsula, is similar to the Prince William Sound drowned fiord system, except that it is more exposed to the Gulf, and the submarine depths are mostly less than 100 fathoms (180 m).

In contrast, the shoreline between Cape Fairweather and the Copper River Delta is rather uniform, with indentations at only three isolated locations: Dry Bay, Yakutat Bay, and Icy Bay (Fig. 1). Also, instead of rising directly from the shore, the mountains rise some 2 to 40 miles (3 to 64 km) back from the coast, and the sea is relatively shallow for some distance offshore. In this stretch several glaciers, including the large Bering and Malaspina piedmont glaciers, reach or almost reach tidewater.

The Copper River Delta (Fig. 3), which lies between Prince William Sound and the eastern portion of the North Gulf Coast, is complexly different from other coastal areas in the region. It is a relatively flat plain separated from the Gulf of Alaska by a chain of barrier islands that stretches from Point Martin in the east to Hinchinbrook Island in the west, a distance of about 53 miles (85 km). A tidal flat region, the Copper River Flats, stretches across the mouth of the river and extends westerly into most of Orca Inlet and as far as Middle Ground Shoal in Orca Bay. These flats are bordered on the landward side by marshes. The entire lower Copper River Delta is broken by numerous river tributaries and tidal sloughs. Some upper portions of the Copper River Delta are fans of glacial alluvia, and between this area and the marshes is a slope of glacial silt deposits. In some areas the marshes extend some 8 miles (13 km) directly to the bases of the mountains. On the upper Copper River Delta, where the river leaves the mountains, there are extensive sand dunes.

The adjacent Gulf of Alaska waters of the North Gulf Coast-Prince William Sound region lie mostly over a continental shelf of less than 100 fathoms (180 m). The edge of the continental shelf is generally beyond 35 miles (60 km) from the shore; however, the eastern tip of the Aleutian Trench pierces this area with depths in excess of 2,000 fathoms (3,700 m) south of Middleton Island.

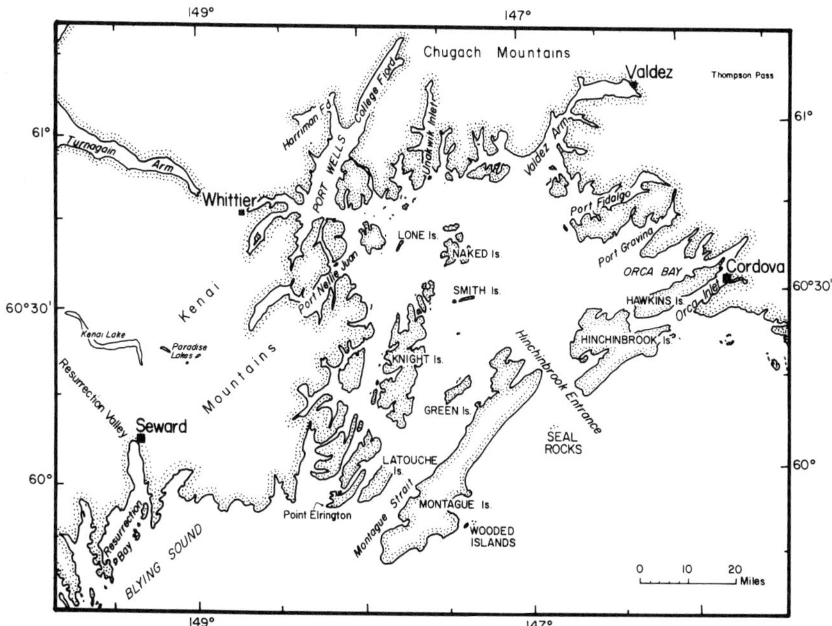

Fig. 2. Map of Prince William Sound and vicinity.

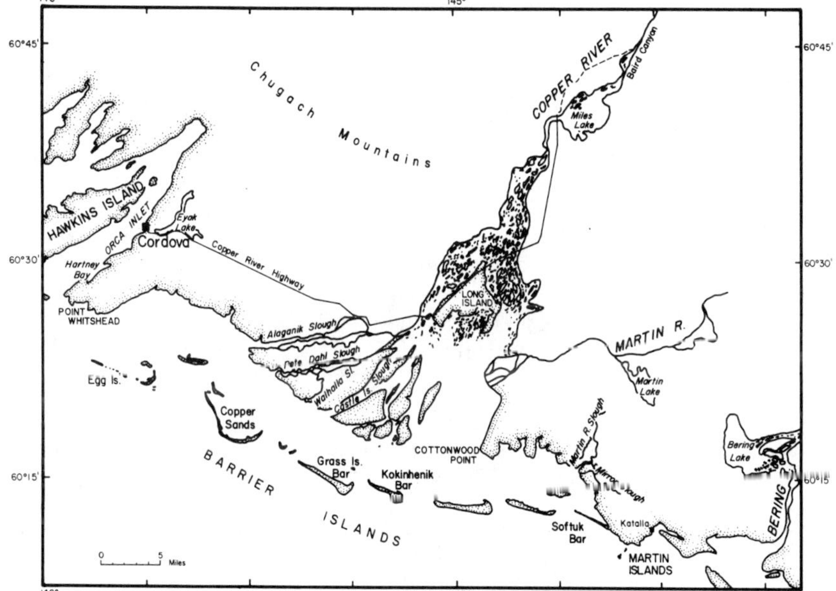

Fig. 3. Map of the Copper River Delta and vicinity.

Case et al. (1966), Moffit (1954), Miller (1958), and Plafker (1967) combine to give a comprehensive description of the geology of the North Gulf Coast-Prince William Sound region, and the following encapsulation is from these sources. The rocks are predominantly marine sediments of the Mesozoic and Cenozoic eras, which have been consolidated, folded, and metamorphosed in varying amounts. They are mostly slates and graywackes, with considerable variation in composition and texture; argillite is common. Igneous rocks, though less prominent, are widely distributed in the region; these are mostly greenstone (altered submarine lava flows, chiefly basalt and diabase) and granitic intrusive rocks, occurring as dikes, sills, batholiths, etc. The rocks underlying the coastal lowland and foothill belt between the Copper River and Cape Fairweather are more recent in origin, being sedimentary rocks of the latter Tertiary and Quaternary age; and they in turn are overlain by Quaternary sediments of silt, sand, and gravel.

The present-day, complex geomorphology of the region is a result of many powerfully active geologic forces over the last 250 million years – the uplifting, folding, crumpling, and shearing of strata to form the mountains; the intrusion of molten rocks into these raised, sedimentary strata; the alternate sinking and flooding and then rising of valley floors; extensive glaciations, heavy precipitation, and other erosion forces wearing down the mountains and redepositing sediments on valley floors and at the mouths of streams and rivers at lower elevations.

The North Gulf Coast-Prince William Sound region is one of the most active seismic regions in the world, and major fault systems extend through it; the epicenter of the great Alaskan earthquake of 27 March 1964 was located in northwestern Prince William Sound at 61°06' N, 147°44' W (Wood, 1966). The 1964 earthquake, with a magnitude of between 8.3 and 8.6 on the Richter Scale, wrought tectonic changes in land levels over probably more than 110,000 sq miles (285,000 km^2) of southcentral Alaska, affecting most of the North Gulf Coast-Prince William Sound region. According to Plafker (1969), tectonic deformations extended along the Gulf of Alaska from the southwest tip of the Kodiak islands, through the Prince William Sound area, to the vicinity of Yakataga. A broad zone of subsidence centered along the axis of the Kodiak-Kenai-Chugach mountains and affected most of the Kenai Peninsula and the northern and western parts of Prince William Sound. A zone of major uplift occurred on the seaward side of this axis, extending from the coast onto the sea floor and affecting all but the extreme northwestern and northern parts of the Prince William Sound area and affecting the coastal belt as far as Yakataga. A zone of slight uplift occurred on the landward side of the axis, extending northward into the Alaska and Aleutian ranges. In all, some 48,000 sq miles (125,000 km^2) subsided an average of about 2.5 ft (.76 m) and some 60,000 sq miles (155,000 km^2) uplifted an average of about 6 ft (1.8 m). Vertical movements ranged from as much as 7.5 ft (2.3 m) of subsidence on the south coast of the Kenai Peninsula to 38 ft (11.6 m) of uplift on southwestern Montague Island.

These tectonic shifts have caused extensive alterations in the natural environment and biota (see Committee on the Alaska Earthquake, 1971); but, owing to the resilience of nature, most of the effects on the avifauna appear to be transitory. The potential effect on the waterfowl, however, appears more serious. Waterfowl habitats are concentrated on the delta marshes at the mouths of the rivers in the eastern parts of the region, the portion uplifted by the earthquake; the Copper River Delta, for instance, was raised 6.2 ft (1.89 m), and some of the most productive marshes near the flats are currently more than 1 m above Mean High

Water and are no longer inundated even by storm tides. This environmental change is causing habitat changes which in turn may profoundly affect the waterfowl utilization of the area (Crow, 1968).

CLIMATE

The weather of the North Gulf Coast-Prince William Sound region is maritime, with moderate temperature ranges, high humidity, frequent overcast and fog, and high levels of precipitation. A semi-permanent low pressure trough, the "Aleutian Low," is located over the Gulf of Alaska/North Pacific annually from October through March, forming the main breeding ground for cyclonic storms over the Northern Hemisphere. During the winter more lows are found in the Gulf of Alaska than in any other part of this hemisphere (U. S. Coast and Geodetic Survey, 1964). The "Aleutian Low" dissipates or is forced northward with the building of a large "Pacific High" in late May or early June (ibid.).

Because of the prevalence of cyclonic storms in the region, low stratus or cumulus clouds and accompanying mists are regular and frequent phenomena in the region, as are haze, fog, rain, and snow. Visibility is often limited by snow squalls from November to May and by fogs of varying geographic extents and densities, mainly from June through September.

Temperature. Summers are cool and winters mild. Normal annual extremes at many coastal points are lows near 0°F (-18°C) and highs near 75°F (24° C), although local temperature extremes may get as low as about -30°F (-34°C) in winter and up to about 85°F (29°C) in summer. Mean annual temperatures for the port cities are 40.0°F (4.4°C) at Yakutat, 40.1°F (4.5°C) at Cordova, 35.7°F (2.1°C) at Valdez, 38.7°F (3.7°C) at Whittier, and 39.5°F (4.2°C) at Seward (U. S. Environ. Sci. Serv. Admin., 1971).

Precipitation. The region is exposed to an easterly movement of cyclonic storms from the Pacific Ocean, winds that are warm and heavily-laden with moisture after having passed over the central Pacific. The outer coastal points and islands receive considerably less precipitation than the heads of some of the deeply incised fiords and the mountains. Mean annual precipitation is 131.81 inches (334.80 cm) at Yakutat, 167.68 inches (425.91 cm) at Cordova*, 62.37 inches (158.42 cm) at Valdez, 175.28 inches (445.21 cm) at Whittier, and 67.35 inches (171.07 cm) at Seward (U. S. Environ. Sci. Serv. Admin., 1971). Record rainfalls of over 14 inches (36 cm) in 24 hours have been recorded at Cordova, but precipitation is usually distributed over extended periods. Much of the precipitation falls as snow — between late August and May in the mountains, and from October to April at or near sea level. Mean annual snowfall is 219.6 inches (557.8 cm) at Yakutat, 116.7 inches (296.4 cm) at Cordova*, 244.5 inches (621.0 cm) at Valdez, 263.8 inches (670.1 cm) at Whittier, and 80.6 inches (204.72 cm) at Seward. Maximum recorded snow depths on the ground have been 95 inches (241 cm) at Cordova, 135 inches (343 cm) at Valdez, 141 inches (358 cm) at Whittier, and 41 inches (104 cm) at Seward (U. S. Environ. Sci. Serv. Admin., 1971).

*In contrast to these precipitation recordings at the city of Cordova, recordings at the Cordova Airport, on the upper Copper River Delta 13 miles (21 km) east of Cordova, show a mean annual precipitation of only 80.98 inches (205.69 cm), including 89.3 inches (226.8 cm) of snowfall.

Wind. For most of the year, prevailing wind direction is easterly, winds being especially strong along the coast where they are intensified because of being blocked and diverted by the mountains. Seasonally and locally, westerly winds are common in summer and northerly winds in winter.

Winds exceeding gale force (32-63 mph, 51-101 kph) occur regularly along the coasts from September until June, and hurricane force (75+ mph, 120+ kph) winds are recorded annually — often, in some years. A unique, wind-building situation may develop over southcentral Alaska anytime from fall to early spring: a high pressure area over mainland Alaska and Canada will cause steep pressure gradients toward the Gulf of Alaska, and the ensuing air movement is usually funneled down the numerous mountain passes, most notably the Copper River Valley. These northwesterly or northerly winds, according to pilot reports, frequently attain and sustain velocities well in excess of 65 mph (105 kph). Wind measurements taken by the Copper River and Northwestern Railway from July 1908 to December 1909 near Miles Lake (Mile 50 Copper River Highway) on the Copper River showed an average daily maximum velocity for this period of 25 mph (41 kph), with the highest monthly average daily maximum velocity being 59 mph (95 kph) in January, including 10 days with a maximum of 70 mph (113 kph) or more (Ellsworth and Davenport, 1915). These local winds are the force building the sand dunes along the upper Copper River Delta and the Copper River.

OCEANOGRAPHY

The water circulation in the Gulf of Alaska is dominated by the Alaska Current, a counterclockwise eddy of the Subarctic Current.

Temperature and Salinity. Seawater temperatures in the region vary from seasonal and local extremes of 18°C (64°F) to -2°C (28°F), with annual means at Yakutat, Cordova, and Seward, respectively, of 7.7°C (45.9°F), 6.4°C (43.5° F), and 7.2°C (45.0°F) (U. S. Nat. Ocean Survey, 1970).

The mean annual seawater salinity (in parts per 1000 at 15°C [59°F]) at the port cities is as follows: Yakutat, 20.6; Cordova, 21.8; Whittier, 18.8; and Seward, 16.8 (U. S. Nat. Ocean Survey, 1970). Salinities at these coastal ports are highest during winter when freshwater discharge from land is at a minimum; at this season, salinities compare closely with those of the open Gulf of Alaska, roughly 32.

Ice Conditions. During the winter, ice forms locally in the heads of some bays and fiords, especially those receiving substantial freshwater discharges from land. Drift-ice at or near the numerous outfalls of valley glaciers, usually within bays and fiords, is normal throughout the year; drift-ice on the open continental shelf waters is unusual and local. During the winter, particularly in a period of decreasing tidal ranges, ice often accumulates on beaches and tidal flats. With increasing tidal ranges and/or storm waves and tides, this ice disappears.

Tides. Diurnal tidal ranges in the Gulf of Alaska average from 3.1 m (10.2 ft) along the outer points and islands to 3.8 m (12.5 ft) in the waters of Prince William Sound. At Cordova, during the spring tides, the range may be as great as 5.5 m (18.2 ft), with other coastal stations within the region showing similar increases (U. S. Nat. Ocean Survey, 1972). The normal tide range is often greatly modified by strong winds or storms within the Gulf, producing differences of 1 m (39.4 inches) or more between indicated and actual high or low tide levels.

Strong tidal currents cause rapid mixing of river water with seawater at entrances to bays, inlets, and fiords and in most coastal areas. Tide rips occur at many coastal points, with maximum turmoils present along the coast between Gore Point, Kenai Peninsula, and the Chugach Islands, where they are caused by the greater tidal ranges of the adjacent Cook Inlet region.

Ocean Currents. Westerly or southwesterly set currents predominate along the North Gulf Coast. Some of these currents reach high velocities, e.g., the southwesterly set current outside Hinchinbrook Entrance has been reported at 2.5 knots (4.6 kph) (U. S. Coast and Geodetic Survey, 1964). Commercial fishermen have reported that velocities well in excess of 2.5 knots (even up to 5+ knots [9 kph]) sometimes occur when waters are influenced simultaneously by Gulf storms and spring tides, e.g., off the barrier islands off the Copper River Delta, where they may be further influenced by the discharge from the Copper River.

Waves. Swells are predominantly from the southwest. High seas, associated with storms, are mostly from the southeast.

Avian Habitats

The North Gulf Coast-Prince William Sound region is phytogeographically a part of the Sitka Spruce-hemlock coastal/subalpine forests of the Pacific Coast. A great variety of habitats is available to and utilized by birds within the region, the variety being enhanced by the proximity of inshore and offshore waters and by the presence of major mountain systems. For the purposes of this publication, fourteen avian habitats are recognized:

Tundra
Shrub thickets
Hemlock-Sitka Spruce forests
Bogs
Mixed deciduous-spruce woodlands
Marshes
Lacustrine waters
Fluviatile waters
Cliffs, bluffs, and screes
Moraines, alluvia, and barrier islands
Beaches and tidal flats
Rocky shores and reefs
Inshore waters
Offshore waters

These habitats have been differentiated and described on the basis of the life-form of the vegetation, topography, and the physical nature of the substrate. More detailed descriptions of some of the region's vegetation may be found in Cooper (1942) and Crow (1968).

Representative views of the habitats are shown in Figs. 4-12, and cross-sectional diagrams in Fig. 13 illustrate the relative positions of the habitats and their major subdivisions to each other.

Some birds are restricted sharply in the habitats they utilize, while others show considerable flexibility. Many species, of course, show an affinity for one habitat type for nesting and others for courting, mating, resting, or foraging; and affinities may shift with seasons. Table 1 is a complete checklist of the birds of the North Gulf Coast-Prince William Sound region and indicates the species' primary and secondary habitat preferences. A primary preference (XX) is indicated if a major segment of the population of the species uses the habitat at any time of the year for any of its activities. A secondary preference (X) is indicated if the habitat is used by a minor segment of the population or as an alternate if the primary habitat is unavailable for any reason. Minor habitat utilization has not been indicated.

Scientific names for the plants in the following habitat descriptions follow Hultén (1968).

TUNDRA

A major portion of the North Gulf Coast-Prince William Sound region's land mass is covered by ice fields, glaciers, and high, steep mountain slopes that are little used by birds. Upland cliffs and screes (see below) and tundra, however, are used by a few species (see Table 1). In this region, the tundra is alpine in distribution, occurring mostly above 1500 ft (450 m), both on the mainland and on the islands; for the most part, it is under snow from October to June. Depending upon slope, drainage, and exposure, the vegetation varies from xeric fellfield, through a more moist heath tundra, to a wet sedge-grass tundra in depressions of high water content. Vegetation consists primarily of low, often mat-forming plants. Important species include Crowberry (*Empetrum nigrum*), Alpine and Dwarf blueberries (*Vaccinium uliginosum* and *V. caespitosum*), Mountain Heather (*Phyllodoce aleutica* and *P. glanduliflora*), Alpine Azalea (*Loiseleuria procumbens*), Alaska Moss heather (*Cassiope stelleriana*), sedges, and a number of other herbs and mosses and lichens.

SHRUB THICKETS

Shrubs form extensive thickets in the region, averaging some 10 ft (3 m) in height but attaining 20+ ft (6+ m) in some places. Dense, relatively uniform thickets of Sitka Alder (*Alnus crispa sinuata*) occur extensively between the coniferous forest and the alpine tundra and between the beach and the forest. Also, being a pioneer species, this alder establishes itself quickly in such disturbed areas as avalanche tracts, borders of mountain streams, areas of recent glacial retreat, and cut-over areas. These dense alder thickets are often impenetrable, partly because of the spreading growth of the alder (multi-stemmed with some stems often growing horizontally instead of vertically) and partly because of a dense intermixture of other shrubs such as the spiny Devilsclub (*Echinopanax horridum*) and Salmonberry (*Rubus spectabilis*). Ferns, grasses, sedges, and mosses provide additional ground cover. In damp open spots within the alders, dense growths of Cow Parsnip (*Heracleum lanatum*) and False Hellebore (*Veratrum viride*) may occur.

A somewhat different shrub habitat occurs extensively along the drainage systems at the lower elevations and especially on alluvial floodplains. Here, willows, including some rather large Alaska Willows (*Salix alaxensis*), become prominent, although alders are common, too. This willow-alder association is more open and

Fig. 4. Alpine tundra and scree (foreground) on Montague Island. (Photo by Wallace Watts.)

Fig. 5. Shrub thickets along Richardson Highway near Valdez. (Photo by Meng-Lein Lee.)

hence supports a richer, more varied undergrowth than the dense, uniform alder thickets; this undergrowth commonly includes Sweet Gale (*Myrica gale*), Salmonberry, Devilsclub, Blueberry (*Vaccinium ovalifolium* and *V. alaskensis*), Redberried Elder (*Sambucus racemosa*), Trailing Black Currant (*Ribes laxiflorum*), and various herbs.

Hemlock-Sitka Spruce Forests

The dense, coniferous forests of the region extend from sea level to altitudes varying from a few 100 ft (30 m) to nearly 2,000 ft (600 m). Because of the steep topography in much of the region, the forest is confined to a relatively narrow strip bordering most of the coastal areas and extending up the valleys. Mountain Hemlock (*Tsuga mertensiana*) is the major constituent of most of the coniferous forests, although Sitka Spruce (*Picea sitchensis*) is somewhat more widely distributed. Western Hemlock (*Tsuga heterophylla*) is abundant in the eastern portions of Prince William Sound and the North Gulf Coast, but becomes scarce to the westward; Alaska Cedar (*Chamaecyparis nootkatensis*) is common locally. The trees in these forests average some 1-2 ft (.3-.6 m) dbh and 40-45 ft (12-14 m) in height, although some exceed 3 ft (.9 m) dbh and 100 ft (30 m) in height. The understory of the coniferous forests commonly includes a variety of shrubs (Blueberry, *Vaccinium ovalifolium* and *V. alaskensis;* Lingonberry, *V. vitis-idaea;* Fool's Huckleberry, *Menziesia ferruginea;* Mountain Ash, *Sorbus sitchensis;* Devilsclub; Red-berried Elder; and, in more open areas, Copperbush, *Cladothamnus pyrolaeflorus;* and Salmonberry). The ground cover is dominated by mosses, especially species of *Hylocomium* and *Rhytidiadelphus loreus;* and there is a wide variety of herbs, including ferns, club-mosses (*Lycopodium* species), Dwarf Dogwood (*Cornus canadensis*), Twisted Stalk (*Streptopus amplexifolius*), Goldthread (*Coptis aspleniifolia*), and Five-leaved Bramble (*Rubus pedatus*).

Bogs

Within the region, bogs (known locally as "muskegs") develop in depressions, flat areas, and on gentle slopes where drainage is poor; they are usually associated with the coniferous forests. The substrate is essentially sedge-moss peat, covered by thick mats of various *Sphagnum* species, sedges (especially *Carex* and *Eriophorum*), shrubs and sub-shrubs (Sweet Gale; Bog Cranberry, *Oxycoccus microcarpus;* Alpine and Dwarf blueberries; Labrador Tea, *Ledum palustre decumbens;* Crowberry; Bog Rosemary, *Andromeda polifolia;* Cloudberry, *Rubus chamaemorus;* etc.), Grass-of-Parnassus (*Parnassia palustris* and *P. fimbriata*) and other herbs, and fruticose and foliose lichens. In the driest areas of the bogs, the heath may invade the herbaceous mat, and a few, scattered, slow-growing, poorly-formed conifers may be found at the edges. Numerous small ponds often occur within the bogs, supporting some aquatic plants (Pondweeds, *Potamogeton* species; Bur Reeds, *Sparganium* species; Yellow Pond Lily, *Nuphar polysepalum;* Buckbean, *Menyanthes trifoliata;* etc.).

Mixed Deciduous-Spruce Woodlands

Stands of Black Cottonwood (*Populus balsamifera trichocarpa*) are extensive along some of the rivers, across the higher portions of their deltas, and on moraines. These are intermixed to varying degrees with Sitka Spruce, Paper Birch

Fig. 6. Hemlock-Sitka Spruce forest, and rocky shores along Kings Bay, Port Nellie Juan. (Photo by Meng-Lein Lee)

Fig. 7. Bog habitat on Latouche Island. (Photo by U.S. Forest Service.)

(*Betula papyrifera* and *B. kenaica*), and tall shrubs of Alaska Willow and Dwarf Birch (*Betula nana*). The stands have an undergrowth of luxuriant grasses, Horsetails (*Equisetum* species), Fireweed (*Epilobium* species), and other herbs; and medium-to-tall shrubs, including Salmonberry, Prickly Rose (*Rosa acicularis*), High-bush Cranberry (*Viburnum edule*), and willows. Alder frequently forms an understory, especially where these woodlands grade into alder thickets at higher and/or drier locations.

MARSHES

Brackish and freshwater marshes are found on the Copper River Delta and, to a lesser extent, adjacent to the tidal flats at the mouths of other rivers and streams. On the Copper River Delta, the marsh vegetation is composed primarily of sedges (*Carex*, especially *C. lyngbyaei*), grasses (especially *Deschampsia beringensis, Festuca rubra,* and *Calamagrostis inexpansa*), Arrow Grass (*Triglochin maritimum*), and Spike Rush (*Elocharis kamtschatica*), with Wild Pea (*Lathyrus palustris*), Pacific Silverweed (*Potentilla egedii*), Seaside Crowfoot (*Ranunculus cymbalaria*), and Hedysarum (*Hedysarum alpinum americanum*) being common forbs and the Arctic Willow (*Salix arctica*) a common, prostrate shrub. In drier areas, such as on low, natural levees, mixed forb-low shrub communities develop, which in turn grade into the shrub thickets of better drained areas.

LACUSTRINE WATERS

With the exception of the very small ponds found in the bogs and marshes, all lakes and ponds and their shorelines are included as lacustrine waters. Countless shallow ponds of various sizes occur within the marshes. Those nearest the coast are shallow and may be brackish. They support a relatively uniform plant community dominated by stands of Mare's Tail (*Hippuris tetraphylla*), sedges, Pondweed (*Potamogeton filiformis*), and Water Milfoil (*Myriophyllum spicatum*). With increasing distance from the coast, the ponds deepen and support a more diverse vegetation, including *Hippuris vulgaris,* which replaces *H. tetraphylla,* Bur Reeds (*Sparganium* species), Yellow Pond Lily, and sometimes dense stands of Horsetail (*Equisetum* species). The deeper, upland lakes may or may not have emergent plants along the shorelines.

FLUVIATILE WATERS

Fluviatile waters comprise all flowing freshwater surface waters — streams and rivers.

CLIFFS, BLUFFS, AND SCREES

Upland cliffs and screes are extensive in the region, due to the steep topography and recent glaciation, but they are only sparsely utilized by birds. Raptors and some swallows use the cliffs, and Gray-crowned Rosy Finches, Snow Buntings, and probably Marbled Murrelets use the screes for nesting. Lowland bluffs (including cutbanks, coastal rocks and sea stacks, and islets, as well as coastal bluffs) are utilized much more extensively, especially those along the mainland coast and on some of the islands where they are used as nesting and resting sites by seabirds and some raptors. The coastal bluffs are most frequent in Prince William Sound and along the western portions of the North Gulf Coast.

Fig. 8. Hemlock-Sitka Spruce forest, Black Cottonwood stand, and alluvium, Kings Bay, Port Nellie Juan. (Photo by Meng-Lein Lee.)

Several species of birds that utilize this habitat under natural conditions now also are utilizing similar habitats provided by artificial structures of human habitation — wharves, buildings, bridges, etc. Several swallows have thus adapted themselves, Dippers nest under river bridges, etc.

MORAINES, ALLUVIA, AND BARRIER ISLANDS

Unvegetated glacial deposits; alluvial deposits of gravel, sand, and silt; and barrier islands above the effects of tides are included in this habitat. Glacial and alluvial deposits are common, especially in the larger valleys and along the larger rivers of the region. A series of sandy barrier islands has been formed seaward of the mouth of the Copper River; these islands are sparsely vegetated, with Beach Rye (*Elymus arenarius mollis*) and Beach Fleabane (*Senecio pseudo-arnica*) the most conspicuous plants.

BEACHES AND TIDAL FLATS

This habitat is subject to regular tidal inundations. Sandy and pebbly beaches occur primarily where there is surf action along the outer coasts. These areas, plus adjacent areas of sparse vegetation (predominantly Beach Rye) within the upper reaches of storm tides, form a unique habitat utilized by a few birds, i.e., Savannah Sparrows, Arctic Terns, and Glaucous-winged Gulls. Tidal flats, formed primarily of glacial silt, mud, and sand mixtures, occur on the Copper River Delta and to a lesser extent at the mouths of other rivers and streams and on the shallows of numerous bays and lagoons. Fertile, exposed flats extend for vast distances at low tide.

Fig. 9. Marsh area at the mouth of Gravina River. (Photo by U.S. Forest Service.)

Fig. 10. Grass flats of the Copper River Delta Marshes. (Photo by Wallace Watts.)

ROCKY SHORES AND REEFS

Shorelines of rock and rubble, inundated regularly by tides, are common along the western North Gulf Coast. This habitat supports a rich food source, including Blue Mussels (*Mytilus edulis*), barnacles (*Balanus* species, *Chthamalus dalli*), limpets (*Acmaea* species), periwinkels (*Littorina* species), isopods (*Idothea* species), gammarid amphipods, several species of polychaete worms, etc.

INSHORE WATERS

Inshore waters include all waters of Prince William Sound and those of the North Gulf Coast within 3 nautical miles (5.6 km) to seaward of all outer coastal points and islands. Waters within this zone retain a shore influence, with even land birds flying over these expanses of water with some regularity. Waters in much of the area are shallow enough for birds to feed on or near the bottom.

OFFSHORE WATERS

Waters seaward of 3 nautical miles (5.6 km) compose the offshore habitat. These waters are beyond most shore influences and are essentially pelagic; oceanic birds usually do not venture in numbers any closer to the coast.

OTHER ECOLOGICAL FORMATIONS

Within the region there are several areas which differ substantially, ecologically, from the rest of the region: the Copper River Delta, the Resurrection Valley drainage system near Seward, the end moraine of the Malaspina Glacier, and Middleton Island. These ecologically different areas explain some of the avian distribution and abundance patterns found in the region.

The Copper River Delta is unique in the region for its great expanse (400 sq miles [1,000km^2]) of flat, open wetlands and fertile tidal flats. (See Crow [1968] for a detailed description of the plant ecology of the Copper River Delta.) Somewhat similar ecological conditions exist at the mouths of several of the other large rivers of the region, notably the Bering, Situk, and Alsek rivers, but nowhere else are the areas as extensive. The presence of these vast and fertile habitats attracts great numbers of waterfowl and shorebirds to the Copper River Delta for resting and feeding during migration and for nesting.

The drainage system of Resurrection Valley is unique chiefly for two reasons. First, it is close to the edge of the interior boreal forest communities of the western Kenai Peninsula-Cook Inlet region, and there are no real physical barriers, especially between Upper Russian River and Resurrection Valley. Thus, some boreal forest taxa extend into the valley and intermix with those of the coastal vegetation, e.g., the interior forms of the Paper Birch (*Betula papyrifera humilis*) and Alder (*Alnus crispa crispa*), Dwarf Birch (*Betula nana*), Shrubby Cinquefoil (*Potentilla fruticosa*), and the Littletree Willow (*Salix arbusculoides*). Second, the climate is drier and temperatures more extreme than elsewhere along the coast, because the valley is at the head of deeply-incised Resurrection Bay and is protected from the main coastal influences by the surrounding Kenai Mountains. Several boreal forest birds follow the "interior" influences into the Resurrection Valley area. Harlan's Hawks, Swainson's Thrushes, Myrtle Warblers, and Blackpoll Warblers breed here but not elsewhere in the North Gulf Coast-Prince William Sound region.

Fig. 11. Coastal bluffs, sea stacks and islets, and rocky shores and reefs. (Photo by Wallace Watts.)

Fig. 12. Tidal flats in Orca Inlet. (Photo by U.S. Forest Service.)

The Malaspina Glacier, together with its end moraine, appears to be a significant factor in bird distribution along the eastern North Gulf Coast, although we are not very familiar with the area and more information is needed. The massive glacier itself has long served as a physical barrier to the movement of some species, and the type of habitats (mixed deciduous-spruce woodlands and shrub thickets) on the end moraine also inhibits the expansion of the ranges of some birds. The range of the Spruce Grouse, for example, seems to be limited on the east by the Malaspina Glacier, and several species from southeastern Alaska have been recorded in the vicinity of Yakutat (Shortt, 1939) but not beyond, e.g., Screech Owl and Western Flycatcher. This area also shows an influence from the interior, apparently coming from interior Canada via the Alsek River; this is the only area besides Resurrection Valley where Dwarf Birch reaches the region, and the only summer records of Rough-legged Hawk and Gray-cheeked Thrush in the region are from here. Another note of interest is the apparent nesting of large numbers of Kittlitz's Murrelets in the end moraine of Malaspina Glacier; this is the only place along the outer coasts of the region where they are common, and they are present in summer by the thousands in the waters at the front of the glacier.

Middleton Island, in the Gulf some 65 miles (105 km) south of Hinchinbrook Entrance, is different from other islands in the region. Geologically, it contains marine glacial sediments similar to the Tertiary sediments underlying the lowlands of the eastern North Gulf Coast and appears to be related to that formation (Miller, 1953). The climate, of course, is maritime, but mean annual temperatures (42.3°F [5.7°C]) are warmer and precipitation (58.02 inches [147.37 cm]) is less than at adjacent mainland localities (U. S. Environ. Sci. Serv. Admin., 1971). The flora appears to have been derived from the islands and mainland to the north (Thomas, 1957), but the life-form of the vegetation more closely resembles that of the coastal tundras of southern Kodiak Island, the Alaska Peninsula, and the Aleutians. Middleton Island is the only known nesting area in the region for Lapland Longspurs, probably because of the tundra-like vegetation on the upper terraces (Rausch, 1958). This island is also the site of the easternmost breeding colony of the Thick-billed Murre (ibid.). Also, Snowy Owls may occur here more or less regularly, but only erratically in the rest of the region.

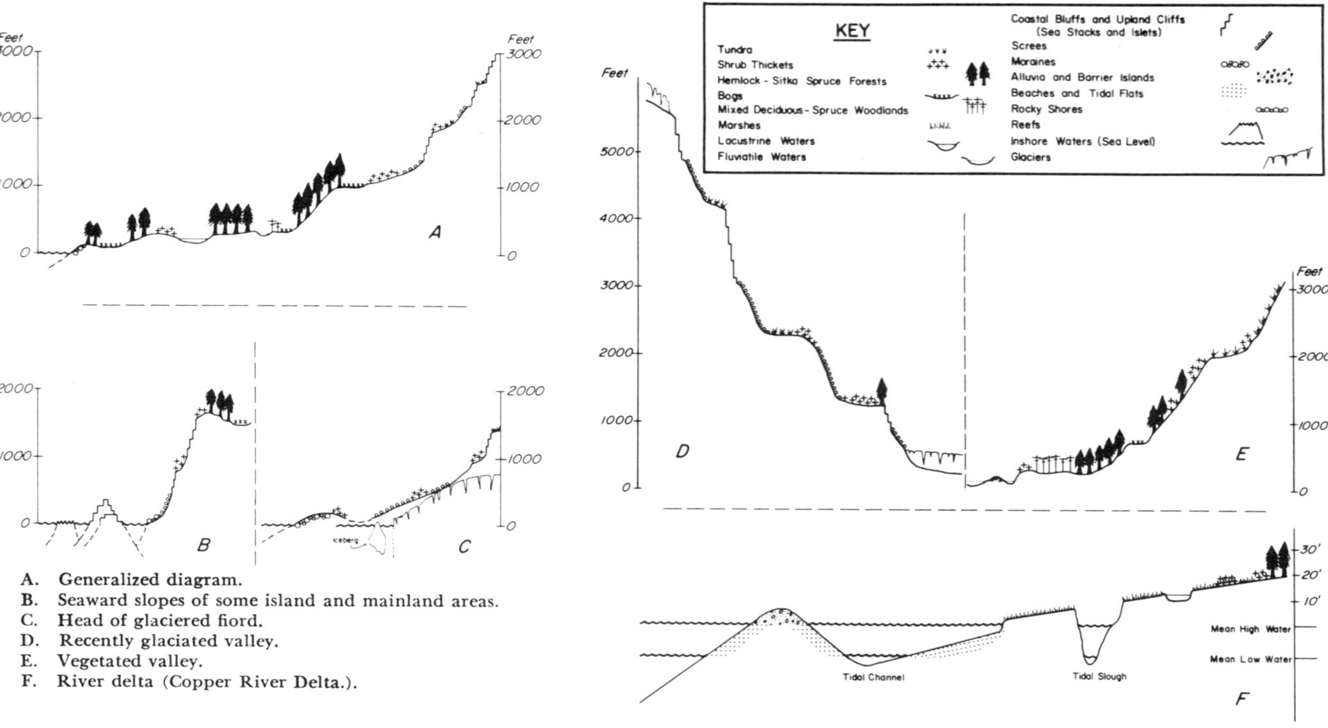

A. Generalized diagram.
B. Seaward slopes of some island and mainland areas.
C. Head of glaciered fiord.
D. Recently glaciated valley.
E. Vegetated valley.
F. River delta (Copper River Delta.).

Fig. 13. Cross-sectional diagrams showing relative positions of the various habitats in the North Gulf Coast – Prince William Sound region.

Table 1. Checklist of the birds of the North Gulf Coast – Prince William Sound Region. Primary preferences—XX; secondary preferences—X; minor habitat utilization is not indicated, nor are preferences of species accidental to the region. Key: * breeding record(s); # probable breeding; + possible breeding; ° casual or accidental.

	Tundra	Shrub thickets	Hemlock-Sitka Spruce forest	Bogs	Mixed deciduous-spruce woodlands	Marsh	Lacustrine waters	Fluviatile waters	Cliffs, bluffs, and screes	Moraines, alluvia, and barrier islands	Beaches and tidal flats	Rocky shores and reefs	Inshore waters	Offshore waters
Common Loon							XX*						XX	X
Yellow-billed Loon													XX	X
Arctic Loon													XX	X
Red-throated Loon							XX*						XX	X
Red-necked Grebe													XX	X
Horned Grebe							XX*						XX	
Short-tailed Albatross°														XX
Black-footed Albatross													X	XX
Laysan Albatross														XX
Fulmar													X	XX
Pink-footed Shearwater													X	XX
Pale-footed Shearwater°													X	XX
Sooty Shearwater													X	XX
Slender-b Shearwater													X	XX
Scaled Petrel°														XX
Fork-tailed Petrel									XX*				XX	XX
Leach's Petrel														XX
Double-c Cormorant							X		XX*			XX	XX	X
Brandt's Cormorant°									XX*			XX	XX	
Pelagic Cormorant									XX*			XX	XX	X
Red-faced Cormorant									XX*			XX	XX	X
Great Blue Heron			XX*			X	X	X		X	XX	XX		

Table 1. — continued

	Tundra	Shrub thickets	Hemlock-Sitka Spruce forest	Bogs	Mixed deciduous-spruce woodlands	Marsh	Lacustrine waters	Fluviatile waters	Cliffs, bluffs, and screes	Moraines, alluvia, and barrier islands	Beaches and tidal flats	Rocky shores and reefs	Inshore waters	Offshore waters
Whistling Swan						XX	XX	X			X		XX	
Trumpeter Swan						XX	XX*	X		X	X		X	
Canada Goose	X	X*	X*	XX		XX*	XX#	X		XX*	XX	X	X	X
Black Brant						X				X	XX	X	XX	XX
Emperor Goose						X				X	XX	X	XX	
White-fronted Goose						XX				X	XX	X	X	X
Snow Goose						XX				X	XX		XX	X
Mallard		X*		X		XX*	XX	XX		X	XX	X	XX	
Gadwall						XX*	XX	X			XX		X	
Pintail		X*				XX*	XX	X		X	XX	X	XX	X
Green-winged Teal		XX*	X*	X		XX*	XX	XX		X	XX	X	XX	
Blue-winged Teal						XX#					X		X	
European Widgeon°						XX							X	
American Widgeon						XX*	XX	X		X	XX	X	X	X
Shoveler						XX*	X	X		X	XX	X	X	
Redhead°						XX	X							
Ring-necked Duck						X	XX							
Canvasback						XX*	XX				X		X	
Greater Scaup						XX*	XX	X		X	XX	X	XX	
Lesser Scaup						X+	XX							
Common Goldeneye			X+				XX	X			X	X	XX	
Barrow's Goldeneye			XX*		XX*		XX	XX			X	X	XX	

Table 1. – continued

	Tundra	Shrub thickets	Hemlock-Sitka Spruce forest	Bogs	Mixed deciduous-spruce woodlands	Marsh	Lacustrine waters	Fluviatile waters	Cliffs, bluffs, and screes	Moraines, alluvia, and barrier islands	Beaches and tidal flats	Rocky shores and reefs	Inshore waters	Offshore waters
Bufflehead			X+				XX	X			X		XX	
Oldsquaw							X*						XX	X
Harlequin Duck		X*	X*					XX		X	X	XX	XX	
Steller's Eider											X	X	XX	
Common Eider												X	XX	
King Eider												X	XX	
White-winged Scoter							X*				X	X	XX	X
Surf Scoter							X*				X	X	XX	X
Common Scoter											X	X	XX	X
Hooded Merganser							XX	X					X	
Common Merganser		X*					XX	XX		X	X	X	XX	
Red-breasted Merganser						X*	X	X			X	X	XX	X
Goshawk		X	XX*		XX*	X					X			
Sharp-shinned Hawk	X	XX	XX*		XX*	X					X			
Red-tailed Hawk°					XX+									
Harlan's Hawk					XX*									
Rough-legged Hawk	XX+	X				XX				X				
Golden Eagle	XX								XX#					
Bald Eagle	X		XX*		XX*	XX	X	XX	XX*	XX	XX	XX	X	
Marsh Hawk	X	X		X		XX*				X	X			
Osprey					X*	XX	XX	X					X	
Gyrfalcon	XX								X+		X			

Table 1. — continued

	Tundra	Shrub thickets	Hemlock-Sitka Spruce forest	Bogs	Mixed deciduous-spruce woodlands	Marsh	Lacustrine waters	Fluviatile waters	Cliffs, bluffs, and screes	Moraines, alluvia, and barrier islands	Beaches and tidal flats	Rocky shores and reefs	Inshore waters	Offshore waters
Peregrine Falcon						X			XX*	X	X	X	XX	
Pigeon Hawk	X	XX	XX#		X	X					X			
Sparrow Hawk		X			XX	X								
Spruce Grouse		X	XX*		XX*									
Willow Ptarmigan	X	XX*	X	X	X	XX								
Rock Ptarmigan	XX*	XX	X						XX					
White-tailed Ptarmigan	XX+	XX							XX*					
Sandhill Crane	X					XX+				X	XX			
American Coot°						X	X						X	
Black Oystercatcher									XX*	X	X	XX		
Semipalmated Plover										XX*	X	X		
Killdeer°										XX	X			
American Golden Plover	X					XX				X	XX	X		
Black-bellied Plover						XX				X	XX	X		
Surfbird											X	XX		
Ruddy Turnstone										X	X	XX		
Black Turnstone										X	X	XX		
Common Snipe	X	X		XX+	X	XX*				X	X			
Whimbrel						X				X	XX	X		
Bristle-thighed Curlew°											XX			
Spotted Sandpiper						X	XX*			XX*	XX	X		
Solitary Sandpiper				XX		XX	XX				X			

Table 1. – continued

	Tundra	Shrub thickets	Hemlock-Sitka Spruce forest	Bogs	Mixed deciduous-spruce woodlands	Marsh	Lacustrine waters	Fluviatile waters	Cliffs, bluffs, and screes	Moraines, alluvia, and barrier islands	Beaches and tidal flats	Rocky shores and reefs	Inshore waters	Offshore waters
Wandering Tattler	X#			X						XX*	X	XX		
Greater Yellowlegs				XX*		XX#	X			XX	XX	X		
Lesser Yellowlegs				XX*		XX#	X			XX	XX	X		
Knot										X	XX	X		
Rock Sandpiper											X	XX		
Sharp-tailed Sandpiper°						X					XX			
Pectoral Sandpiper						XX				X	XX	X		
Baird's Sandpiper						XX				X	XX			
Least Sandpiper				X		XX*	X			XX	XX	X		
Dunlin						XX				X	XX	XX		
Short-billed Dowitcher						XX*				X	XX	X		
Long-billed Dowitcher						XX				X	XX	X		
Semipalmated Sandpiper						XX				X	XX			
Western Sandpiper	X			X		XX+				X	XX	X		
Bar-tailed Godwit											XX			
Hudsonian Godwit						XX+				X	XX	X		
Sanderling										X	XX			
Red Phalarope											X	X	X	XX
Northern Phalarope				X		XX*	XX	X		X	XX	X	XX	XX
Pomarine Jaeger						X				X	X		XX	XX
Parasitic Jaeger				X		XX*				XX+	XX	X	XX	XX
Long-tailed Jaeger											X		XX	XX

Table 1. — continued

	Offshore waters	Inshore waters	Rocky shores and reefs	Beaches and tidal flats	Moraines, alluvia, and barrier islands	Cliffs, bluffs, and screes	Fluviatile waters	Lacustrine waters	Marsh	Mixed deciduous-spruce woodlands	Bogs	Hemlock-Sitka Spruce forest	Shrub thickets	Tundra
Skua°	XX	X												
Glaucous Gull	X	XX	X	XX	X		X		X					
Glaucous-winged Gull	XX	XX	XX	XX	XX*	XX*	XX	X	XX*					
Herring Gull	X	XX	XX	XX	X+				X+					
Mew Gull	XX	XX	XX	XX	X*	X	XX	X	XX*			X*		
Bonaparte's Gull	X	XX	X	XX	X		X	X	X			X*		
Black-legged Kittiwake	XX	XX	XX	XX	X	XX*			X					
Sabine's Gull	XX	X		X										
Arctic Tern	XX	XX	XX	XX	XX*	XX*	X	X	XX*		X			
Aleutian Tern	X	XX		X	X				XX*					
Common Murre	XX	XX				XX*								
Thick-billed Murre	XX	XX				XX*								
Pigeon Guillemot	X	XX	X			XX*								
Marbled Murrelet	XX	XX				X#						X+		
Kittlitz's Murrelet	XX	XX				X#								
Ancient Murrelet	XX	XX												
Cassin's Auklet°	X	X												
Parakeet Auklet	X	XX				XX*								
Crested Auklet	XX	X												
Rhinoceros Auklet		XX				XX#								
Horned Puffin	XX	XX				XX*								
Tufted Puffin	XX	XX				XX*								

Table 1. – continued

	Tundra	Shrub thickets	Hemlock-Sitka Spruce forest	Bogs	Mixed deciduous-spruce woodlands	Marsh	Lacustrine waters	Fluviatile waters	Cliffs, bluffs, and screes	Moraines, alluvia, and barrier islands	Beaches and tidal flats	Rocky shores and reefs	Inshore waters	Offshore waters
Mourning Dove°						X					X			
Screech Owl°			X+											
Great Horned Owl		X	XX*		XX*	X			X					
Snowy Owl	X	X				XX			X	X		X		
Hawk Owl		X	XX+		XX#	X								
Pygmy Owl°			X+											
Great Gray Owl			XX+		XX*									
Short-eared Owl	X	X		X		XX*				XX	X			
Boreal Owl		X	X		XX#									
Saw-whet Owl		X	XX#		X+									
Common Nighthawk°						X								
Anna's Hummingbird°														
Rufous Hummingbird		X	XX*		X									
Belted Kingfisher						X	X	XX	XX*	X	X	X	X	
Yellow-shafted Flicker			X		XX									
Red-shafted Flicker°					X									
Hairy Woodpecker			X		XX*									
Downy Woodpecker		X	XX#		XX*									
Black-backed 3-t Woodpecker°			X		XX									
Northern 3-t Woodpecker			X		XX*									
Say's Phoebe°	X								XX+					
Traill's Flycatcher		XX*	X		X	X								

Table 1. – continued

	Tundra	Shrub thickets	Hemlock-Sitka Spruce forest	Bogs	Mixed deciduous-spruce woodlands	Marsh	Lacustrine waters	Fluviatile waters	Cliffs, bluffs, and screes	Moraines, alluvia, and barrier islands	Beaches and tidal flats	Rocky shores and reefs	Inshore waters	Offshore waters
Western Flycatcher°			X		X									
Western Wood Pewee					XX									
Olive-sided Flycatcher		X	X		XX									
Horned Lark	XX#									X				
Violet-green Swallow	X			X	X	XX	XX	X	XX*	X	XX		X	
Tree Swallow			X		XX*	XX	XX	X	X+	X	XX		X	
Bank Swallow						XX	X	X	XX*	X	X		X	
Barn Swallow						XX	X	X	XX*	X	X		X	
Cliff Swallow						XX	X	X	XX*		X		X	
Purple Martin°														
Gray Jay		X	X		XX*									
Steller's Jay		X	XX*		X						X			
Black-billed Magpie	X	XX*	X	X	XX*	X			X	X	X	X		
Common Raven	X	X	XX*	X	XX	XX	X	X	XX*	X	XX	X	X	
Northwestern Crow			XX*		X	X			X	XX	XX	XX	X	
Black-capped Chickadee		X	X		XX*									
Boreal Chickadee		X			XX#									
Chestnut-b Chickadee		X	XX*											
Red-breasted Nuthatch		X	XX#		XX#									
Brown Creeper			XX*		XX									
Dipper							X	XX	XX*	XX				
Winter Wren		XX*	XX#		X									

Table 1. – continued

	Tundra	Shrub thickets	Hemlock-Sitka Spruce forest	Bogs	Mixed deciduous-spruce woodlands	Marsh	Lacustrine waters	Fluviatile waters	Cliffs, bluffs, and screes	Moraines, alluvia, and barrier islands	Beaches and tidal flats	Rocky shores and reefs	Inshore waters	Offshore waters
Robin	X	XX*	XX*		XX*	X			XX#	X	X			
Varied Thrush	X	XX*	XX*	X	XX*	XX			X	X	XX	X		
Hermit Thrush	X	XX*	XX*	X	XX*	X			X	X	X	X		
Swainson's Thrush		X	X		XX*									
Gray-cheeked Thrush		X	X		XX*									
Wheatear	XX#													
Golden-crowned Kinglet		X	XX#		XX+									
Ruby-crowned Kinglet		XX	XX*		XX*									
Water Pipit	XX*			X		XX				XX	XX	X		
Bohemian Waxwing		X	X		XX*									
Northern Shrike	X	XX*	X		XX*	XX								
Starling											X			
Red-eyed Vireo°														
Orange-crowned Warbler		XX*	XX*		XX*	X						X		
Yellow Warbler		XX*			X	X								
Myrtle Warbler		X	X		XX*									
Townsend's Warbler		X	XX*		XX*									
Blackpoll Warbler		X	XX*											
Northern Waterthrush		XX#			X									
Yellowthroat°														
Wilson's Warbler		XX*	X		XX									
Red-winged Blackbird°		X				XX								

Table 1. — continued

	Tundra	Shrub thickets	**Hemlock-Sitka Spruce forest**	Bogs	Mixed deciduous-spruce woodlands	Marsh	Lacustrine waters	Fluviatile waters	Cliffs, bluffs, and screes	Moraines, alluvia, and barrier islands	Beaches and tidal flats	Rocky shores and reefs	Inshore waters	Offshore waters
Rusty Blackbird		XX*	X	X	X	XX				X	X			
Common Grackle°														
Pine Grosbeak		X	XX*		XX+									
Gray-c Rosy Finch	X				X				XX*	X	X			
Hoary Redpoll		XX			X	X								
Common Redpoll	X	XX*	X		XX*	X								
Pine Siskin		XX	XX*		XX	X								
Red Crossbill			XX#		XX+									
White-winged Crossbill			XX#		XX+									
Savannah Sparrow	XX*	XX*	X	X	X	XX*				X	X	X		
Slate-colored Junco	X	XX#	XX*		XX*	X								
Oregon Junco	X	X	XX#		XX*	X								
Tree Sparrow	X	XX*				X								
White-crowned Sparrow		XX*			XX	X								
Golden-c Sparrow		XX*	X	X	X	X						X		
White-throated Sparrow°														
Fox Sparrow	X	XX*	XX*	X	XX*	X						X		
Lincoln's Sparrow	X	XX*		X	X	XX*								
Song Sparrow		XX*	X		X	XX*					XX	XX		
Lapland Longspur	XX*			X		XX				X	XX	X		
Snow Bunting	XX					X			XX*	XX	X	X		

Utilization of the Region by Birds

Two hundred nineteen species of birds have been recorded in the North Gulf Coast-Prince William Sound region; 72 occur in numbers exceeding tens of thousands, 10 in the millions. Of the total, 111 species are primarily water-related. There is a high seasonal turnover, but of those species occurring regularly, 181 occur in the spring, 163 in the summer, 180 in the fall, and 109 in the winter. Largely because of the maritime climate and year-round ice-free waters, 101 species are resident throughout the year.

Below is a summary of the highlights of the seasonal utilization of the region by these birds. For ease of discussion, the various avian habitats have been combined into four major geographic areas: Offshore, Inshore, Tidal (Beaches and Tidal Flats, and Rocky Shores and Reefs), and Land (the remaining habitats, including Lacustrine and Fluviatile waters).

The Offshore and Inshore areas are delineated in the same way as the respective habitats (see p. 17). Within these areas, birds congregate where food is particularly abundant, such as where an "edge effect" is created by convergent waters (ocean currents, tidal action, wind action, freshwater outflows, upwelling, etc.). Small aquatic organisms and floating seaweeds are found in bands on the surface — sometimes extending for miles — along these convergence lines. Here often are found large congregations of feeding petrels, shearwaters, Fulmars, gulls, terns, and phalaropes.

The Tidal area is the zone between low and high tides; it is the most heavily utilized area in the region, especially the tidal flats which are used for feeding and resting by spectacular numbers of resident and migrant waterfowl, shorebirds, and gulls.

The Land area of the region is varied (see Avian Habitats) and is used by a broad spectrum of migrant, visitant, and breeding birds.

SPRING

From an ornithological viewpoint, spring is the most dramatic time of year in the North Gulf Coast-Prince William Sound region, primarily because of the millions of birds that are concentrated in the region for the limited period of migration. Several factors contribute to the spectacular concentrations found during this period: 1) Geographically, the region is along the main Pacific route of northern latitude breeders migrating to the northwestern limits of the North American continent. 2) The high, rugged topography of the coastal mountain systems, coupled with the northern arc of the Gulf of Alaska, forces the great majority of migrants to funnel through the region along a narrow coastal corridor. 3) Restriction of certain avian habitats within the region accounts further for phenomenal concentrations in a few specific areas, especially in the Copper River Delta. And, finally, 4) concentrations are enhanced by the fact that the duration of the migration period is telescoped at these northern latitudes, with the main passage extending over little more than five weeks.

Spring migrants actually reach the North Gulf Coast-Prince William Sound region from almost all points of the compass (Fig. 14). At least two species arrive from the west, the Aleutian Tern and the Wheatear. Some trans-Pacific migrants appear to arrive from the south, some probably first making landfall in the North Gulf Coast-Prince William Sound region, i.e., American Golden Plover, Bristle-thighed Curlew, Wandering Tattler, Ruddy Turnstone, and, to a lesser extent,

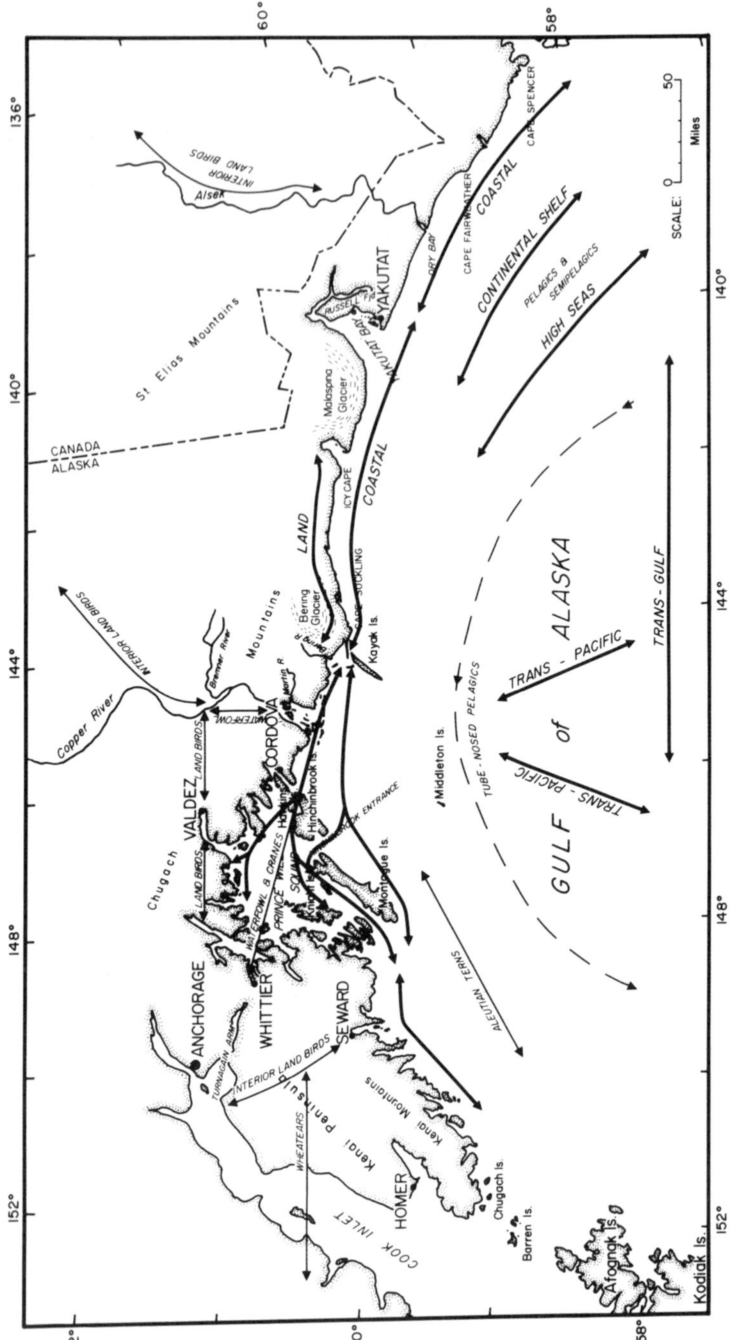

Fig. 14. Main routes of migrants in the North Gulf Coast — Prince William Sound region.

possibly the Pintail, American Widgeon, Black-bellied Plover, and Sanderling. Most pelagic species also enter the region from southerly directions, e.g., Fulmar, Black-legged Kittiwake, Long-tailed Jaeger, Red Phalarope, etc.

Migrants arriving from the north generally include land species that reach Alaska via the interior of the continent and then move south into the region through the mountain passes and river valleys – Alsek, Copper, and Resurrection (see discussion under Avian Habitats).

The vast majority of spring migrants arrive from easterly directions. Most land birds follow the narrow coastal corridor between the mountains and the sea, but some venture regularly over tidal areas and inshore waters within sight of land. In addition, during late May there is a surprising passage of passerines moving westward in fair numbers through snow-free alpine tundra areas. Tremendous numbers of waterbirds follow what might be called the coastal migration route, encompassing inshore and tidal areas and to some extent the edges of the land corridor. These migrants parallel the eastern North Gulf Coast west to the Copper River Delta (the only heavily utilized staging area for Whistling Swans and numerous other waterfowl and shorebirds), where some migrants continue along the outer coast, bound for breeding areas in adjacent western Alaska, but where most move into and across Prince William Sound (Fig. 14). These Prince William Sound migrants fan out into three main paths across the Sound, one along the northern periphery, one across the center, and one along the southern periphery, ultimately entering upper, central, and lower portions, respectively, of adjacent Cook Inlet after passing over the Chugach and Kenai mountains. A few of the northern periphery migrants appear to strike directly over the mountains to the northward (e.g., Oldsquaws and scoters).

Still other migrants from the east migrate through the offshore waters. These migrants are divisible into the "continental shelf migrants" that generally move along the coast between 3 nautical miles from shore and the edge of the continental shelf (e.g., Arctic Tern, Parasitic Jaeger, and Pomarine Jaeger) and the "high seas migrants" which apparently arrive from distances in the North Pacific Ocean (e.g., Black-legged Kittiwake, Long-tailed Jaeger, and Red Phalarope). In addition, there is some evidence that a trans-Gulf movement occurs, but this is more evident in the fall than in the spring.

To give a "feel" for the utilization of the region by birds, some details of seasonal activities of residents as well as migrants are described in the following paragraphs.

After months of relative quiet, the forests of the region burst into life with startling suddenness during the latter half of April with the arrival of the Ruby-crowned Kinglet and other songsters. During May, thrushes, warblers, and sparrows are especially abundant; they occur in such numbers during migration that they are common throughout a wide variety of habitats, from alpine areas high in the mountains to ships at sea. At the same time, the marshes are inundated by a myriad of waterfowl and shorebirds, and shortly thereafter the skies overhead are filled with thousands of swallows.

The tremendous concentrations of arriving and migrating waterfowl and shorebirds utilizing the tidal and marsh areas are hard to imagine unless one has observed them. Densities of more than 250,000 shorebirds per square mile fed on the tidal flats of the Copper River Delta in early May 1964. Between 25 April and 20 May each year, the 200+ sq mi (500+ km^2) tidal flats of the Copper River Delta are host to more than 20 million birds, mostly shorebirds and waterfowl. A great percentage of Alaska's populations of several species of waterfowl and shorebirds pass through this area in the spring: White-fronted Geese, Pintails, Western Sandpipers, Knots, Dunlins, Short- and Long-billed dowitchers, and Least Sandpipers. Knots occur here by the tens of thousands each spring, but are rare elsewhere along Alaska's southern coast.

Throughout the afternoon of 27 April 1971, approximately 5,500 Pintails per hour and 500 Whistling Swans per hour passed just north of Strawberry Point, entering Prince William Sound along a migratory route heavily utilized in late April and early May. Similar numbers continued to pass by for several days.

During this same period, rocky tidal areas (rocky shores and reef habitat) host at least 250,000 shorebirds of different species: Ruddy and Black turnstones, Surfbirds, Whimbrels, Wandering Tattlers, and American Golden and Black-bellied plovers. Some passerines appear more or less regularly during migration along these rocks and reefs, as well as at other outer coastal points and on ships at sea; most regular are Varied Thrushes, Savannah Sparrows, Golden-crowned Sparrows, Fox Sparrows, Wilson's Warblers, and Orange-crowned Warblers.

In the inshore areas, loons, grebes, waterfowl, hawks, eagles, cranes, shorebirds, and gulls follow the coastline in a seemingly endless stream, some remaining as visitants and others moving on along the outer coast or into Prince William Sound. Glaucous-winged, Mew, and Bonaparte's gulls, Black-legged Kittiwakes, White-winged, Surf, and Common scoters, Oldsquaws, Greater Scaup, and cormorants appear in large numbers, sometimes many thousands, to linger for a time in these inshore waters, feeding on spawning Pacific Herring (*Clupea harengus pallasi*) and their eggs at several locations along the coast during April and May.

Enormous numbers of birds move into and through the offshore area in spring – trans-Pacific migrants, continental shelf migrants, high seas migrants, and possibly trans-Gulf migrants; included are waterfowl, kittiwakes, alcids, phalaropes, terns, petrels, jaegers, and several of the strong-flying shorebirds. In addition, southern latitude tube-nosed pelagics (albatrosses and shearwaters) wander into waters of the Gulf of Alaska; their wanderings tend to be oriented in a westerly direction, probably related to the counterclockwise eddy of the Subarctic Current in the Gulf.

SUMMER

During the summer the land areas are heavily utilized by all of the nesting species. Summering passerines numbering in excess of hundreds of thousands of individuals include Varied Thrushes, Hermit Thrushes, Ruby-crowned Kinglets, Orange-crowned Warblers, Savannah Sparrows, and Fox Sparrows – the Hermit Thrush probably present by the millions.

Alcids, Black-legged Kittiwakes, cormorants, Glaucous-winged Gulls, and Arctic Terns are the most abundant birds found on the coastal bluffs, rocks, sea stacks, islets, and barrier islands. Kittiwakes number in excess of a million birds and Tufted Puffins and Glaucous-winged Gulls are present in similar numbers. Several large colonies of Fork-tailed Petrels, Pelagic and Red-faced cormorants, and Arctic Terns are also present. Most of the large (10,000+) bird colonies are located from the Copper River Delta westward, through Prince William Sound and along the North Gulf Coast; among the largest colonies (100,000+) are ones at the mouth of Resurrection Bay and in the Chiswell Islands. Several species of non-colonial seabirds nest along the coast: Pigeon Guillemots nest abundantly along the rocky shorelines, and Marbled and Kittlitz's murrelets apparently nest in mountain screes and moraines. Breeding Peregrine Falcons are associated with several seabird colonies; 12 to 20 pairs breed in the region. Eighteen hundred to 2,000 pairs of Bald Eagles nest in the North Gulf Coast-Prince William Sound region, mainly along the coasts and river systems. The marshes have a tremendous number of nesting waterfowl, gulls, terns, and shorebirds, particularly the marshes of the Copper River Delta, where there are tens of thousands of nesting Canada Geese, Glaucous-winged Gulls, and Northern Phalaropes. Nearly the entire North American population of 35,000+ "Dusky" Canada Geese (*B. c. occidentalis*) breeds here, where densities in prime habitat have exceeded 100 nests per square mile (Hansen, 1962). The Copper River Delta marshes also support a sizable (150 to 250 pairs) nesting population of the little-known Aleutian Tern, possibly the largest number in one area in North America. The Copper River Delta and adjacent North Gulf Coast area is an important breeding ground for the Trumpeter Swan. On a late summer survey in 1968, 1,022 of these swans were counted just inland on the marsh ponds and lakes from Yakataga to Cordova (Hansen et al., 1971).

During the summer, as well as throughout the year, large concentrations of gulls are attracted to wastes produced by fish processing plants. Yakutat, Cordova, and Seward have plants operating year-round. Beginning in spring and continuing into fall, several other processing plants are active, including some mobile (shipboard) operations. Over 10,000 gulls are semi-resident about the Cordova waterfront during June, July, and August; in addition to many non-breeding gulls, breeding gulls are attracted from as far away as the Copper River Delta, some 20 miles (32 km), by the unnatural abundance of food.

The tidal area is utilized for feeding throughout the summer by breeding and non-breeding shorebirds, gulls, and waterfowl. Immature and other non-breeding gulls are particularly abundant wherever concentrated food sources are available, either natural or otherwise. Non-breeding Black-bellied Plovers and several species of sandpipers feed in numbers on the mud flats and sand beaches of the Copper River Delta throughout the summer, as do similar numbers of breeding Black Oystercatchers and non-breeding Surfbirds on rocky shores and reefs throughout the region.

Inshore areas are heavily utilized during the summer by birds breeding along the coast. Locally, huge concentrations of cormorants, gulls, and alcids occur adjacent to sites of seabird colonies. During U. S. Fish and Wildlife Service surveys taken 21 July - 4 August 1972, Marbled Murrelets represented the largest avian biomass in Prince William Sound, numbering 250,000 birds. Large non-breeding populations of several species summer in the inshore area, some south of their breeding range. Most noticeable are White-winged, Surf, and Common scoters which, altogether, number several thousands during this season, often in flocks of several hundred each.

Offshore waters seaward of nesting colonies of kittiwakes, puffins, murres, murrelets, and petrels are heavily utilized for feeding by these birds. In addition, offshore waters are host to large numbers of petrels, shearwaters, and albatrosses. A concentration of Sooty Shearwaters off the Barren Islands in June 1965 was estimated by Roseneau (unpubl. notes) to consist of at least 2,600,000 individuals. The rare and endangered Short-tailed Albatross has been recorded in the Gulf of Alaska several times, and careful examination of white-bodied albatrosses in the region could reveal additional occurrences in the region.

FALL

Migration is an important aspect of fall utilization of the region, though it is less dramatic than in spring. Many migrants pass through on their way southward, but movement is more diffuse and less hurried, extending from July to November. For the most part, fall migration routes tend to be the reverse of the spring routes; however, there is apparently a sizable trans-Gulf movement of waterfowl – mainly Black Brant, Canada Geese (Cackling), and White-fronted Geese – from the Alaska Peninsula-Kodiak regions to British Columbia, Washington, Oregon, and California (Einarsen, 1965; R. D. Jones, pers. comm.; Nelson and Hansen, 1959; Gabrielson and Lincoln, 1959), a movement that in most years largely by-passes the North Gulf Coast-Prince William Sound region.

In the land areas, fall migration begins in July, with swallows and shorebirds moving first. Peak movements of most passerines occur between mid-August and mid-September, but thrushes and Fox Sparrows are still moving in October. In years when they occur, mass movements of siskins and crossbills take place in mid-October. During September and October large movements of migrating cranes, hawks, and eagles pass along the narrow band of land between the mountains and the coast; on clear days with light westerly winds, a nearly continuous stream of Bald Eagles, Marsh Hawks, and Sharp-shinned Hawks moves easterly along the coast on updrafts and thermals. During late September 1963, Steven R. Smith, local fisherman/photographer/biologist, (pers. comm.) estimated that over 500,000 Sandhill Cranes passed southeastward over the eastern Copper River Delta during the daylight hours over a 5-day period.

Again, during the fall, tidal and marsh areas are heavily utilized by migrating waterfowl, gulls, terns, and shorebirds. Shorebirds and terns migrate from July to September; waterfowl, from August to November, but especially from mid-September to mid-October. A concentration of over 10,000 Arctic Terns remained for several days on the east side of Yakutat Bay, near Ocean Cape, during the last week of July 1968. Estimated concentrations of 100,000 White-fronted Geese were seen along the Martin River on 5 September 1928 (Gabrielson and Lincoln, 1959) and on the Bering River Delta 1-4 September 1957 (Solf, pers. comm.).

Severe southeast storms and considerable precipitation occur in September and October; some storms, especially along the coast, are accompanied by prolonged winds of hurricane force. These severe storms restrict migratory movements, and, as a result, large numbers of ducks, geese, swans, and cranes often pile up on the Copper and Bering river deltas. Following such storms, a tremendous lift-off and mass exodus occurs. At times a buildup of birds occurs west of the region, in Cook Inlet and/or in western Alaska, and, depending on the lateness of the season, birds arrive at the marsh and tidal areas of the Copper River Delta in large numbers, to stop or pause only briefly, if at all.

In late summer and fall, thousands of gulls, eagles, and fish-eating ducks gather at the many salmon streams and intertidal spawning areas. There are several hundred short-run and intertidal spawning streams within the North Gulf Coast-Prince William Sound region, all of which have these attendant feeders on dying and dead salmon. During the latter half of August and in September, much of the Glaucous-winged, Herring, and Mew gull population is located in and about salmon-spawning locations.

Almost every year, associated with the southeast storms mentioned above, a wave of migrating Fork-tailed Petrels moves into the inshore waters. This petrel migrates mostly in offshore waters and is present only in small numbers moving southeastward over inshore waters; but, if a storm occurs, thousands are blown into the inshore area, and they may become common even to the heads of bays, inlets, and fiords of Prince William Sound.

Peak utilization of offshore areas occurs during the fall. Large numbers of shearwaters and albatrosses are still present when post-breeding individuals of many species, such as kittiwakes, gulls, terns, jaegers, and phalaropes, disperse from land-based breeding locations to the offshore area for feeding preparatory to migration. Phalaropes utilize this area by the millions in the early fall, as do petrels and kittiwakes in the late fall.

WINTER

The land area is utilized during the winter by relatively few bird species, most of which are resident: raptors, ptarmigan and other grouse, and several passerines, notably corvids and fringillids. Some fringillids, especially Pine Siskins, crossbills, and redpolls, vary greatly in abundance from year to year, numbering in tens of thousands some years but being essentially absent in others.

Tens of thousands of shorebirds (Rock Sandpipers, Dunlins, Surfbirds, Black Turnstones, and Black Oystercatchers), in local flocks, frequent the rocky shores and reefs of the tidal area during the winter; and Bald Eagles, ravens, crows and gulls use the tidal flats and beaches as primary foraging sites. U. S. Fish and Wildlife Service surveys conducted 24 March-4 April 1972 estimated 2,000 Bald Eagles within Prince William Sound, in or near tidal areas. During winters of heavy snowfall, many landbirds and mammals are forced to the tidal area to forage. In Prince William Sound in late winter, Sitka Black-tailed Deer (*Odocoileus hemionus sitkensis*) often are confined by deep snow to the beaches where they feed on kelp, mostly *Fucus distichus* and *Laminaria* species, cast up on the beaches by storms. During severe winters Bald Eagles, ravens, magpies, and gulls congregate on these same beaches to feed on dead deer.

Large numbers of waterfowl and gulls overwinter within the inshore areas, especially along the shores of bays and inlets. Mallards, Greater Scaup, Common and Barrow's goldeneyes, Buffleheads, Oldsquaws, Harlequin Ducks, White-winged, Surf, and Common scoters, and Common and Red-breasted mergansers total in the hundreds of thousands during this season. Loons, grebes, cormorants, and alcids account for similar numbers of birds, including at least several hundred Yellow-billed Loons. Concentrations are usually in areas of 50 fathoms (90 m) depth or less, specifically near tidal flats and reefs.

Gulls and alcids form the bulk of wintering birds utilizing the offshore area during the winter. Little is known about their winter densities. Isleib censused 18 birds per square mile in a 15 sq mi (39 km^2) block (a 1-mile-wide strip) between 12 and 27 nautical miles (22-50 km) southeast of Hinchinbrook Island on 27 December 1972; 40% of the birds were Glaucous-winged Gulls, the rest were Black-legged Kittiwakes, Mew Gulls, and a variety of alcids. Several hundreds of apparently storm-killed murrelets and murres were found on the outside beaches of Montague Island in January 1970 (Kenneth Mitchell, U. S. Forest Service, pers. comm.), suggesting that the wintering populations within the offshore area are substantial, though limited to relatively few species.

Annotated List of Birds

Over the years, 219 species of birds have been recorded within the defined limits of the North Gulf Coast-Prince William Sound region. These species are listed below with annotations regarding their seasonal status, abundance, and distribution in the region. Common and scientific names are those of the American Ornithologists' Union (1957), except as otherwise indicated. We have avoided, insofar as possible, discussions at the subspecific level, in spite of the fact that many tantalizing systematic-biogeographic problems exist in the region; our primary contributions are from field observations, and specimens were not collected for taxonomic studies.

In describing the status of a given species, we have used the following basic terminology:

resident — a species represented within the region throughout the year.

migrant — a seasonal transient through the region.

breeder — a species with known or probable breeding populations within the region.

visitant (mainly summer or winter) — a species having populations that may remain in the region for a period of time, but which is not adequately described by the preceding terms.

The following abundance terms have beeen utilized:

abundant — species occurs repeatedly in proper habitats, with available habitat heavily utilized, and/or the region regularly hosts great numbers of the species.

common — species occurs in all or nearly all proper habitats, but some areas of presumed suitable habitat are occupied sparsely or not at all and/or the region regularly hosts large numbers of the species.

fairly common — species occurs in only some of the proper habitat, and large areas of presumed suitable habitat are occupied sparsely or not at all and/or the region regularly hosts substantial numbers of the species.

uncommon — species occurs regularly, but utilizes very little of the suitable habitat, and/or the region regularly hosts relatively small numbers of the species; not observed regularly even in proper habitats.

rare — species occurs, or probably occurs, regularly within the region, but in very small numbers.

casual — species has been recorded no more than a few times, but irregular observations are likely over a period of years.

accidental — species has been recorded only a time or two; it is so far from its usual range that further observations are considered unlikely.

Another abundance expression that we have found useful is "# to # of birds per time period in proper habitat"— an indication of the usual numbers of a given species to be expected when observed from usual land or water transport through the proper habitats.

In addition to relative abundance classifications, at the end of each species account we have provided an estimate of the total populations utilizing the North Gulf Coast and Prince William Sound region. These admittedly long-shot "guesstimates" are Isleib's, based on his extensive and intensive field experience in the region, on a few censuses he performed on non-randomly selected sites, and on the results of his participation in the U. S. Fish and Wildlife Service Prince William

Sound waterbird surveys. The funneling of the major migratory movements through the region, caused by topography, and the restriction of some of the major habitats within the region contribute to making such estimation attempts feasible.

A large number of geographic locations are mentioned in the text. The more significant localities are shown on the maps in Figs. 1 - 3, and a list of all localities with regional designations and showing latitudes and longitudes is given in the Appendix.

Gavia immer — Common Loon

The Common Loon is a common resident of the North Gulf Coast-Prince William Sound region.

Spring migrants are common throughout inshore waters and on larger lakes from mid-April to mid-May (20 to 100 per day in proper habitat). Appearances and disappearances of numbers of these loons in the northern and western portions of Prince William Sound suggest that these waters function as a migration route for birds moving to and from inland summering areas.

Breeders occur on most of the larger, upland lakes within the forests and woodlands of the region, where several pairs may nest on a single lake, especially if fish are abundant. Shortt (1939) saw Common Loons on Yakutat Bay, Russell Fiord, and Situk Lake in 1936, finding them frequently about Khantaak Island, where young were seen with adults on 20 August. Common Loons are fairly common on saltwater adjacent to their coastal breeding lakes, apparently visiting the coast for feeding and resting.

Fall migrants appear along the coast during September and are common from early October through early November (20 to 100+ per day in proper habitat).

The Common Loon is fairly common in winter in the more sheltered bays and inlets (6 to 20+ per day in proper habitat).

Estimates of populations utilizing the North Gulf Coast and Prince William Sound: migration, a few, probably several, 1,000's; summer, a few, possibly several, 100's; winter, a few, probably several, 100's.

Gavia adamsii — Yellow-billed Loon

The Yellow-billed Loon is a resident of the North Gulf Coast-Prince William Sound region, occurring seasonally as a rare migrant, a rare summer visitant, and a fairly common winter visitant.

Spring migrants are difficult to separate from winter visitants, but birds observed along the outer coasts (0 to 5 per day in proper habitat) from late March to June are probably migrants.

While observed only irregularly, summer visitants are probably regular in small numbers along the North Gulf Coast and in Prince William Sound (0 to 10+ per season in proper habitat). These birds are non-breeders, both breeding-plumaged and sub-adult birds. Isleib saw one breeding-plumaged and two first-year birds on numerous occasions during July and August 1971 in Port Fidalgo, PWS, and has seen other Yellow-billed Loons in Valdez Arm, Port Gravina, Port Nellie Juan, Unakwik Inlet, and Orca Bay, PWS. Shortt (1939) saw a single Yellow-billed Loon, either a late migrant or summer visitant, well out to sea off the Malaspina Glacier on 25 May 1936. There are no reports of this loon on freshwater in the region.

Fall migrants move through the region from late September through mid-November; locally, in eastern Prince William Sound, they may be fairly common (20 to 100+ per day in proper habitat).

Winter visitants are fairly common (6 to 20+ per day in proper habitat), distributed widely along the coast and in Prince William Sound, generally in habitats similar to those preferred by Common Loons. Counts made along the Cordova waterfront showed 16 Yellow-billed Loons and 48 Common Loons on 27 December 1969 and 27 Yellow-billed Loons and 18 Common Loons on 29 December 1971.

Estimates of populations utilizing the North Gulf Coast and Prince William Sound: migration, a few, probably several, 100's; summer, a few 10's; winter, several 100's, probably a few 1,000's.

Gavia arctica — Arctic Loon

The Arctic Loon is a resident of the North Gulf Coast-Prince William Sound region, occurring seasonally as a common migrant, an uncommon summer visitant, and a common winter visitant; it usually remains on saltwater.

Spring migrants are common, especially along the outer coasts, from late April through mid-May (100+ per day in proper habitat). A regular stream of migrants passed westward around the Kenai Peninsula (25+ per hour off Gore Point) on 15 and 16 May 1963. Shortt (1939) found it the most common loon during May 1936 in the Yakutat Bay area; he saw it in "some numbers" throughout the summer but found no evidence of breeding.

Summer visitants, usually in breeding plumage, occur especially in the bays and fiords of Prince William Sound. The U. S. Fish and Wildlife Service survey 21 July - 4 August 1972 estimated over 1,600 Arctic Loons along the northern periphery of Prince William Sound, from Port Wells to Port Gravina. These summer observations suggest possible breeding in some adjacent freshwater lakes, but there are no substantiating records.

Fall migrants are common along the coasts from late September through early November (100+ per day in proper habitat).

From November to May, winter visitants are usually common along the coasts and in the bays and fiords, regularly in flocks of 50 to 100 birds and occasionally in large aggregations of 100's of birds. Arctics are the only loons that form large, tight aggregations in the region. A few 1,000 birds lingered in Orca Inlet during late November and early December 1969; 263 were counted there on 27 December 1969; but only 14 were there on 23 December 1972. A flock of a few to several hundred Arctic Loons winters annually in Sheep Bay, PWS.

Estimates of populations utilizing the North Gulf Coast and Prince William Sound: migration, a few 10,000's; summer, a few 1,000's; winter, a few, probably several, 1,000's.

Gavia stellata — Red-throated Loon

The Red-throated Loon is a resident of the North Gulf Coast-Prince William Sound region, occurring seasonally as a common migrant, a locally common breeder, and an uncommon, sometimes fairly common, winter visitant.

Spring migrants move along the outer coasts from mid-April to late May (20 to 100+ per day in proper habitat), generally as scattered individuals or loose flocks. They occur regularly in association with Arctic Loons, at times in about equal numbers.

Breeders are common on the shallow ponds of the Copper River Delta and locally elsewhere along the North Gulf Coast. Shortt (1939:5) recorded it as "a not uncommon summer resident of Yakutat Bay and vicinity" and found immatures with adults in late July 1936 in Russell Fiord. Shepherd (pers. field notes) recorded two downy chicks at Pete Dahl Slough, CRD, on 22 June 1959. The shallow ponds used by Red-throated Loons for breeding, unlike the larger, deeper lakes used by Common Loons, contain few, if any, fish, and the adults regularly fly to the coast to feed.

Fall migrants are fairly common along the outer coast from early September until early November (20 to 100 per day in proper habitat).

Red-throated Loons are regular winter visitants, but their abundance varies greatly from year to year. During the winters of 1968-69 and 1971-72, for example, the Red-throated Loon was second in numbers only to the Arctic Loon; during the winters of 1969-70 and 1970-71 it was the least common loon in the region; and during 1972-73 it was the most common. It has not been observed in large, tight wintering aggregations such as Gabrielson observed in 1944 in Southeastern Alaska (Gabrielson and Lincoln, 1959). Counts made along the Cordova waterfront showed 3 Red-throated Loons on 27 December 1969, 61 on 29 December 1971, and 97 on 23 December 1972.

Estimates of populations utilizing the North Gulf Coast and Prince William Sound: migration, a few 10,000's; summer, a few 1,000's; winter, a few 100's to probably several 1,000's.

Podiceps grisegena — Red-necked Grebe

The Red-necked Grebe is a resident of the North Gulf Coast-Prince William Sound region, occurring seasonally as a common migrant, an uncommon summer visitant, and a fairly common winter visitant.

Spring migrants are numerous from late April through mid-May (20 to 100+ per day in proper habitat) along the coast and in Prince William Sound, usually occurring in small flocks of 5 to 20 individuals; they are rare in freshwater.

Summer visitants are uncommon, occurring as scattered individuals, especially in Prince William Sound. U. S. Fish and Wildlife Service boat surveys 21 July-4 August 1972 estimated a total of about 240 Red-necked Grebes in Prince William Sound. There are no known breeding records in the region, but it breeds regularly in the adjacent Cook Inlet-Kenai Peninsula region and should be looked for as a possible breeder at lakes along the western North Gulf Coast and the western portions of Prince William Sound.

Fall migrants are common (100+ per day in proper habitat), especially in Prince William Sound, from late August to late October. The U. S. Fish and Wildlife Service aerial surveys 5-12 October 1971 estimated in excess of 4,500 Red-necked Grebes within 220 yards (200 m) of the shoreline of Prince William Sound; most of these birds were in small groups and may have been family units.

Winter visitants are fairly common in sheltered coastal waters and in Prince William Sound, usually as scattered individuals and small groups in waters of less than 50 fathoms (90 m); they are especially numerous along the shores of Knight Island. Censuses taken along the Cordova waterfront produced counts of 19 on 27 December 1969 and 28 on 29 December 1971.

Estimates of populations utilizing the North Gulf Coast and Prince William Sound: migration, a few 10,000's; summer, a few 100's; winter, several 1,000's, possibly 10,000's.

Podiceps auritus — Horned Grebe

The Horned Grebe is a resident of the North Gulf Coast-Prince William Sound region, occurring seasonally as a common migrant, an uncommon local breeder and summer visitant, and a fairly common winter visitant.

Spring migrants are common (20 to 100+ per day in proper habitat), especially in the sheltered waters of bays and inlets, and, unlike Red-necked Grebes, they occur regularly on the lakes and ponds of the region. Migrants appear in late April and occur commonly through the third week of May, being most numerous during the second week of May.

Summer visitants and breeders are uncommon on freshwater ponds in the Copper River Delta and locally elsewhere in the region (0 to 10+ per summer on Copper River Delta). Shepherd (pers. field notes) recorded two downy young in the vicinity of Pete Dahl Slough, CRD, on 29 June 1959 and another brood at Castle Slough, CRD, on 6 July 1959; Yocom (1963) recorded an adult with two half-grown young along the Copper River Highway on 11 June 1962; and Ruth Isleib (pers. comm.) saw an adult with two half-grown young near Alaganik Slough, CRD, in late July 1972.

Fall migrants appear in September and are common until early November (20 to 100 per day in proper habitat) on freshwater and along the shores of sheltered coastal waters.

Winter visitants are fairly common (6 to 50+ per day in proper habitat) as scattered individuals and small groups of two to ten individuals in the bays and inlets, often in shallow water and near tidal flats.

Estimates of populations utilizing the North Gulf Coast and Prince William Sound: migration, several 1,000's, probably 10,000's; summer, probably a few 10's; winter, a few, probably several, 1,000's.

Diomedea albatrus — Short-tailed Albatross

The Short-tailed Albatross formerly ranged fairly commonly throughout the pelagic waters of the North Pacific Ocean (Sanger, 1972). Today, however, it is a rare and endangered species, and only two observations have been recorded in the Gulf of Alaska over the past 25 years: Kenyon (1950) saw what appears to have been an immature Short-tailed Albatross in the offshore waters approximately 50 miles (80 km) southeast of Cape St. Elias on 25 November 1947, and Sanger (1964:47) reported a sight record by Hewitt Jackson of "a black-footed albatross with a pink beak" about 60 miles (96 km) southwest of Cape Spencer (57°30' N, 139°14' W) on 15 May 1956. These records, plus the observation by Wahl (1970) of one on 3 May 1970 off Washington State and the one by Gruchy et al. (1972), 24-26 June 1971, at Ocean Station Papa (50° N, 145° W) suggest the possibility of its continued occurrence in waters adjacent to Alaska's North Gulf Coast.

Diomedea nigripes — Black-footed Albatross

The Black-footed Albatross is a fairly common visitant in the offshore waters along the North Gulf Coast-Prince William Sound region. It apparently occurs regularly in these offshore waters between May and October and irregularly at other seasons.

Gabrielson (Gabrielson and Lincoln, 1959:74) probably has had more field experience in the high seas portions of the Gulf of Alaska than any other ornithologist in recent years, and he reported that the " 'goony' is a familiar sight in the offshore coastal waters of the north Pacific. Nearly every boat crossing the Gulf of Alaska has an escort of these birds . . . " Daniel D. Gibson and Richard J. Gordon (Gibson, pers. comm.) saw 73 Black-footed Albatross in 5 hours while crossing the Fairweather Bank off Cape Fairweather on 30 July 1970. Humberg (pers. comm.) reported seeing these albatrosses regularly in the area beyond the 12-mile U. S. contiguous zone during the summer and irregularly during the winter months in 1968 and 1969, observing as many as 15 in a 1-hour watch on 16 September 1969 some 50 miles (80 km) off Cape Fairweather. Shortt (1939) saw one as close as 1 mile (1.6 km) offshore of Yakutat Bay on 5 July 1936.

Estimates of populations utilizing the offshore waters along the North Gulf Coast: summer, probably several 1,000's, possibly 10,000's; winter, a few individuals, possibly 100's.

Diomedea immutabilis — Laysan Albatross

The Laysan Albatross is a rare or uncommon visitant in the offshore waters along the North Gulf Coast-Prince William Sound region.

Gabrielson and Lincoln (1959) suggested that some of the reported observations of Short-tailed Albatross in the Gulf of Alaska may refer to this species instead. Gabrielson (Gabrielson and Lincoln, 1959) saw a "white-bodied albatross" in the Gulf of Alaska on 9 June 1940, and Scheffer (Murie, 1959) saw a Laysan Albatross off Cape Hinchinbrook on 23 September 1938. Kenyon identified a Laysan Albatross about 230 miles (370 km) due east of Kodiak on 13 October 1948, and he quoted the ship's Captain Carlson as telling him that "during his five round trips to the Pribilofs each year, he quite often sees 'one or two of the white albatrosses with the black wings and back at about this same place while crossing the Gulf between Kodiak and Cape Spencer . . .' " (Kenyon, 1950: 100). Humberg (pers. comm.) saw several "white-bodied" albatrosses in offshore waters of the region in 1968 and 1969, mostly in the spring and fall. He was close enough to identify one behind a trawler on the Fairweather Bank on 16 September 1969 as a Laysan Albatross.

Estimates of populations utilizing the offshore waters along the North Gulf Coast: yearly, probably 100's.

Fulmarus glacialis — Fulmar

The Fulmar is a common migrant and a common visitant in the North Gulf Coast-Prince William Sound region. Throughout most of the year it is common in the offshore waters of the North Gulf Coast, and in summer it is also common in inshore waters to within about a mile of the outer coastline; it is an uncommon summer visitant and rare winter visitant in Prince William Sound.

Most ornithologists crossing the Gulf of Alaska in waters near the North Gulf Coast have seen Fulmars. Gabrielson (Gabrielson and Lincoln, 1959) saw them on various occasions, June-October, 1940-1946. Laing (1925) saw a dozen or more off Cape St. Elias on 13 March 1924. Shortt (1939) saw them fairly regularly off the coast near Yakutat during the summer of 1936. Humberg (pers. comm.) saw Fulmars commonly in the offshore waters throughout the year in 1968 and 1969, although less commonly during the winter than at other seasons. Surveys by the U. S. Fish and Wildlife Service 21 July - 4 August 1972 estimated a total of about 10,000 Fulmars in a strip about 12 miles (19 km) wide around the Gulf Coast side of Montague Island.

Fulmars occur regularly as singles or in small groups within Prince William Sound during the summer (May-September), but generally not within a mile of shore. The only winter observation within Prince William Sound is of one seen by Isleib on 27 February 1970 in Orca Bay.

There are no known breeding colonies within the region, although it apparently breeds in the closely adjacent Barren Islands (Sowl, pers. comm., and American Ornithologists' Union, 1957).

Estimates of populations utilizing the North Gulf Coast and Prince William Sound: yearly, a few, probably several, 10,000's.

Puffinus creatopus — Pink-footed Shearwater

The Pink-footed Shearwater appears to be an uncommon summer visitant in the inshore and offshore waters along the North Gulf Coast-Prince William Sound region.

Isleib saw several shearwaters on 26 June 1964 between 1 and 2 miles off Kokinhenik Bar, CRD, and identified two that came close as Pink-footed Shearwaters. On 21 June 1968 he saw one with several Sooty Shearwaters near the same location. Humberg (pers. comm.) tentatively identified a few Pink-footed Shearwaters offshore along the North Gulf Coast during the summers of 1968 and 1969, and he identified some 20+ of them among numerous other shearwaters on the Fairweather Bank on 16 September 1969. Sowl (pers. comm.), while flying U. S. Fish and Wildlife Service surveys in August 1971, saw a few Pink-footed Shearwaters a few miles off Latouche Island.

The above observations extend the known range of the Pink-footed Shearwater north to 60° N along the Alaskan coast, where it apparently wanders regularly into the waters of the North Gulf Coast from June through September.

Estimates of populations utilizing the waters along the North Gulf Coast: summer, a few, probably several, 100's.

Puffinus carneipes — Pale-footed Shearwater

The Pale-footed Shearwater is a casual summer visitant in the inshore and offshore waters along the North Gulf Coast-Prince William Sound region.

Pete and Ruth Isleib closely observed a single Pale-footed Shearwater 2 miles (3 km) off Ocean Cape on 21 July 1968. This individual was flying steadily westward paralleling the coast and passed within 200 ft. (60 m) of their vessel, giving excellent views of its field marks and flight characteristics.

Sowl (pers. comm.) saw one and possibly two others a few miles off Latouche Island during aerial surveys of Prince William Sound by the U. S. Fish and Wildlife Service in August 1971.

Closely adjacent to the region, 5-10 miles (8-16 km) off the southwest tip of the Kenai Peninsula, Dick Veit of New York City (in litt. to D. D. Gibson, 1972 and 1973) watched a Pale-footed Shearwater on 5 or 6 August 1972 sitting on the water 20-30 ft (6-9 m) from the ferry he was riding; "It was an entirely dark bird, having a pale, pinkish bill that was definitely that of a shearwater."

The above observations extend the known range of the Pale-footed Shearwater north to 60° N along the Alaskan coast.

Puffinus griseus — Sooty Shearwater

The Sooty Shearwater is an abundant summer visitant in the offshore waters along the North Gulf Coast, occurring less commonly in inshore waters and in Prince William Sound.

The most numerous southern latitude pelagic occurring in the region, this shearwater occurs regularly in the offshore waters, numbering from a few individuals to tremendous concentrations totaling millions of birds.

One concentration of Sooty Shearwaters between the Chugach Islands and the Barren Islands on 1 July 1965 was estimated at a minimum of 2,600,000 birds (Roseneau, unpubl. notes). A similar concentration of "square miles of sitting birds" was observed by Solf in Hinchinbrook Entrance during June 1965.

Isleib has seen Sooty Shearwaters uncommonly near the coast at Yakutat, Cape Suckling, Copper River Delta, and in the Prince William Sound area, the largest concentration on these inshore waters being 3,000+ birds in a fog near Southeast Breakers off Cape Suckling on 19 July 1968. Sowl (pers. comm.) found them fairly commonly in the waters about Montague Island during the U. S. Fish and Wildlife Service aerial surveys in August 1971.

Estimates of populations utilizing the North Gulf Coast and Prince William Sound: summer, 100,000's—in some years, 1,000,000's.

Puffinus tenuirostris — Slender-billed Shearwater

The Slender-billed Shearwater is an uncommon summer visitant in the inshore and offshore waters of the North Gulf Coast-Prince William Sound region.

Gabrielson and Lincoln (1959) cited numerous records and specimens from Kodiak Island westward and mentioned that the species occurs with some regularity in the Gulf of Alaska and south along the coast of western North America. The Slender-billed Shearwater is difficult to distinguish among the great flocks of similar Sooty Shearwaters that are often present. Isleib has seen the Slender-billed Shearwater only rarely—during late June, July, and August among Sooty Shearwaters off the Copper River Delta and during July and August in inshore and offshore waters off Montague Island. Sowl (pers. comm.) saw them more commonly among pelagics in the waters of Montague Strait during U. S. Fish and Wildlife Service aerial surveys of Prince William Sound in August 1971. Humberg (pers. comm.) saw them irregularly in offshore waters during the summers of 1968 and 1969, but found them numerous only once: on 16 September 1969, it was the most common pelagic about a trawler on the Fairweather Bank where Humberg saw hundreds in a hour, with only a few Sooty Shearwaters among them.

Slender-billed Shearwaters occur most frequently between May and September, but a specimen (UA 3322) collected 6 miles (10 km) north of Hinchinbrook Island in Orca Bay on 29 January 1970 indicates its occurrence, at least irregularly, outside of the summer season.

Estimates of populations utilizing the North Gulf Coast and Prince William Sound: summer, a few, possibly several, 1,000's.

Pterodroma inexpectata — Scaled Petrel

The Scaled Petrel is a casual summer visitant in the waters off the North Gulf Coast-Prince William Sound region.

Until recently, this southern latitude pelagic had been reported only twice in waters adjacent to the region of the North Gulf Coast: one at Kodiak, 11 June 1882, and one near Sitka, 17 May 1908 (Gabrielson and Lincoln, 1959). On 16 September 1969, however, Humberg (pers. comm.) observed three birds on the Fairweather Bank, which, based on his description, were probably Scaled Petrels. Richard J. Gordon, Alaska Department of Fish and Game, (in litt. to D. D. Gibson, 1970) saw one on the Fairweather Bank on 30 July 1970.

These petrels are probably more common than observations to date would indicate, perhaps annual in occurrence; they apparently are regular and common in the vicinity of the Alaskan Gyre, 500 miles (800 km) south of the North Gulf Coast-Prince William Sound region, where Gerald A. Sanger, University of Washington, (in litt. to D. D. Gibson, 1969) found during summer 1969 that "Peak abundance occurred about 350 miles [560 km] SSE of Kodiak Island, when they were present in densities of over 1 bird per linear mile . . . for a distance of 27 miles [45 km]."

Oceanodroma furcata — Fork-tailed Petrel

The Fork-tailed Petrel is a resident of the North Gulf Coast-Prince William Sound region, occurring seasonally as an abundant migrant, an abundant summer visitant-breeder, and a rare or irregular winter visitant.

Spring migrants apparently move north well offshore in the Gulf of Alaska and are not seen in inshore waters until May.

From May throughout the summer, Fork-tailed Petrels occur regularly in both the inshore and offshore waters of the region, being abundant from the outer coasts of Prince William Sound westward along the western North Gulf Coast. U. S. Fish and Wildlife Service surveys by boat 21 July-4 August 1972 estimated a total of almost 19,000 Fork-tailed Petrels in Prince William Sound and in the closely adjacent outer coastal waters; a large percentage of these petrels were in Prince William Sound, especially in the area of Montague Strait. The only known breeding colony in the region was located on 23 July 1972 by Isleib and Sowl on the Wooded Islands, PWS; colony size was undetermined. Other breeding sites undoubtedly exist between Cape St. Elias and the western North Gulf Coast, with the Chiswell Islands being a most likely locality. Roseneau (unpubl. notes) found this petrel breeding by the 10,000's in June 1965 on East Amatuli Island of the adjacent Barren Islands.

Fall migrants move mostly in offshore waters between mid-September and mid-November, but small numbers move southeast over the inshore waters. Storms in the Gulf of Alaska at this season regularly produce strong winds along the coastal areas which occasionally exceed 100 knots (185 kph), displacing thousands of Fork-tailed Petrels into the inshore waters. The birds then become common even to the heads of the bays, fiords, and inlets of Prince William Sound. The average date of these storm-induced movements into inshore waters is 10 October.

Robert Ingebo, Cordova resident who was mate on the Prince William Sound mail boat at the time, reported that Fork-tailed Petrels came aboard ship in mid-winter on several occasions between 1958 and 1962, apparently attracted by deck lights; these occurrences were most frequent after storms in the Gulf of Alaska between December and March and when the boat was anchored in the Montague Island-Latouche Island area. Isleib and George J. Divoky, U. S. Fish and Wildlife Service, observed a Fork-tailed Petrel between Lone Island and Naked Island on 30 March 1973.

Estimates of populations utilizing the North Gulf Coast and Prince William Sound: migration, several 100,000's, probably 1,000,000's; summer, a few, probably several, 10,000's; winter visitants, largely unknown, possibly a few 100's.

Oceanodroma leucorhoa — Leach's Petrel

The Leach's Petrel is probably an uncommon visitant, at least in summer, in the offshore waters of the North Gulf Coast-Prince William Sound region.

Although only a few of these petrels have been reported from the region, they are probably more common than the number of records would indicate; they are common both to the west and east of the region, although the North Gulf Coast-Prince William Sound region appears to be within a hiatus between the breeding ranges of the two subspecies (Gabrielson and Lincoln, 1959). On a 2-day cruise across the Gulf of Alaska, from Cape Spencer to Kodiak Island, D. D. Gibson (pers. comm.) saw four Leach's Petrels in the vicinity of the Fairweather Bank on 30 July 1970 and 15+ in the vicinity of the Portlock Bank on 31 July 1970. According to Gabrielson and Lincoln (1959), Alexander Wetmore saw "dark-colored petrels" between 29 May and 4 June 1911 in the Gulf of Alaska; and VanKammen (1916:172) saw a small flock of "whale birds" off of Yakutat on 25 May [year not given] which were "if my identification be correct, Leach's Petrel."

From closely adjacent areas, there is a skin of a Leach's Petrel in the Leningrad Museum from Kodiak collected 1 August 1843 (Gabrielson and Lincoln, 1959); and Gabrielson (1944), on 13 June 1940 between the Barren Islands and Afognak Island, saw a "dark-bodied bird" among Fork-tailed Petrels that he thought was probably a Leach's Petrel.

Estimates of populations utilizing the North Gulf Coast and Prince William Sound: summer, 100's, possibly 1,000's.

Phalacrocorax auritus — Double-crested Cormorant

The Double-crested Cormorant is a common resident along the North Gulf Coast and in Prince William Sound.

Spring migrants move along the coast from late March through May (most common in late April and early May), augmenting the numbers of wintering birds.

This cormorant is common during the summer and breeds at several locations along the North Gulf Coast. A few pairs breed at the large kittiwake colonies in Boswell Bay and along the seaward sides of Hinchinbrook and Wooded islands; Shortt (1939) found them fairly commonly in the Yakutat Bay area during the summer of 1936, with breeding colonies in Russell and Nunatak fiords; and, according to Shaffer, two pairs have bred for a number of years since 1962 at Caines Head in Resurrection Bay. Double-crested Cormorants, especially summering, nonbreeding immatures and subadults, are frequent visitants to freshwater.

Fall migrants are common from August until November along the coast, and they occasionally visit freshwater.

The number of winter visitants varies to some extent with the severity of weather during late fall and early winter. Censuses along the Cordova waterfront produced counts of 108 Double-crested Cormorants on 27 December 1969 after a mild and wet autumn and only 4 on 29 December 1971 after a normal autumn with occasional prolonged harsh weather conditions.

Estimates of populations utilizing the North Gulf Coast and Prince William Sound: migration, a few, possibly several, 10,000's; summer, several 1,000's; winter, a few 1,000's.

Phalacrocorax penicillatus — Brandt's Cormorant

The Brandt's Cormorant is a casual breeder in the North Gulf Coast-Prince William Sound region.

The only record of this cormorant in the region is of a small breeding colony at Seal Rocks, Hinchinbrook Entrance, located by Isleib and Sowl on 22 July 1972. Thirteen breeding-plumaged adults, four of them sitting on nests, were present among a colony of some 275 pairs of Black-legged Kittiwakes. No other species of cormorants were in the colony area.

In view of the fact that this record is the second for Alaska (first was a specimen taken by Grinnell at Forrester Island on 2 June 1917 [Gabrielson and Lincoln, 1959]) and the first breeding record, it is of interest to note that the site being utilized by the colony (Seal Rocks) was made habitable by uplift resulting from the 1964 earthquake; prior to the earthquake, these rocks were too heavily storm-washed for nesting birds.

Phalacrocorax pelagicus — Pelagic Cormorant

The Pelagic Cormorant is an abundant resident along the North Gulf Coast and in Prince William Sound.

This cormorant is abundant in the coastal waters throughout the year, usually occurring as scattered individuals and small flocks along the storm-washed, rugged coasts and in the larger bays and fiords, especially near good feeding areas and roost sites. Occasionally they congregate in groups of several hundreds. U. S. Fish and Wildlife Service surveys of Prince William Sound in both 1971 and 1972 estimated over 10,000 wintering cormorants, mostly Pelagics. Summering cormorants of all species in 1972 totaled an estimated 32,000+ individuals.

Considerable migratory movement and population shifts occur among Pelagic Cormorants along the outer coasts in April and again in September and October.

Shortt (1939) found Pelagic Cormorants abundant in the Yakutat area in 1936, with breeding colonies at Cape Enchantment and in Nunatak Fiord and numerous roosting sites throughout the area. Isleib has observed numerous small colonies in Prince William Sound, often associated with Black-legged Kittiwake colonies. Rausch (1958) reported it the second most abundant species of cliff-nesting bird (after Black-legged Kittiwake) on Middleton Island in 1956. Sowl (pers. comm.), while flying a survey of seabird colonies during August 1971, found numerous colonies totaling several 10,000's of cormorants along the coastline between Resurrection Bay and the Chugach Islands, most of which were undoubtedly this species.

Estimates of populations utilizing the North Gulf Coast and Prince William Sound: migration, probably several 10,000's; summer, several 10,000's; winter, a few, possibly several, 10,000's; total annual utilization, a few 100,000's.

Phalacrocorax urile — Red-faced Cormorant

The Red-faced Cormorant is an uncommon, local resident of the North Gulf Coast-Prince William Sound region.

Although they had not been identified in the region prior to 1969*, Red-faced Cormorants may make up a significant portion of the cormorant population along the western North Gulf Coast between southwestern Prince William Sound and the Chugach Islands; outside the breeding season, sightings have been recorded as far east as Cordova.

*The Red-faced Cormorant breeds in the Semidi Islands (Gabrielson and Lincoln, 1959); in Kukak Bay, Shelikof Strait (Gibson, 1970); in Kachemak Bay, southern Cook Inlet (pers. obs.); and is common and undoubtedly breeds in Chiniak Bay, northeastern Kodiak Island (Gibson, pers. comm.).

The species was first recorded in the region on 27 February 1969 when Isleib identified an adult among numerous wintering cormorants in Port Gravina, PWS; additionally, on 27 December 1969, he saw two roosting with numbers of Pelagic and Double-crested cormorants on Spike Island off the Cordova waterfront. He tentatively identified several Red-faced Cormorants between 25 February and 1 March 1971 in the southwestern portion of Prince William Sound while flying surveys with the U. S. Fish and Wildlife Service, and he saw one adult and an immature on the Cordova waterfront on 23 December 1972. Solf saw an adult in Port Etches, Hinchinbrook Island, on 15 September 1972.

A colony of Red-faced Cormorants was discovered at Pt. Elrington in southwestern Prince William Sound on 23 July 1972. Isleib and Sowl counted about 75 nests and estimated that there were about 300 Red-faced Cormorants at the colony, including both breeders and non-breeders. Only five Pelagic Cormorant nests were noted at the colony, and Red-faced outnumbered the Pelagics in the general area.

Estimates of populations utilizing the North Gulf Coast and Prince William Sound region: yearly, a few, probably several, 1,000's.

Ardea herodias – Great Blue Heron

The Great Blue Heron is an uncommon resident of the North Gulf Coast-Prince William Sound region.

The summer distribution of adults and the presence of immature birds in late summer suggest that small "heronries" (one to fewer than six pairs) occur in the coniferous forests near various sheltered, isolated lagoons and inlets and on islands well removed from human activities. The only verified report of nesting in the region, however, is that of J. B. Clock, lifelong resident of Prince William Sound, (pers. comm.) who found two nests at a forest-bog edge about a quarter of a mile (.4 km) from the head of St. Matthews Bay, Port Gravina, PWS, in the 1950's in early summer. The stick platforms were located in the tops of stunted, 6-inch (15-cm) dbh Sitka Spruce, and each held five eggs. In addition, Shortt (1939) was informed by local residents that there was a heronry near Humpback Creek near Yakutat in 1936, but he had no opportunity to verify its existence.

Great Blue Herons occur regularly throughout the North Gulf Coast-Prince William Sound region during post-breeding dispersal, when they appear regularly on the upper portions of the Copper River Delta, along the outer coasts, and extend irregularly to adjacent Cook Inlet. Shortt (1939) collected two and reported that they "became conspicuous" about Yakutat in late July and August 1936. U. S. Fish and Wildlife Service surveys in both 1971 and 1972 estimated approximately 100 resident Great Blue Herons in Prince William Sound.

Isleib watched a surprisingly hardy Great Blue Heron fly across the head of Resurrection Bay near Seward on 20 December 1961 when the temperature was -23°F (-31°C) and gale force winds were blowing out of the north!

Estimates of populations utilizing the North Gulf Coast and Prince William Sound: yearly, a few 100's.

Olor columbianus – Whistling Swan

The Whistling Swan is a common migrant and a casual summer and winter visitant along the North Gulf Coast and in Prince William Sound.

Spring migrants pass through the region from mid-April through mid-May (earliest, 12 on 15 April 1969 at Cordova). The peak of their northbound migration through the region is during the last days of April, at which time they become locally abundant. On the afternoon of 27 April and morning of 28 April 1971, an hourly average of approximately 500 Whistling Swans passed between Hawkins and Hinchinbrook islands, entering Prince William Sound from the Copper River Delta-eastern North Gulf Coast. Most of the spring migrants fly parallel to the eastern North Gulf Coast west to the Copper River Delta (the only heavily utilized staging area for Whistling Swans) and then utilize all three of the main migration paths across Prince William Sound. The upper and central paths are utilized most heavily, with relatively few birds following along the western portion of the North Gulf Coast around the Kenai Peninsula.

Shepherd (pers. comm.) has observed individuals and small groups of Whistling Swans lingering as summer visitants on the marshes of the Copper River Delta; these swans were non-breeders which remained until the fall migration. Shaffer watched two non-breeding adults from 25 May until 25 June 1963 on a pond at Mile 13 Seward Highway.

Fall migration is from mid-September until early November, with peak movements during the first half of October. Mostly, the swans use migration routes similar to those of the spring migration, but Kenneth Roberson, Alaska Department of Fish and Game, (pers. comm.) has reported seeing swans in the Chitina area migrating down the Copper River toward the delta. At least some of these swans were probably Whistling Swans rather than the locally breeding Trumpeter Swans, because some of Roberson's observations were during October and Trumpeters normally leave the upper Copper River Valley by late September.

Winter visitants are apparently casual. Local outdoorsmen have reported that Whistlers occasionally overwinter, but the only recent record is of an adult which attempted overwintering with Trumpeter Swans at the outflow of Eyak Lake during the winter of 1970-71 and was found dead in mid-February 1971.

Estimates of populations utilizing the North Gulf Coast and Prince William Sound: migration, a few 10,000's; summer and winter, a few individuals.

Olor buccinator — Trumpeter Swan

The Trumpeter Swan is a locally common resident of the freshwater areas of the eastern North Gulf Coast, an uncommon migrant and visitant in Prince William Sound, and casual along the western North Gulf Coast.

During much of this century, this large swan was considered a vanishing and endangered species, although individuals were probably never as few as was widely reported in the 1930's and 1940's. In the mid-1950's the Trumpeter Swan was "rediscovered" as the breeding swan in southcentral Alaska (Monson, 1956). The population along the eastern North Gulf Coast drainages has increased during the past 30 years, and late summer surveys by the U. S. Fish and Wildlife Service in 1968 yielded counts of 660 adults and 362 cygnets in an estimated 2,080 sq miles (8,030 km^2) from Yakataga to and including the Copper River Delta (Hansen et al., 1971).

The first spring migrants usually arrive on the Copper River Delta during the last week of March, and they are common by the second week of April. A few flocks of Trumpeter Swans and mixed flocks of swans migrate across Prince William Sound between mid-April and early May, usually at lower elevations than the pure flocks of Whistling Swans.

Nesting is confined largely to the coastal plains and drainages from Yakataga west through the Copper River Delta, possibly to the Gravina River

Valley, PWS. Most breeding pairs are at their nest sites by early May. Hansen et al. (1971) found the mean size of 53 completed clutches to be 4.9 eggs, with the date of the first egg varying in different years from 28 April to 11 May; first hatching dates varied from 16 to 29 June. Small flocks of non-breeding birds (immatures, subadults, and unmated adults) occur regularly during the summer on Bering Lake and the lacustrine waters of the Copper River Delta.

In late summer and early fall, large numbers of Trumpeter Swans congregate on ponds and marshes along the coast. Most of them depart by mid-October, but in some years numbers remain until freeze-up in November. Some of the swans migrating across Prince William Sound during September are probably Trumpeter Swans, as they appear as family group-sized flocks prior to the large flights of those identified as Whistling Swans.

A few family groups winter on the open, freshwater outlets of Eyak Lake and Martin Lake and locally elsewhere if suitable conditions exist. Shaffer watched an immature Trumpeter Swan along the Seward waterfront 14 - 30 January 1972. These swans are temporarily driven to saltwater during extremely cold periods when freshwater locations freeze. Some 10 to 40 birds have wintered annually at these locations in recent years, and it appears that there is not enough additional area for an enlarged wintering population without utilization of saltwater.

Estimates of populations utilizing the North Gulf Coast and Prince William Sound: migration, a few 1,000's; summer, a few 1,000's; winter, a few 10's.

Branta canadensis — Canada Goose

The Canada Goose is a resident of the North Gulf Coast-Prince William Sound region, occurring seasonally as an abundant migrant, locally abundant breeder, and locally uncommon winter resident.

Behaviorally, there appear to be four identifiable populations of Canada Geese utilizing the region; three of these apparently represent reasonably distinct subspecific taxa (as described by Delacour, 1951), but the fourth remains an enigma.

Spring migrants are present from late March to late May. *B. c. occidentalis,* the main breeding population, begin arriving during the last days of March or the first days of April, and they are abundant on the Copper River Delta by late April. Migrant *B. c. taverneri* are fairly common from mid-April through early May. A few flocks of *B. c. minima* occur from late April to late May, associated at times with Black Brant. *B. c. minima* are the only ones that regularly migrate offshore and around the Kenai Peninsula. At times, migrant flocks are composed of what appears to be a variety of birds with visually different subspecific characteristics.

Canada Geese nest from the Bering River area and the Copper River Delta and their drainages westward through Prince William Sound to the adjacent upper Cook Inlet region. They appear to be largely absent from the western North Gulf Coast, although Shaffer reported six breeding pairs at Lost Lake, Resurrection Valley, and two breeding pairs at Paradise Lake in June 1969. Shortt (1939) saw migrant flocks as late as 16 May 1936 in the Yakutat area, but he found no evidence of breeding, although natives claimed that they nested in the Situk Lake area. Hansen (1962) reported that a few non-breeding *B. c. occidentalis* utilize a few bays near Yakutat for molting, but apparently do not breed there.

A large segment of the estimated 35,000+ population (see Chapman et al., 1969) of *B. c. occidentalis* breeds on the Copper River Delta, where densities in prime habitat have been recorded at 108 nests per sq mile (Hansen, 1962). The peak of nesting on the Copper River Delta in 1959 was between 21 May and 6 June (Hansen, 1962), with the major hatching occurring between 11 and 22 June (Trainer, 1959). An uplift of 6.2 ft (1.89 m) of the main Canada Goose nesting areas on the Copper River Delta, caused by the 1964 earthquake, seems likely to result in progressively more restricted nesting habitat, at least over the next few decades, and hence possibly a reduced breeding population (Crow, 1971).

Fall migration occurs from September to mid-November. *B. c. occidentalis* begin leaving the Copper River Delta in late September and most are gone by the end of October. Fall migrant *B. c. taverneri* are fairly common in the Copper River Delta area during September and, for a short period of time, usually in early October, they are abundant. Shaffer has seen numbers stopping to rest in Resurrection Valley, both in spring and fall. Fall migrant *taverneri* enter the region in greatest numbers from the upper and central portions of Cook Inlet through the Kenai and Chugach mountains. A few flocks, presumably of *B. c. taverneri,* occur irregularly in November (latest, flock of 120 on 18 November 1971 at Cordova, migrating eastward). The diminutive *B. c. minima* is uncommon during September but occasionally, especially during poor weather in the Gulf of Alaska, becomes fairly common in early October, arriving on the North Gulf Coast from both the Cook Inlet region and the Kodiak-Alaska Peninsula region; it rarely lingers. Most migrant *B. c. minima* apparently are trans-Gulf migrants, flying over the open seas between the Alaska Peninsula and their southern wintering grounds (Nelson and Hansen, 1959).

The fourth population utilizing the region (i.e., in addition to *B. c. occidentlias, B. c. taverneri,* and *B. c. minima*) is found in Prince William Sound. For years, on the basis of geographic distribution, these birds have been presumed to be *B. c. occidentalis.* Behaviorally, however, they show striking similarities to *B. c. fulva,* the resident Canada Goose of southeastern Alaska. A population of perhaps a few thousand birds nests in the coniferous forests at or near the coast of the mainland and larger islands of Prince William Sound and summers on nearby upland meadows — habitat niches nearly identical to those used by *B. c. fulva.* A few to several hundred wintering Canada Geese, apparently the northernmost wintering geese in North America, remain on the tidal flats of several of the bays, inlets, and fiords of Prince William Sound — habitation more typical of *B. c. fulva* than of the highly migratory *B. c. occidentalis.* Four specimens collected on 27 May 1970 by Julius Reynolds, Alaska Department of Fish and Game, and examined by John W. Aldrich, U. S. Fish and Wildlife Service, proved to be larger than typical *B. c. occidentalis,* and Aldrich has suggested that they may be intermediates between *B. c. fulva* and *B. c. occidentalis* (in litt. to Phillip D. Havens, 1971). The problem of the identity and discreteness of this Prince William Sound population offers a potentially rewarding opportunity for future study.

Estimates of populations utilizing the North Gulf Coast and Prince William Sound: migration, several, 10,000's, possibly 100,000's; summer, a few 10,000's; winter, a few to several 100's; total annual utilization, several 10,000's, possibly 100,000's.

Branta nigricans — Black Brant

The Black Brant is a fairly common spring migrant, a rare summer visitant, and a rare fall migrant in the North Gulf Coast-Prince William Sound region.

Most spring migrants apparently by-pass the North Gulf Coast by flying directly across the Gulf of Alaska, although many pass through the region's offshore waters between early April and early May (reported by several crab fishermen in these waters at this time in 1972). Some reach these offshore waters weeks before they show up closer to the coast. A movement through inshore waters occurs during late April and early May (earliest, 40 on 18 April 1973 at Port Chalmers, Montague Island, by Solf, and 19 on 23 April 1969 at Hartney Bay, Orca Inlet), during which time they are fairly common along the North Gulf Coast and range uncommonly into the bays and fiords of Prince William Sound. Some apparently cross the Kenai Mountains into adjacent upper Cook Inlet, where they are seen occasionally in spring (L. J. Peyton, pers. comm.; and pers. obs.).

In many years, this coastal migration is essentially completed by 20 May, with only a few flocks observed thereafter. In some years, however, substantial numbers of migrants pass through during late May and early June. During 1963, for example, numerous flocks of hundreds of brant, totaling an estimated 8,000 to 10,000 birds, flew westward along the barrier islands of the Copper River Delta between 20 and 24 May, and an estimated 3,000 to 5,000 birds passed between 26 May and 1 June. Similar numbers of late migrants were present during 1967, 1968, and 1971. Many of these late birds are undoubtedly subadults and non-breeders, and some are mixed in flocks with Snow and Canada geese that stop regularly to rest and feed on the tidal flats and marshes of the delta. Between late May and mid-June 1971, Shaffer saw flocks of late migrants at Seward and a pair inland at Moose Pass on the Kenai Peninsula.

A few stragglers may remain in the region as summer visitants. Rausch (1958) saw two brant on 11 June and again on 12 June, three on 16 June, and a single bird on 27 June 1956 on Middleton Island. Brant regularly linger along the barrier islands of the Copper River Delta after mid-June, usually in flocks of fewer than ten birds. Most of these late birds appear eventually to move westward along the coast and are probably very late, non-breeding stragglers from spring migration; occasional individuals, however, spend the summer in the region.

Fall migrants along the North Gulf Coast are rare, most brant apparently flying directly across the North Pacific (Robert D. Jones, U. S. Fish and Wildlife Service, pers. comm.). A few occur in offshore waters, irregularly along outer coastal points, and along the barrier islands off the Copper River Delta from mid-August to October. Isleib shot one at the head of Resurrection Bay on 28 October 1962, and, according to local hunter Les Maxwell (pers. comm.), hunters on the marshes of the Copper River Delta see or shoot an occasional brant during October.

There are no records of wintering Black Brant along the North Gulf Coast, but Gabrielson and Lincoln (1959) reported winter records from the adjacent Cook Inlet and Kodiak regions; hence, an occasional winter occurrence along the western portion of the North Gulf Coast can be expected.

Estimates of populations utilizing the North Gulf Coast and Prince William Sound: migration-spring, a few, probably several, 10,000's; migration-fall, 10's, possibly 100's; summer, 10's.

Philacte canagica — Emperor Goose

The Emperor Goose is a rare migrant and rare winter visitant along the North Gulf Coast and in Prince William Sound.

Over the years, in late April and early May, small numbers of spring migrants, mixed with other migrant waterfowl, have been reported by several local outdoorsmen, making it appear that they are probably regular in small numbers during this period. West, Peyton, and Isleib saw three Emperors with a flock of

100+ White-fronted Geese on 4 May 1970 on Egg Island, CRD. Peter Fridgen, Alaska Department of Fish and Game, (pers. comm.) saw six at Grass Island Slough, CRD, on 10 May 1970. Solf saw a pair of adults on a brackish-water pond near Martin River Slough, CRD, during early July 1954. This last observation is unusually late and may represent summering non-breeders.

Fall hunters reportedly have shot or seen occasional (once or twice in 10 years) Emperor Geese at various localities throughout the region during October and November. Three Emperor Geese were shot by local hunters Frank L. Hoover and Sam Manuel near Eyak River on the Copper River Flats on 1 October 1954 (Les Maxwell, pers. comm.). An adult male and two immature males, "recently shot" near Seward, were brought to Shaffer on 21 November 1971. Gabrielson and Lincoln (1959:130) reported a winter record on the basis of a 13 November 1930 letter by Terhune which stated that "a large flock was noted 'recently' on the Copper River Flats and that 'a number' were secured." This 1930 flock, however, was more likely a migrant flock in early or mid-October, because the Copper River Flats are not habitable for wintering geese and are mostly devoid of waterfowl after the third week of October.

Wintering birds were reported by O'Farrell and Sheets (1962) on Middleton Island, where five were seen on 25 and 26 February 1961. Isleib observed two overwintering birds that were present from January until the second week of March 1969 on the tide flats of Orca Inlet. Also, fishermen and trappers reportedly have seen others irregularly in winter along the outer islands and coasts of Prince William Sound and the North Gulf Coast.

The cumulative observations do not add up to many birds but do indicate that the Emperor Goose may occur at almost any time from October through mid-May along the North Gulf Coast.

Estimates of populations utilizing the North Gulf Coast and Prince William Sound: migration and winter, a few individuals, probably a few 10's.

Anser albifrons — White-fronted Goose

The White-fronted Goose is a common migrant along the North Gulf Coast and in Prince William Sound, where it utilizes almost exclusively the Bering River and Copper River delta areas.

Spring migrants arrive in late April (earliest, 37 on 23 April 1969), are locally common during early May, and usually have departed by the end of the third week of May. A late flock of 40 birds lingered on the Copper River Delta, however, on 28 May 1963, and Gabrielson (Gabrielson and Lincoln, 1959) saw five there on 10 June 1940. The spring migrants usually linger only briefly on their northward flight, and they do not build up large concentrations as they do in the fall.

The spring migration route of the White-fronted Goose (known locally as "Yellow-legs") through the region is principally along the eastern North Gulf Coast to the Copper River Delta, thence west and northwest across Prince William Sound, over the Kenai and Chugach mountains, and into adjacent Cook Inlet.

The only summer report is of one flushed from Whiskey Pete Slough, CRD, on 22 July 1962 by Yocom (1963). White-fronts may breed occasionally on the Copper River Delta, since they have been recorded breeding in a similar habitat along Turnagain Arm in Cook Inlet (Gabrielson and Lincoln, 1959; Phillip D. Havens, Alaska Department of Fish and Game, pers. comm.).

Many fall migrants follow the reverse of their spring migration routes through the region, but others utilize the trans-Gulf route over the offshore waters of the Gulf of Alaska and the North Pacific (Gabrielson and Lincoln, 1959). Fall migrants begin arriving on the Copper River Delta during the first half of August (earliest, a small flock on 1 August 1959 at Pete Dahl Slough, CRD [Shepherd, pers. field notes]); and the majority pass through the region within 10 days of 1 September, rarely being seen after mid-September (latest, three shot mid-October 1957, two shot mid-October 1958, and one shot 22 October 1969, all on the Copper River marshes [Les Maxwell, pers. comm.]). Every fall large numbers of White-fronted Geese congregate on the marshes of the eastern portion of the Copper River Delta and, to a lesser extent, on the Bering River flats. Gabrielson and Lincoln (1959: 135) cite "a concentration estimated at 100,000 birds . . . along the east bank of the Martin River [CRD] . . . on September 5, 1928." The only reported concentration in recent years exceeding 30,000 birds is that by Solf of approximately 100,000 White-fronted Geese on the flats of the Bering River between 1 and 4 September 1957; this concentration built up during a period of easterly winds and departed en masse on 4 September when the winds shifted to the west.

Estimates of populations utilizing the North Gulf Coast and Prince William Sound: migration-spring, a few to several 10,000's; migration-fall, a few to several 10,000's — in some years, 100,000's.

Chen hyperborea — Snow Goose

The Snow Goose is a common migrant along the North Gulf Coast and in Prince William Sound.

Spring migrants are commonly seen on and over the Copper River Delta between 20 April and 5 May (earliest, several hundred birds in two flocks on 15 April 1973, 15 miles off the Copper River Delta, and 37 on 17 April 1969 over the Copper River Delta). Occasionally, a few large flocks appear later (70 on 23 May 1963); irregularly, singles or a few individuals occur into early June (one with Black Brant on 29 May 1963 on the Copper River Delta; three with migrating Canada [Cackling] Geese on 7 June 1968 offshore from the Copper River Delta). Steven R. Smith, local fisherman/photographer/biologist, (pers. comm.) saw numerous flocks of geese, including this species, migrating over the Situk River-Yakutat area during the first week of May 1969. Gabrielson and Lincoln (1959: 139) reported that Snow Geese have been observed "moving up the Copper River as far as Copper Center" (upper Copper River Valley). Migrant Snow Geese in the region principally utilize the route along the eastern North Gulf Coast to the Copper River Delta, thence west across Prince William Sound, over the Kenai Mountains, and into adjacent Cook Inlet. Fall migration reverses this route.

Fall migrants rarely are present before late September (earliest, three on 26-28 August 1971 at Cottonwood Point, CRD, by Les Maxwell and Peter Fridgen [pers. comm.], and seven on 14 September 1967 at Grass Island Slough, CRD) and are locally abundant (numbers dependent on weather conditions to the north and west) on the Copper River Delta sometime between late September and mid-October (latest, 31 on 27 October 1968 over Cordova). Their arrivals and departures are often paralleled by similar numbers of Whistling Swans. Most fall migrants on the Copper River Delta prefer the outer grass flats, where, at times, they congregate in large flocks of a few to several thousand birds.

Estimates of populations utilizing the North Gulf Coast and Prince William Sound: migration, a few 10,000's — in some falls, several 10,000's.

Anas platyrhynchos — Mallard

The Mallard is a common resident of the North Gulf Coast-Prince William Sound region; it is an abundant migrant, a fairly common breeder, and a common winter visitant.

The Mallard, while not as numerous as some of the other dabbling ducks, is more regularly encountered in a wider range of habitats than any of the others. Spring migrants are abundant during late April-early May.

Shepherd (1959) found six nests (av. clutch, 8.0 eggs) and six broods (av. size of four Class I broods, 5.3 chicks) on the Copper River Delta in 1959; nesting began during the first week of May and the peak of hatch was 10 June. Gabrielson (Gabrielson and Lincoln, 1959) saw a female with 11 young that were about 10 days old on 10 June 1940 on the Copper River Delta. Yocom (1963) saw several females with young in the same area on 11 and 12 July 1962. The Alexander Expedition (Grinnell, 1910a) reported a few Mallards at the head of Cordova Bay (Orca Inlet) and thought there was good evidence of breeding. Shortt (1939) thought it bred during the summer of 1936 at Situk Lake and on Russell Fiord, where he collected two immature males on 5 August 1936. Shaffer has found it breeding in the vicinity of Seward, where it is resident throughout the year.

Fall migrants are common from late August until mid-October. During winter months the Mallard is conspicuous in flocks on the tidal flats and beaches of the bays, fiords, and inlets in Prince William Sound and along the North Gulf Coast. It also winters in freshwater areas that remain unfrozen.

U. S. Fish and Wildlife Service surveys of Prince William Sound estimated some 15,000 Mallards during the first week of May 1971, a few hundred during late July-early August, approximately 8,000 during the first week in October, and in excess of 3,000 wintering birds in February 1972.

Estimates of populations utilizing the North Gulf Coast and Prince William Sound: migration, a few, possibly several, 10,000's; summer, a few 1,000's; winter, several 1,000's, possibly a few 10,000's.

Anas strepera — Gadwall

The Gadwall is a fairly common local resident along the North Gulf Coast and in Prince William Sound.

Spring migrants are fairly common on the grass flats of the Copper River Delta and uncommon on the tidal flats and marshes elsewhere in the region. Migrants pass through the region from the third week of April until mid-May and are usually associated with other dabbling ducks.

Gadwalls are fairly common throughout the summer in several areas on the grass flats of the Copper River Delta. Olson (1953) reported on observations of two nests and four broods found in the Pete Dahl Slough area, CRD, during June and July 1953. The eleven eggs of one nest all hatched successfully on 7 July, but one chick died before leaving the nest; only four chicks were with the hen on 18 July. Of two broods enumerated on 30 July 1953, one contained four chicks and the other, eleven. Isleib flushed young barely able to fly in the Grass Island Slough area in mid-August 1968 and in the Copper Slough area in mid-August 1970. Yocom (1963) saw Gadwalls fairly commonly on the Copper River Delta during July 1962 but did not see broods. A few Gadwalls may breed also in Prince William Sound, possibly near where they winter regularly at Port Fidalgo and Port Wells. Shaffer found a pair and nest at Thumb Cove, Resurrection Bay, on 16 May 1970.

Although common on the Copper River Delta during the fall, the Gadwall is uncommon or rare elsewhere along the North Gulf Coast. Gabrielson (Gabrielson and Lincoln, 1959) found it common on the grass flats of the Copper River Delta on 27 September 1941, ranking it next to American Widgeon in total numbers. Lingering regularly into October, they are one of the latest dabbling ducks to migrate.

Large flocks winter at Coghill Flats in Port Wells and at the head of Port Fidalgo. A few occur less regularly in winter at Orca Inlet, Port Gravina, Unakwik Inlet, and at other locations in Port Wells.

Estimates of populations utilizing the North Gulf Coast and Prince William Sound: migration, a few 1,000's; summer, several 100's, possibly a few 1,000's; winter, several 100's.

Anas acuta – Pintail

The Pintail is a resident of the North Gulf Coast-Prince William Sound region, occurring seasonally as an abundant migrant, a common breeder, and a rare winter visitant.

Spring migration extends over a longer period than with other waterfowl. The Pintail is one of the earliest migrants, arriving regularly in early April; flocks are still moving northwestward in early June, making them also one of the latest spring migrants. During the height of movement in late April and early May, it is by far the most abundant species of waterfowl in the region. Isleib counted 5,500 birds per hour passing along a migratory path through Hawkins Cutoff throughout the afternoon of 27 April 1971, and he has seen several hundreds per hour utilizing this route as late as the first week of June. Large numbers of Pintails migrate far offshore, and apparently many migrate westward off the North Gulf Coast and around the Kenai Peninsula. This offshore route is seldom used by other migrant dabbling ducks.

The Pintail is one of the most common breeding dabblers on the Copper River Delta, and it is a regular, though less common, breeder elsewhere within the region. In 1959, on the Copper River Delta, Shepherd (1959) located 76 nests (av. clutch, 6.5 eggs) and 36 broods (av. size 22 Class I broods, 4.5 chicks; 10 Class II, 5.8 chicks); nesting began during the first week of May 1959, and the peak of hatch was 10 June. Rausch (1958) saw Pintails frequently on a large pond on Middleton Island in 1956 and saw two broods on 11 June. Shortt (1939) considered it the commonest dabbling duck in the Yakutat area during the summer of 1936.

A few males, possibly local birds, appear on the outer beaches and tidal flats in mid-June and are regularly seen in flocks by early July. Flocks, composed mostly of males, are fairly common along the outer coasts through July and early August. During mid- and late August the flocks become abundant, and they include increasing numbers of females and/or juveniles during late August and early September.

Although Pintails are abundant during the fall on the marshes of the Copper River Delta, most of the large migrant flocks pass swiftly through the region and utilize the tidal flats and beaches if they stop. Pintails are abundant locally until mid-October, and most of the fall migrants have departed by early November.

Small numbers winter in Prince William Sound, usually associated with larger numbers of Mallards and Gadwalls on the tidal flats at Orca Inlet, Port

Fidalgo, Unakwik Inlet, Port Wells, and probably elsewhere along the North Gulf Coast in sheltered bays and inlets.

Estimates of populations utilizing the North Gulf Coast and Prince William Sound: migration, several 100,000's, probably 1,000,000's; summer, a few, probably several, 1,000's; winter, a few 100's.

Anas carolinensis — Green-winged Teal

The Green-winged Teal is a resident of the North Gulf Coast-Prince William Sound region, occurring seasonally as an abundant migrant, a fairly common breeder, and a rare winter visitant.

Spring migrants are abundant or common through most of the region's tidal flats and marshes. Migration begins in mid-April (earliest, two on 16 April 1969 at Hartney Bay, Orca Inlet) and extends into late May. They are most numerous in late April on the marshes of the Copper River Delta, occurring as pairs and small flocks.

The Green-winged Teal breeds as scattered pairs throughout most of the region's suitable habitats, but it is probably most common on the upper grass flats and the willow-alder brush flats of the Copper River Delta. Shortt (1939) saw males almost daily in the Situk River area in June 1936. Gabrielson (Gabrielson and Lincoln, 1959) saw it as a "particularly plentiful bird" in the Copper River drainage areas on many occasions. Rausch (1958) saw a pair and several adults on many occasions in June 1956 on Middleton Island and believed it was breeding. Shepherd (pers. field notes) found a nest on Pete Dahl Slough, CRD, with six eggs on 10 June 1959; later that summer, he saw three broods, including one of seven downies on 6 July on Castle Slough, CRD. Isleib has seen a few teal broods during late June and early July between Mile 7 and Mile 23 of the Copper River Highway east of Cordova.

Small groups of males regularly frequent the outer tidal flats of the Copper River Delta after mid-July, becoming fairly common in August. Most migrants appear in late August and early September on the tide flats and occasionally occur in flocks totaling a few to several hundred birds. A large flock of over 1,200 birds was present in Shipyard Bay, Orca Inlet, on 11 September 1971. Fall migrants become uncommon by late September - early October, and most Green-winged Teal have departed by late October.

Winter visitants are rare in Prince William Sound. They occur as occasional individuals and small flocks mixed with other dabbling ducks wintering on the tide flats in Port Wells, Unakwik Inlet, Port Fidalgo, Orca Inlet, and probably elsewhere along the North Gulf Coast in sheltered bays and inlets.

Estimates of populations utilizing the North Gulf Coast and Prince William Sound: migration, a few, probably several, 10,000's; summer, a few, possibly several, 1,000's; winter, several 10's, probably a few 100's.

Anas discors — Blue-winged Teal

The Blue-winged Teal is a rare migrant and probable breeder in the North Gulf Coast-Prince William Sound region.

A few spring observations of this teal have been reported: Solf saw a male at Cannery Creek, Unakwik Inlet, with a group of Green-winged Teal during the first week of May 1959. Isleib saw three Blue-winged Teal flying westward near Montague Point, Montague Island, on 17 May 1963. Johnson (pers. field notes) observed a flock of eight at the Yakutat Airport on 8 June 1966 and an adult male was collected (UA 2478). Shaffer saw an adult male at Seward on 12 June 1971.

There are no breeding records within the region, but Shepherd (pers. field notes) saw a pair on the Copper River Delta on 29 June 1959, and Shaffer observed a pair that successfully raised four young in 1971 at Mile 13 Seward Highway, one mile outside the region.

Hunters report Blue-winged Teal every fall on the Copper River Delta. Fisherman Richard Jennings (pers. comm.) found them fairly common near Cottonwood Point in late August-early September 1969, when he remembers shooting "a bag limit" of these teal during the first week of September. Blue-winged Teal are occasionally taken by hunters in other portions of the Copper River Delta's grass flats, and in 1969 it was reported from many areas on these marshes. The latest fall report is of a female shot by Dean Curran, local hunter, on 18 October 1971 on the Copper River Delta.

Estimates of populations utilizing the North Gulf Coast and Prince William Sound: migration-spring, a few individuals, possibly 10's; migration-fall, several 10's — in some years, a few 100's.

Mareca penelope — European Widgeon

The European Widgeon is a casual (perhaps rare) migrant through the North Gulf Coast-Prince William Sound region.

Isleib observed a lone male on 23 April 1961 on the tide flats at the head of Resurrection Bay near Seward and a male, in company with American Widgeons, on 4 May 1971 in Harrison Lagoon near the entrance of Harriman Fiord, PWS. Shepherd (in litt., 1973) reported seeing a male about 5 May 1958 on Big Glacier Slough, CRD.

Les Maxwell, local hunter, (pers. comm.) reported that, over a period of many years, hunters have shot an occasional European Widgeon on the Copper River Delta. The only specific record, however, is of a male shot on the Copper River Flats during the first week of October 1960 (Jim H. Branson, U. S. Fish and Wildlife Service, pers. comm.).

Estimates of populations utilizing the North Gulf Coast and Prince William Sound: migration, probably a few individuals.

Mareca americana — American Widgeon

The American Widgeon is a resident of the North Gulf Coast-Prince William Sound region, occurring seasonally as an abundant migrant, a fairly common breeder, and a rare winter visitant.

Spring migrants arrive as early as mid-April (earliest, seven on 16 April 1969 at Hartney Bay, Orca Inlet), are abundant in late April and early May, and are fairly common until late May. The American Widgeon is regularly mixed with the more numerous Pintail and utilizes the same migration paths, a few even occurring in the flocks of Pintails that migrate off the coast.

Shortt (1939) found it an uncommon breeder in the Yakutat area; Gabrielson (Gabrielson and Lincoln, 1959) reported it as a fairly common breeder on the Copper River Delta; Shepherd (1959) recorded three broods on the Copper River Delta in 1959; and Isleib found two broods, one of five and one of eight downy young, on 14 June 1968 along Grass Island Slough, CRD.

Fall migrants appear on the tide flats of the Copper River Delta in mid-August and are abundant in September. Post-breeding widgeon, in compact flocks of several hundred birds, appear on the Copper River Delta in mid-September and are common until mid-October; a few small flocks are regular until early November. American Widgeon occur regularly as fall migrants, in flocks of up to 100 birds, at the head of Resurrection Bay during September (Shaffer, pers. comm.).

A few individuals and small flocks winter with other dabbling ducks on the tidal flats in Prince William Sound (mostly on the tidal flats at the head of Port Fidalgo and at Coghill River in Port Wells) and rarely elsewhere.

Estimates of populations utilizing the North Gulf Coast and Prince William Sound: migration, a few, probably several, 10,000's; summer, several 100's, possibly a few 1,000's; winter, a few 100's.

Spatula clypeata – Shoveler

The Shoveler is a fairly common migrant and a locally common breeder along the North Gulf Coast and in Prince William Sound.

Spring migrants arrive on the Copper River Delta as early as the third week of April (earliest, two on 21 April 1969 at Mile 21 Copper River Highway), and are fairly common from early May until early June. Migrant Shovelers often occur in mixed flights with Pintails and Mallards.

In summer, Shovelers are conspicuous and are among the most numerous breeding dabblers on the marshes of the Copper River Delta. They were reported as common by both Gabrielson (Gabrielson and Lincoln, 1959) in 1940 and Yocom (1963) in 1962, and Shepherd (1959), in 1959, found 13 nests (av. clutch, 8.9 eggs) and 15 broods (av. size 14 Class I broods, 6.7 chicks). Shepherd (ibid.) estimated the earliest nesting began on 25 May 1959 and recorded the peak of hatch as 10 July. On 27 June 1959 he recorded (pers. field notes) a flock composed of 70 male and 2 female Shovelers. These 1959 dates appear relatively late for this species, especially in view of its spring arrival time.

Isleib has observed scattered pairs, probably breeding, in Prince William Sound during the summer. Grinnell (1910a), however, did not list it from Prince William Sound in 1908, nor did Shortt (1939) record it from the Yakutat area in 1936. Possibly this species is more widespread at present than earlier in this century.

Fall migrants begin appearing on the tidal flats along the coast in mid-August. They are fairly common until early October on the Copper River Delta (latest, three in Port Wells, PWS, on 10 October 1971, and two on the Copper River Delta on 21 October 1968). During early September it is one of the most frequently shot waterfowl on the Copper River Delta.

Although no Shovelers have yet been reported during winter, it seems likely that a few may winter occasionally with other dabblers on the fiord tidal flats of Prince William Sound.

Estimates of populations utilizing the North Gulf Coast and Prince William Sound: migration, a few, probably several, 1,000's; summer, several 100's, mostly on the Copper River Delta.

Aythya americana – Redhead

The Redhead is casual, reported in the North Gulf Coast-Prince William Sound region only from the Copper River Delta.

Shepherd (pers. field notes) saw a pair of Redheads and collected the female at Pete Dahl Slough, CRD, on 26 May 1959 (Wash. State Univ. 59-404). Les Maxwell, local hunter, (pers. comm.) reported that three Redheads were shot in this same area in early October 1969.

Aythya collaris — Ring-necked Duck

The Ring-necked Duck is a rare spring migrant in the North Gulf Coast-Prince William Sound region.

A few pairs or individuals have appeared every spring since 1966 (earliest, two on 26 April 1969 at Mile 11 Copper River Highway; largest number, eight on 7 May 1969 at Eyak Lake; latest, one on 23 May 1971 at Eyak Lake).

The Ring-necked Duck recently has been reported breeding in adjacent upper Cook Inlet (two females with broods July 1971, Willard A. Troyer, U. S. Fish and Wildlife Service [pers. comm.]) and should be looked for as a possible breeder in the North Gulf Coast - Prince William Sound region.

A few Ring-necked Ducks probably occur as fall migrants, although they have escaped notice thus far. Other than Canvasback and "scaup," *Aythya* rarely are differentiated by the hunters on the Copper River Delta.

Estimates of populations utilizing the North Gulf Coast and Prince William Sound: migration-spring, a few to several individuals, probably a few 10's.

Aythya valisineria — Canvasback

The Canvasback is an uncommon migrant and a local breeder in the North Gulf Coast-Prince William Sound region.

Small flocks of spring migrants occur uncommonly on freshwater lakes and in saltwater bays and fiords during the first three weeks of May, most frequently in mid-May. Shortt (1939) saw a few individuals at Yakutat on 18 and 19 May 1936. Lyon et al. (unpubl. notes) saw a flock of 16 at Whittier on 16 May 1954. Johnson (pers. field notes) saw a flock of 20+ at Martin Lake east of the Copper River 16-18 May 1968.

Breeding in the region has been reported only from the Copper River Delta, where apparently substantial numbers occur on the marshes of the Pete Dahl Slough area. During late June 1971, while flying several times over the area in a light aircraft, Isleib saw several small flocks, mostly of males, and one flock of about 60 males. Shepherd (1959), working in this area in 1959, found nine nests (av. clutch, 7.4 eggs) and four broods (av. four Class I broods, 5.8 chicks); he reported that earliest nesting began 25 May and that the hatching peak came 10 July. Yocom (1963) saw a female with a brood of two young about 3 weeks old on 21 July 1962 on these same marshes.

Fall migrants also have been reported only from the Copper River Delta-Cordova area, and, again, mostly from the Pete Dahl Slough marsh area. Most of the local breeders appear to leave during the first days of September. Migrant Canvasbacks appear in late September and early Ocotber, and, according to Peter Fridgen, Alaska Department of Fish and Game, (pers. comm.) they generally depart by mid-October. During the first week of October 1969, hunters shot 53 Canvasbacks from a flight of several hundred on the Walhalla Slough marshes of the Copper River Delta (ibid.).

Estimates of populations utilizing the North Gulf Coast and Prince William Sound: migration, several 100's; summer, a few 100's.

Aythya marila — Greater Scaup

The Greater Scaup is a resident of the North Gulf Coast-Prince William Sound region, occurring seasonally as an abundant migrant, a locally common breeder, and a common winter visitant.

Spring migrants are abundant from late April to mid-May in the Copper River Delta-eastern Prince William Sound area, but they are generally less numerous elsewhere in the region, except that large flocks occasionally occur at the head of Valdez Arm and in Port Wells.

Breeding has been reported primarily from the Copper River Delta. Here it is probably the most numerous breeding duck near the outer marsh ponds from west of Grass Island Slough to the outlet of Eyak River. Shepherd (1959), during his work on the Copper River Delta in 1959, found 18 nests (av. clutch, 6.9 eggs) and 21 broods (av. 14 Class I broods, 6.7 chicks); he reported that nesting began 25 May 1959 and that the peak of hatching occurred 10 July. Yocom (1963) saw five scaup broods in this area on 24 July 1962. On Bering Lake, on 9 August 1972, Isleib saw several Greater Scaup and one brood.

During the summer, Greater Scaup are rare elsewhere in the region. U. S. Fish and Wildlife Service surveys 21 July - 4 August 1972 produced a count of only 31 Greater Scaup along tidal flats in bays and fiords of Prince William Sound, probably non-breeders. Grinnell (1910a) did not list it for Prince William Sound in 1908. Shortt (1939) did not observe it in the Yakutat area in 1936, nor did Isleib in 1968.

Fall migrants move through the region from early September until early November, being most numerous in late September and early October. Flocks of several hundred were present in the outlet of Coghill Lake, Port Wells, on 6 October 1971.

Wintering Greater Scaups are common in several of the bays and fiords of Prince William Sound and in protected waters near unfrozen tidal flats along the North Gulf Coast. Censuses taken along the Cordova waterfront yielded counts of 67 Greater Scaup on 27 December 1969 and 209 on 29 December 1971.

Estimates of populations utilizing the North Gulf Coast and Prince William Sound: migration, several 10,000's; summer, a few, possibly several, 1,000's; winter, a few, probably several, 1,000's.

Aythya affinis — Lesser Scaup

The Lesser Scaup is a rare migrant in the North Gulf Coast-Prince William Sound region, having been reported only from the Copper River Delta-Cordova area.

Shepherd (in litt., 1973) reported having seen a few Lesser Scaup on the Copper River Delta in early May during spring migration.

None has been identified during the breeding season.

Lesser Scaup may occur with some regularity in small numbers during fall migration. They were first noticed in 1971 when Isleib, between 29 September and 3 October, saw several small groups, totaling about 30 birds (three were shot), at ponds in the grass-shrub flats on the east side of Alaganik Slough. Paying special attention in 1972, Isleib saw 5 Lesser Scaup on 2 October at Long Island, upper Copper River Delta; 8 on 3 October at Eyak Lake, near Cordova; and 32, in company with 149 Greater Scaup, from 9 to 12 October at Eyak Lake.

Estimates of populations utilizing the North Gulf Coast and Prince William Sound: migration-fall, a few 10's, possibly 100's.

Bucephala clangula — Common Goldeneye

The Common Goldeneye is a resident of the North Gulf Coast-Prince

William Sound region, occurring seasonally as a common migrant, a rare summer visitant and probable breeder, and an abundant winter visitant.

Spring migrants are common throughout most of the region on both freshwater and saltwater from late March through early May, being abundant in mid- and late April. Large numbers remain in the northern fiords of Prince William Sound until mid-May.

Summer visitants, probably mostly subadults or non-breeders, occur regularly from late May through mid-September. A few may breed along the northern fiords of Prince William Sound and in some of the timbered valleys along the North Gulf Coast, although no definite breeding observations have been recorded. There are records, however, in immediately adjacent areas: Shepherd (pers. comm.) saw three broods of week-old young, numbering five, six, and nine, respectively, on 26 June 1958 in the Bremner River region up the Copper River, and Shaffer located a pair nesting 60 ft (18 m) above the water in a Black Cottonwood during June 1970 on Ptarmigan Creek near Kenai Lake.

Fall migrants appear along the outer coasts in mid-September and are common by early October. It is difficult to separate migrants from winter visitants, but most of the migrants appear to have passed through the region by mid-November.

Winter visitants are common throughout the region and are locally abundant in some of the bays, fiords, and inlets both along the North Gulf Coast and in Prince William Sound. The fiord arms of the Port Wells area, for example, contain numerous small flocks totaling thousands of Common Goldeneyes, and occasionally a single flock may contain hundreds of birds.

Estimates of the populations utilizing the North Gulf Coast and Prince William Sound: migration, several 1,000's, probably 10,000's; summer, a few 100's; winter, a few 10,000's.

Bucephala islandica – Barrow's Goldeneye

The Barrow's Goldeneye is a resident of the North Gulf Coast-Prince William Sound region, occurring seasonally as a common migrant, a common breeder, and an abundant winter resident.

The Barrow's Goldeneye outnumbers the Common Goldeneye, except locally along the coast in migration and in some of the fiords in winter.

Spring migrants are fairly common along the outer coasts from late March to early May, being most numerous in mid- and late April as pairs and small flocks.

The Barrow's Goldeneye breeds throughout most of the region. During the summer of 1936, Shortt (1939) saw it commonly in the Yakutat area and observed numerous young on the Situk River, at Disenchantment Bay, and in Russell Fiord. Isleib has seen numerous broods at many localities throughout the North Gulf Coast-Prince William Sound region. There is some difficulty distinguishing the females of Barrow's and Common goldeneyes during late July and August, but, with one possible exception, all of the goldeneye broods identified by Isleib have been Barrow's.

From mid-September until late October, Barrow's Goldeneyes, apparently migrants, are fairly common along the outer coasts.

Winter visitants are abundant throughout most of the region's numerous sheltered bays and fiords.

Estimates of populations utilizing the North Gulf Coast and Prince William Sound: migration, several 1,000's, possibly 10,000's; summer, a few, probably several, 1,000's; winter, a few 10,000's.

Bucephala albeola — Bufflehead

The Bufflehead is a resident of the North Gulf Coast-Prince William Sound region, occurring seasonally as an abundant migrant, a rare summer visitant and breeder, and a common winter resident.

Spring migrants move along the coasts from late March to late May, being abundant during mid-April. These birds usually congregate in numerous small flocks at good feeding areas along the migration route, but on 16 April 1970 at Hartney Bay, Orca Inlet, Isleib watched a migrant flock of over 1,000 Buffleheads.

Buffleheads are absent from most of the region during the summer, although occasional birds occur in freshwater areas or at the heads of the fiords along the mainland coasts. Gabrielson and Lincoln (1959) reported that Clarke P. Streator in 1895 and A. K. Fisher in 1899 found Buffleheads breeding in the Yakutat Bay area and that Dufresne believed that its breeding range included Prince William Sound. Shortt (1939), however, apparently did not see them in the Yakutat area during the summer of 1936. There appears to be no positive recent evidence of breeding within the North Gulf Coast-Prince William region, except Shepherd's (pers. comm.) observation of females with broods along the Copper River below Baird Canyon and in the adjacent Bremner River Valley.

Fall migrants occur in small numbers in early September and are common, even abundant, locally, between late September and early November.

Winter visitants are common throughout most of the bays, inlets, and fiords of the region, and, in some sheltered areas, they are abundant. Counts taken along the Cordova waterfront showed 180 Bufflehead present on 27 December 1969 and 111 on 29 December 1971, indicating this species to be the third and fourth most numerous duck along the waterfront during those respective winters.

Estimates of populations utilizing the North Gulf Coast and Prince William Sound: migration, a few 10,000's; summer, a few, possibly several, 10's; winter, a few 10,000's.

Clangula hyemalis — Oldsquaw

The Oldsquaw is a resident of the North Gulf Coast-Prince William Sound region, occurring seasonally as a common migrant, an uncommon summer visitant and rare local breeder, and a common winter visitant.

Spring migrants are common throughout inshore waters and somewhat less common in offshore waters; they are most common from late April to mid-May, but may be locally abundant any time between late March and late May. During the last two weeks of May 1963, many flocks of 20 to 100 birds and many more flocks of 3 to 20 birds were present over the Copper River Delta's tidewaters, altogether totaling several thousand Oldsquaws. Some migrants, when leaving the region, fly directly inland over the Chugach mountains.

Non-breeders are regular during the summer throughout the inshore waters, being locally common in some years. Grinnell (1910a) reported several flocks of non-breeders in June 1908 near Cordova, and Shortt (1939) saw a few summer visitants in 1936 in the Yakutat Bay area. Although there are several breeding observations (Isleib and Shaffer) in closely adjacent Cook Inlet drainages, the only breeding record within the region is Shaffer's observation at Lost Lake in upper

Resurrection Valley in early June 1971 of six breeding-plumaged adults and two broods of downy young.

Fall migrants do not become apparent until the latter half of September; they are fairly common as scattered small flocks in the inshore waters during October and November. Oldsquaws never seem as numerous during the fall as in the spring; perhaps many migrate offshore.

Winter visitants are common in small flocks along the coasts and in the bays and fiords. Censuses taken along the Cordova waterfront produced counts of 148 Oldsquaw on 27 December 1969 and 78 on 29 December 1971.

Estimates of populations utilizing the North Gulf Coast and Prince William Sound: migration, a few 10,000's; summer, several 100's, probably a few 1,000's; winter, several 1,000's, possibly a few 10,000's.

Histrionicus histrionicus — Harlequin Duck

The Harlequin Duck is an abundant resident of the North Gulf Coast-Prince William Sound region.

During the fall, winter, and spring, the Harlequin Duck is conspicuous along the rocky shores of bays, fiords, and islands, and most ornithologists visiting the region, whatever the time of year, have listed the Harlequin Duck as common or abundant. During the nesting season, Harlequins may be briefly less common in inshore waters, when many move to the mountain streams and up the river systems. Grinnell (1910a) described a nest found by Joseph Dixon on 1 July 1908 on Hinchinbrook Island, and Isleib has seen scores of broods during July and August along the shorelines, especially in Prince William Sound.

Characteristically, Harlequin Ducks occur as pairs and small flocks, but occasionally large, compact flocks contain hundreds of birds. Shaffer saw a summer flock of more than 500 males in Eldorado Narrows, Resurrection Bay, on 20 July 1961. Outside the breeding season, in Prince William Sound, Isleib has counted pairs and small flocks every few yards along the rocky shores, at times totaling well in excess of a hundred birds per mile of shoreline. The U. S. Fish and Wildlife Service survey, 5-12 October 1971, estimated in excess of 10,000 Harlequin Ducks in Prince William Sound.

Estimates of populations utilizing the North Gulf Coast and Prince William Sound: yearly, a few 10,000's.

Polysticta stelleri — Steller's Eider

The Steller's Eider is a rare winter visitant along the North Gulf Coast and in Prince William Sound, occurring along the western North Gulf Coast and eastward into Prince William Sound.

Isleib saw 11 Steller's Eiders (1 male, 10 females) at Double Bay, Hinchinbrook Island, on 19 March 1970; and, during the last week of February 1971, while observing on U. S. Fish and Wildlife Service aerial surveys, he saw several small flocks, totaling about 60 birds, in Prince William Sound. One small flock of about 15 birds was observed as far into the northern fiords as Jonah Bay, Unakwik Inlet, and another as far east as Double Bay, Hinchinbroook Island. A breeding-plumaged pair, viewed from a boat, was still present in Double Bay on 27 April 1971, and it was seen again a week later during further aerial surveys.

Estimates of populations utilizing the North Gulf Coast and Prince William Sound: winter, including some lingering into early spring, several 10's, probably a few 100's.

Somateria mollissima — Common Eider

The Common Eider is a rare visitant along the North Gulf Coast and in Prince William Sound.

This eider breeds in the lower Cook Inlet region and in northern southeastern Alaska (Glacier Bay) (Wik and Streveler, 1968; and pers. obs.), but nobody previously has reported it from the North Gulf Coast-Prince William Sound region. On 12 May 1963 Isleib saw about 20 Common Eiders about the Chugach Islands, and on 13 July 1966, Johnson (pers. field notes) saw a breeding-plumaged male in Coghill Lake, Port Wells. Further field studies will probably reveal this eider as a resident and breeder along the southern edge of the Kenai Peninsula, especially on the outer islands from the mouth of Resurrection Bay to the Chugach Islands.

Shaffer has seen a few Common Eiders on Resurrection Bay nearly every fall and winter. Occasional stragglers occur in winter in Prince William Sound as far east as Cordova: a female on 3 February 1969 and another on 18 January 1970, both at Cordova. Again, this eider, while rare, probably winters more frequently between Resurrection Bay and the Chugach Islands than elsewhere in the North Gulf Coast-Prince William Sound region.

Estimates of populations utilizing the North Gulf Coast and Prince William Sound: yearly, a few individuals, probably a few 100's.

Somateria spectabilis — King Eider

The King Eider is a rare winter visitant along the North Gulf Coast and in Prince William Sound, although it is the most numerous of the eiders.

Identification of the wintering *Somateria* is difficult, because the flocks are made up largely of females and subadults, but most of the identified eider flocks have been King Eiders. This eider occurs in the inshore waters from December until May; observations in Prince William Sound range from February to May. In late February 1971, aerial surveys by the U. S. Fish and Wildlife Service estimated a few hundred birds in Prince William Sound. A flock of approximately 75 females and subadult males still lingered in Blackstone Bay, Port Wells, on 4 May 1971. Isleib saw a female on Resurrection Bay on 20 December 1961, and Shaffer saw a flock of about 19 in the same area in late March 1965.

Estimates of populations utilizing the North Gulf Coast and Prince William Sound: winter, a few, possibly several, 100's.

Melanitta deglandi — White-winged Scoter

The White-winged Scoter is an abundant resident of the North Gulf Coast and Prince William Sound.

Scoters are the most numerous and conspicuous sea ducks in the region throughout the year, the White-winged Scoter being second in numbers to the Surf Scoter, with which it regularly associates.

Migrant White-winged Scoters are numerous along the outer coasts in April and May and again from late September to early November. In spring, many of the migrants appear to leave the North Gulf Coast-Prince William Sound region by flying northward directly over the mountain ranges.

Although less numerous in the summer than at other seasons, non-breeders are nonetheless abundant. Shortt (1939) reported it breeding in Disenchantment Bay, recording adults with half-grown young on 5 August 1936. The only other breeding record is by Shaffer who, in July of both 1969 and 1970, saw a female with a brood on Lost Lake in the Resurrection Valley drainage; he has also seen breeding birds (1968, 1969, and 1970) at Paradise and Summit lakes on adjacent areas of the Kenai Peninsula.

During winter and summer, most White-winged Scoters are in inshore waters of less than 50 fathoms (90 m) and occur regularly in large flocks, at times numbering several hundred birds.

Estimates of populations utilizing the North Gulf Coast and Prince William Sound: migration, several 10,000's; summer, a few 10,000's; winter, a few 10,000's; total annual utilization, several 10,000's, possibly 100,000's.

Melanitta perspicillata — Surf Scoter

The Surf Scoter is an abundant resident in the North Gulf Coast-Prince William Sound region. It is the most numerous scoter, indeed the most numerous sea duck, in the inshore waters at all seasons.

Migrants are numerous along the outer coasts in April and May, and large numbers of courting adults are regular in May off the Copper River Delta and in Prince William Sound; many of these scoters appear to leave the region by flying inland directly over the mountain ranges. Shortt (1939) saw large numbers in Yakutat Bay until 24 May 1936.

There are only two breeding records from the region: Shortt (1939) reported that Surf Scoters were fairly common breeders in Disenchantment Bay and Russell Fiord in 1936, but he did not specifically cite observations of nests, eggs, or young. Isleib saw a female with two half-grown young on 9 August 1972 at Bering Lake. In the closely adjacent region at Summit Lake (45 miles [72 km] north of Seward), Shaffer observed a pair that raised three young during July 1969.

Large numbers of non-breeders remain in the region during the summer, and many move into certain bays and fiords for molting. Summering flocks usually number less than a hundred birds, although flocks numbering from several hundred to thousands are regular in the shallow inshore waters, wherever mollusks are abundant. Yocom (1963) saw a flock of 1,500 to 2,000 Surf Scoters on the Copper River Delta on 13 July 1962.

Fall migrants are numerous along the outer coasts from September through November, and winter visitants are abundant in the inshore waters about islands and in the bays and fiords, especially in waters of less than 50 fathoms (90 m).

Estimates of populations utilizing the North Gulf Coast and Prince William Sound: migration, several 10,000's, possibly 100,000's; summer, a few 10,000's; winter, a few, possibly several, 10,000's; total annual utilization, probably 100,000's.

Oidemia nigra — Common Scoter

The Common Scoter is a resident of the North Gulf Coast-Prince William Sound region, occurring seasonally as a fairly common migrant, an uncommon summer visitant, and a common winter visitant. It is the least numerous of the three scoters.

Common Scoters frequent the same inshore habitats as the other scoters and associate freely with them. They usually occur as scattered birds or small flocks, but occasionally, in migration and during the winter, flocks totaling a few hundred birds occur along the outer coasts and in the western portions of Prince William Sound. At times, along these storm-washed coasts, this scoter becomes locally more abundant than the other scoters, which usually prefer more sheltered waters.

Migrant Common Scoters are apparently present from early April to late May and, in the fall, they first appear in late September; because they occur in numbers at all seasons, however, it is difficult to separate migrants from visitants.

Common Scoters have not been reported breeding in the region, although Gabrielson and Lincoln (1959) reported a female with two downy young on 8 August 1945 on the Karluk River on nearby Kodiak Island.

Estimates of populations utilizing the North Gulf Coast and Prince William Sound: migration, several 1,000's, possibly 10,000's; summer, a few 1,000's; winter, several 1,000's, possibly 10,000's; total annual utilization, a few, possibly several, 10,000's.

Lophodytes cucullatus – Hooded Merganser

The Hooded Merganser is a rare visitant along the North Gulf Coast and in Prince William Sound.

During the twelve-year period from 1961 through 1972, approximately twenty Hooded Mergansers have been reported in the Copper River Delta-Prince William Sound area. They have not been reported every year nor have more than a few birds been reported in any one year. They have been seen on lakes, ponds, and streams near the coast and on tidewaters of sheltered inlets and lagoons. Most of the observations have been from late summer and fall, and no evidence of breeding has been reported. These birds are probably stragglers from southeastern Alaska, where they are uncommon residents and breeders (Gabrielson and Lincoln, 1959).

Shaffer reported that two males were shot by hunters near Cape Cleare, Montague Island, in September 1963. Cordova resident Kenneth Kritchen shot two Hooded Mergansers on Eyak River east of Cordova on 5 October 1969 (one specimen, UA 3321, was an immature male). Pete and Ruth Isleib watched two males that appeared irregularly from May to October 1966 on a small pond at Cordova. A male was present in the Cordova boat harbor for several days 30 December 1969-4 January 1970. Robert Ingebo, Cordova resident, (pers. comm.) who first reported this 1970 bird, has seen a few irregularly over a period of years in the Copper River Delta-Prince William Sound area. Isleib and Haddock saw a female-plumaged Hooded Merganser on 22 March 1973 in Culross Passage, PWS. More extensive field work throughout the region, from Prince William Sound eastward along the North Gulf Coast, will probably discover the presence of this species on an annual basis.

Estimates of populations utilizing the North Gulf Coast-Prince William Sound: yearly, a few individuals, possibly 10's.

Mergus merganser – Common Merganser

The Common Merganser is a common resident of the North Gulf Coast and Prince William Sound region.

Spring migrants, as pairs and small flocks, are fairly common along the outer coasts from late March to early May, and they commonly utilize freshwater as soon as it is partially free of ice.

The Common Merganser breeds throughout the region, especially near freshwater. Shortt (1939) found it a common, well-distributed breeding bird throughout the Yakutat area, and he saw one flock of about a hundred on Situk Lake in July 1936. The Alexander Expedition (Grinnell, 1910a) observed numerous adults with young throughout Prince William Sound during the summer of

1908. During July and August the Common Merganser is the most numerous merganser along the shorelines, occurring regularly in the inlets and bays adjacent to the outflows of streams and rivers. It is common at this time to see females with broods.

Fall migrants occur along the outer coasts from mid-September through November, occasionally occurring in large flocks of hundreds and sometimes mixed with larger numbers of Red-breasted Mergansers.

Winter visitants are most common in protected bays, inlets, and fiords and in freshwater, if any is open. Generally in small flocks in winter, this merganser occasionally is abundant locally in large flocks numbering several hundreds.

Estimates of populations utilizing the North Gulf Coast and Prince William Sound: migration, several 1,000's, probably 10,000's; summer, several 1,000's, possibly 10,000's; winter, several 1,000's, possibly 10,000's; total annual utilization, a few 10,000's.

Mergus serrator – Red-breasted Merganser

The Red-breasted Merganser is a resident of the North Gulf Coast-Prince William Sound region, occurring seasonally as an abundant migrant, an uncommon summer visitant and local breeder, and a common winter visitant.

Spring migrants appear all along the outer coasts as numerous small flocks during April and May; they appear regularly in freshwater and in the sheltered waters of bays and inlets during migration, but they are generally outnumbered in these latter areas by Common Mergansers.

Mergansers breed fairly commonly on the Copper River Delta. Although there is some difficulty in distinguishing the species of female mergansers when glimpsed briefly as a thrashing and splashing bird trailed by an equally splashing brood of young, most of these are Red-breasted Mergansers. Isleib has observed broods during late June and early July, 1966, 1967, and 1969, on the Copper River Delta – on Martin River Slough, Grass Island Slough, and on the Copper River below the 27-Mile Bridge. A few summering individuals and small flocks also occur regularly throughout other portions of the North Gulf Coast and Prince William Sound region. On 23 June 1967 Isleib saw two broods on the Bering River – one of seven and one of nine young with attendant females; and Shaffer has reported seeing broods every summer near Seward.

Fall migrants are common in September and abundant locally along the outer coasts in October and into November. During the first two weeks of November 1964, large migrating flocks of several hundred individuals and one aggregation totaling 2,000+ were present near Cordova.

Winter visitants are common, occurring regularly in small flocks throughout the region. They associate freely with Common Mergansers while in the bays and inlets, but along the outer coasts they usually form pure flocks, Common Mergansers being absent from these waters.

Estimates of populations utilizing the North Gulf Coast and Prince William Sound: migration, a few 10,000's; summer, several 100's, probably a few 1,000's; winter, several 1,000's; total annual utilization, a few 10,000's.

Accipiter gentilis – Goshawk

The Goshawk is a fairly common resident of the North Gulf Coast and Prince William Sound.

Shortt (1939) reported it as "fairly plentiful" about Yakutat during the summer of 1936 and collected two immatures in August. Shaffer has found Goshawks common residents of Resurrection Valley; he located several nests near Seward in the 1960's, including one with three eggs at Fourth of July Creek on 6 June 1969. Kenneth Mitchell, U. S. Forest Service, (pers. comm.) was attacked repeatedly by a nesting pair near Mile 23 Copper River Highway in June and July 1970.

The Goshawk is essentially non-migratory in the region, except for its tendency to disperse and range in winter wherever food sources are readily available.

Estimates of populations utilizing the North Gulf Coast and Prince William Sound: yearly, several 100's, probably 1,000's.

Accipiter striatus – Sharp-shinned Hawk

The Sharp-shinned Hawk is an uncommon resident and a fairly common migrant along the North Gulf Coast and in Prince William Sound.

Spring migrants are most frequent between 25 April and 10 May (earliest, one on 15 April 1969, Mile 16 Copper River Highway).

Sharp-shinned Hawks are uncommon during the summer. Shortt (1939) found a nest 30 ft (9 m) up in a Western Hemlock near Situk Lake on 11 August 1936. Shaffer observed adults carrying food in July 1969, 1970, and 1971 near Seward and saw an adult female with three fledged young on 1 September 1968 at Seward. Isleib saw four fledged young with an adult at Mile 22 Copper River Highway on 16 August 1969.

Individuals are more numerous in the fall than at any other season, and they have been observed in such diverse localities as among the fishing vessels on the Copper River Delta and over alpine ridges at 3,000 ft (900 m). Fall migrants are most frequent between 1 September and 25 September (latest probable migrant, 4 November 1968, Hawkins Island) (20 to 100 per fall season in proper habitat).

Sharp-shinned Hawks winter irregularly on the Copper River Delta: one at Mile 24 Copper River Highway, 29 January 1969, and one at Mile 13 Copper River Highway, 26 February 1966. During the winter of 1963-64 at Seward, local falconer Donald R. Evett (pers. comm.) observed Sharp-shinned Hawks on several occasions.

Estimates of populations utilizing the North Gulf Coast and Prince William Sound: migration, a few 1,000's; summer, a few 100's; winter, in some years, a few individuals, possibly 10's.

Buteo jamaicensis – Red-tailed Hawk

The Red-tailed Hawk is casual in the North Gulf Coast-Prince William Sound region.

Gabrielson and Lincoln (1959) cited a specimen taken by Clarke P. Streator at Yakutat on 17 July 1895. There have been only two subsequent reports of "typical" Red-tailed Hawks in the region. Shortt (1939) saw an adult on the Malaspina Glacier 11 July 1936, and West and Peyton (unpubl. notes) saw an adult on 1 May 1970 on the Copper River Delta.

Isleib saw a "typical" adult Red-tailed Hawk just north of Portage Pass in adjacent Turnagain Arm on 14 May 1961; the bird was flying northwest, probably having crossed the mountains from Prince William Sound.

Buteo harlani — Harlan's Hawk

The Harlan's Hawk is a casual migrant and rare local breeder in the North Gulf Coast-Prince William Sound region.

Shaffer has seen Harlan's Hawks annually in the Seward area, and he watched two pairs nest in Black Cottonwoods of the Resurrection Bay drainage near Seward from June to August 1969. Williamson et al. (1965) listed several nesting observations for Harlan's Hawk in the adjacent Anchorage-northern Kenai Peninsula region, to the exclusion of the "typical" Red-tailed Hawk.

Harlan's Hawks appear normally to migrate to and from southcentral Alaska via the interior valleys; they are regular fall migrants along the Glenn Highway between King Mountain and Sheep Mountain in late September and early October (6+ Harlan's Hawks 11 October 1964). Pete and Ruth Isleib, however, saw a migrant "typical" adult Harlan's Hawk flying eastward on 13 October 1969 at Mile 24 Copper River Highway.

Estimates of populations utilizing the North Gulf Coast and Prince William Sound: migration and summer, 10's.

Buteo lagopus — Rough-legged Hawk

The Rough-legged Hawk is a rare migrant and a casual summer and winter visitant in the North Gulf Coast-Prince William Sound region.

Spring migration extends from mid-April to mid-May (earliest, one on 18 April 1969; latest, one on 12 May 1966; both on the Copper River Delta).

Shortt (1939) observed Rough-legged Hawks twice at the Malaspina Glacier between 6 and 22 July 1936 and collected a dark-phase male on 12 September at the Situk River. Edmund Heller (Grinnell, 1910a) collected a full-grown juvenal male at 2,000 ft (600 m) on Chenega Island, PWS, on 31 August 1908.

Fall migration through the region occurs from late August to late October, with migrants not appearing over the lowlands until about mid-September (earliest, one on 31 August 1908 on Chenega Island [ibid.]; latest, one on 26 October 1968 on the Copper River Delta). Shaffer has recorded fall migrants twice in Resurrection Valley, one in October 1967 and one on 22 September 1971.

The only winter record is from 1969-70 on the Copper River Delta: two light-phase individuals first seen on 7 October 1969 were joined by a third (a sooty-appearing light-phase bird) on 23 November, and all three remained until mid-March 1970.

Estimates of populations utilizing the North Gulf Coast and Prince William Sound: migration, a few, probably several, 10's; winter, in some years, a few individuals; summer, reported only by Shortt (1939).

Aquila chrysaetos — Golden Eagle

The Golden Eagle is rare in the North Gulf Coast-Prince William Sound region, although it is common on the drier north side of the Chugach Mountains, where local falconer George Velikanje and Isleib counted 17 active eyries on a 1¼ hr flight near Anchorage in June 1963.

Several spring observations have been recorded for the North Gulf Coast-Prince William Sound region. Isleib saw two subadults in Port Wells in late March 1972 and two adults soaring over ridges south of Cordova on 26 May 1963. Gibson (unpubl. notes) repeatedly saw two subadults at Thompson Pass on 6 May 1972. West and Peyton (unpubl. notes) saw an immature at Mile 27 Copper River

Highway on 28 and 30 April 1970 and another at Hartney Bay, Orca Inlet, on 1 May 1970.

Shortt (1939:11) observed a pair on three occasions during the summer of 1936 in the Yakutat area and said, "This pair was evidently nesting on high inaccessible cliffs on Mount Tebenkof." Annually, Shaffer has seen a pair, which he presumed to be nesting, in the vicinity of Resurrection Valley; during several Aprils he observed aerial courtship, and he saw the pair throughout the summer. Isleib and Sowl watched a pair of adult Golden Eagles on 24 July 1972 patrolling the ridge above the large Black-legged Kittiwake colony in Icy Bay, PWS.

Further field work in the Thompson Pass area near Valdez and the Copper River Valley above the 27-Mile Bridge, Copper River Highway, may reveal this eagle to be somewhat more regular on the southern slopes of the mountains than is now known.

Estimates of populations utilizing the North Gulf Coast and Prince William Sound: migration and summer, a few 10's.

Haliaeetus leucocephalus — Bald Eagle

The Bald Eagle is an abundant and conspicuous resident of the North Gulf Coast and Prince William Sound region.

Spring migration is apparent throughout April and early May.

Bald Eagles nest commonly throughout the region's coastal areas and river systems. Probably 1,800-2,000 pairs nest within the region, with greatest densities occurring in the Yakutat area (F. C. Robards, U. S. Fish and Wildlife Service, pers. comm.). Most nests are located in old-growth timber — spruce, hemlock, or cottonwood — but occasionally they are placed on the ground on such raised sites as beaver houses, mounds, etc.

Fall migration extends from late August to mid-November. During September and October, on days with light southerly or westerly winds, scores of Bald Eagles pass eastward, soaring the updrafts on the ridges between Mile 21 and Mile 27 Copper River Highway.

From mid-summer to mid-winter (early July to January), large numbers of eagles (at times several hundreds) concentrate at some of the many localities along the North Gulf Coast or in Prince William Sound where spawning and spawned-out, dying and dead salmon are found. On 27 December 1969, Isleib counted 416 eagles feeding on spawned-out salmon at Eyak Lake near Cordova. During severe winters, smaller concentrations occur on several of the islands in Prince William Sound, feeding on winter-killed Sitka Black-tailed Deer. After an unusually cold and harsh winter, the U. S. Fish and Wildlife survey 24 March-4 April 1972 estimated 2,000 Bald Eagles in Prince William Sound.

Estimates of populations utilizing the North Gulf Coast and Prince William Sound: summer, 5,000, including 1,800-2,000 pairs; winter 3,000 to 4,000+; total annual utilization, 10,000 to 15,000.

Circus cyaneus — Marsh Hawk

The Marsh Hawk is a resident of the North Gulf Coast-Prince William Sound region, occurring seasonally as a common migrant, an uncommon local breeder, and a rare winter visitant. It is the second most conspicuous raptor in the region (after Bald Eagle) (over 100 per year in proper habitat).

Spring migrants are common from 25 April to 10 May (earliest, one on 15 April 1969, Mile 16 Copper River Highway).

During the summer Marsh Hawks are uncommon on the Copper River Delta. Yocom (1963) saw a male on 11 and 12 July 1962 at Mile 12 Copper River Highway which he presumed to be a nesting bird. In 1968, 1969, and 1970, after numerous aircraft flights across the Copper River Delta in June and July, Isleib estimated that at least three or four pairs were present and probably nesting in the upper portions of the Delta. Shaffer found a nest with four eggs at the base of a small, stunted spruce in a marshy area near Seward in June-July 1969; the young fledged successfully.

Fall migrants are common from 25 August to 20 September, the highest single-day count being 19 observed on the Copper River Delta on 9 September 1968 (latest probable migrant, one on 3 November 1970, Mile 17 Copper River Highway). During migration Marsh Hawks have been observed in such varied locations as several miles off the coast and the alpine ridges along the ice fields and glaciers of the mountains.

Winter occurrences are irregular (2 or 3 years out of 5). An adult female was present on the Copper River Delta from 17 November 1969 to 11 March 1970, and local trappers have reported others during mild winters which coincide with high rodent populations.

Estimates of populations utilizing the North Gulf Coast and Prince William Sound: migration, several 100's, probably a few 1,000's; summer, a few 10's; winter, in some years, a few individuals.

Pandion haliaetus — Osprey

The Osprey is an uncommon migrant and a rare local breeder in the North Gulf Coast-Prince William Sound region.

The main spring movement occurs during late April and early May (earliest, one on 19 April 1964 at Cordova; latest, two on 13 May 1966, Mile 10 Copper River Highway) (3 to 7 per spring migration in proper habitat on the Copper River Delta).

Shortt (1939) considered it an uncommon breeder in the Yakutat area; he noted a few pairs and collected an adult male from a pair nesting along the Situk River on 29 May 1936. Johnson (pers. field notes) saw one bird at the mouth of the Situk River in early August 1966. Donald Calkins, University of Alaska, (pers. comm.) saw one at Stockdale Harbor, Montague Island, on 28 June 1971 and observed it or another at the same location a week later.

Fall migration occurs from late August to mid-October (earliest, one on 23 August 1970, Egg Island, CRD; latest, one on 13 October 1969, Mile 18 Copper River Highway) (3 to 7+ per fall migration in proper habitat on the Copper River Delta).

Estimates of populations utilizing the North Gulf Coast and Prince William Sound: migration and summer, a few 10's.

Falco rusticolus — Gyrfalcon

The Gyrfalcon is rare, both as a migrant and visitant, to the North Gulf Coast and Prince William Sound.

A Gyrfalcon was identified over Port Wells by George Velikanje, local falconer, (pers. comm.) in early July 1966. An adult male, sitting on the bluff over the large kittiwake colony at the head of Blackstone Bay, Port Wells, was observed closely by Isleib and Thomas Ray, U. S. Fish and Wildlife Service, on 26 July 1972. Port Wells lies in the northwest corner of Prince William Sound and is approximately 40 miles (64 km) from the nearest known Gyrfalcon eyrie in the Chugach Mountains.

A probable migrant, an adult dark-phase female in pursuit of a Green-winged Teal, was seen by Isleib at Dan Bay, Hinchinbrook Island, on 8 October 1971.

Shaffer has seen Gyrfalcons irregularly in the adjacent interior of the Kenai Peninsula and believes that they regularly enter the drainages of the North Gulf Coast on the Kenai Peninsula.

Estimates of populations utilizing the North Gulf Coast and Prince William Sound: yearly, a few, probably several, individuals, possibly 10's.

Falco peregrinus – Peregrine Falcon

The Peregine Falcon is a rare resident of the North Gulf Coast and Prince William Sound region.

On the Copper River Delta, migrants* appear most frequently between 15 April (earliest, 13 April 1969, Mile 21 Copper River Highway) and 5 May (5 to 10 per spring migration on the Copper River Delta).

Between 12 and 20 pairs breed along the North Gulf Coast. Eyries are on or in view of the coast and are generally associated with seabird nesting colonies or waterfowl breeding areas.

Fall migrants are most frequent between 10 September and 15 October (5 to 15 per fall migration on the Copper River Delta). Migratory movements are associated with the mass movements of waterfowl on the Copper River Delta.

Peregrine Falcons are rare but regular along the coasts during the winter*.

Estimates of populations utilizing the North Gulf Coast and Prince William Sound: migration, several 10's; summer,12 to 20 pairs; winter, a few, probably several, individuals.

Falco columbarius – Pigeon Hawk

The Pigeon Hawk is a rare resident and an uncommon migrant in the North Gulf Coast-Prince William Sound region.

Spring migrants are uncommon from late March through early May (5 to 10 per spring migration in proper habitat).

Breeding status is unknown, but on the basis of several July and August observations, it probably breeds locally at or near timberline within the region.

Fall migration occurs between early September and late October (10 to 20 per fall migration in proper habitat).

Wintering Pigeon Hawks are rare; they are most frequent during winters when small passerines are fairly common. Isleib watched an adult feeding on a Black-capped Chickadee at Mile 9 Copper River Highway on 20 November 1971; another adult was present at the same location on 23 December 1972; and Laing (1925) saw one at Cordova on 15 March 1924.

Estimates of populations utilizing the North Gulf Coast and Prince William Sound: migration, a few 100's; summer, a few, possibly several, 10's; winter, several individuals.

*Most birds in the region appear to be *F. p. pealei,* but some migrants and one winter bird (an adult male at Cordova 21 January 1971) show charicteristics of the rare and endangered *F. p. anatum.*

Falco sparverius — Sparrow Hawk

The Sparrow Hawk is a rare fall migrant along the North Gulf Coast and in Prince William Sound.

Occurring annually on the Copper River Delta, mostly along the Copper River Highway between Mile 7 and Mile 27 (3 to 10 per fall migration), this falcon is most frequent between 1 and 15 September (earliest, 22 August 1969; latest, 13 October 1969). The only report outside of the Copper River Delta is of a female seen by Isleib at Double Bay, Hinchinbrook Island, on 13 September 1971.

Estimates of populations utilizing the North Gulf Coast and Prince William Sound: migration-fall, a few 10's.

Canachites canadensis — Spruce Grouse

The Spruce Grouse is a fairly common resident along the North Gulf Coast and in Prince William Sound.

The Spruce Grouse is fairly common throughout the forests and woodlands of the Kenai Peninsula eastward through most of the larger islands and the mainland of Prince William Sound and in the coastal forest to Cape Suckling; it is more common on the Kenai Peninsula than elsewhere in the region. The only reports east of Cape Suckling are from Terry Holiday, local bush pilot (pers. comm.); he reported having seen Spruce Grouse at an airstrip in the forest belt near the north shore of Icy Bay and also that residents of Yakataga have shot a few in that area. Grinnell (1910a) reported that the Alexander Expedition in 1908 found Spruce Grouse generally distributed, though not abundant, about Prince William Sound. Shaffer has found Spruce Grouse nesting commonly in the Seward area, especially on the surrounding forested hillsides; he located nests almost annually between 1960 and 1971 on Fox Island and at Humpy Cove, Resurrection Bay, and he watched two females on nests near Seward during June 1971. The Spruce Grouse does not range east of Icy Bay; apparently the broad expanse of the Malaspina Glacier and its end moraine between Icy Bay and Yakutat Bay is an effective barrier to range expansion.

Estimates of populations utilizing the North Gulf Coast and Prince William Sound: yearly, several 1,000's, possibly 10,000's.

Lagopus lagopus — Willow Ptarmigan

The Willow Ptarmigan is locally a fairly common resident along the mainland portions of the North Gulf Coast and Prince William Sound.

Willow Ptarmigan occur fairly commonly in the headwaters of Resurrection River, at Whittier in Passage Canal, College Fiord, Lowe River Valley to Thompson Pass, and in the lower Copper River Valley-Copper River Delta area. Shortt (1939) reported Willow Ptarmigan common in the Malaspina Glacier, Disenchantment Bay, and Russell Fiord areas near Yakutat in 1936, and he collected five specimens. This ptarmigan is absent from the islands.

During the summer, Willow Ptarmigan occur most regularly in the grassy and brushy, somewhat open, valleys between 1,000 and 2,500 ft (300-750 m) elevation. In some locations, such as College Fiord and Russell Fiord, they occur near sea level, but at others, such as at the heads of the mountain valleys, as high as 3,000 ft (900 m). During most years, Shaffer has found this ptarmigan nesting in fair numbers (perhaps 10 to 30 pairs) on Mt. Marathon and vicinity near Seward. Gabrielson (Gabrielson and Lincoln, 1959) saw several broods of Willow Ptarmigan along the shores of College Fiord, Port Wells, on 13 August 1945.

When not breeding, Willow Ptarmigan are often found in large concentrations. Among the highest counts in Resurrection Valley is one by Shaffer of a flock of about 1,000 birds at Lost Lake on 10 October 1970. The areas of greatest winter abundance include portions of the Copper River Delta and the Martin River Valley and the area between Yakutat and Dry Bay, apparently because the adjacent hills and valleys provide the most extensive breeding habitat in the region. Trappers who have spent considerable time in these areas have reported that, normally, scattered wintering flocks number fewer than 100 birds per flock, flocks being somewhat larger in the Martin River Valley. During the late 1950's, however, they saw concentrations numbering several thousands on the willow-alder flats of the Copper River Delta.

Estimates of populations utilizing the North Gulf Coast and Prince William Sound: yearly, a few 10,000's.

Lagopus mutus – Rock Ptarmigan

The Rock Ptarmigan is a fairly common resident of the mountains of the North Gulf Coast and Prince William Sound.

The Rock Ptarmigan appears to be fairly common in areas of alpine tundra between 1,000 (300 m) and probably 5,000 ft (1500 m). Isleib has seen it regularly above 1,000 ft (300 m) near Seward, Whittier, Thompson Pass, in the mountains near Cordova, and on Hawkins, Hinchinbrook, and Montague islands in Prince William Sound. From an aircraft he saw several small flocks at areas above 3,800 ft (1200 m) along the Cordova Glacier on 14 September 1971, and he saw a single Rock Ptarmigan flying at 2,100 ft (640 m) between Hawkins and Hinchinbrook islands on 9 May 1971. He has seen it only once near sea level in the region: a pair of birds on a 20-ft (6-m) bluff of snow along the shoreline at the head of Blackstone Bay, Port Wells, during the last week of February 1971.

Grinnell (1910a) reported Rock Ptarmigan at elevations above 1,500 ft (450 m) on several of the larger islands in Prince William Sound in 1908, where five adult males were collected. Shortt (1939) found the Rock Ptarmigan less common than the Willow at Yakutat in 1936, but he collected a pair above 2,000 ft (600 m) on 26 May 1936 at Russell Fiord and saw others at 1,400 ft (425 m) near Turner Glacier, Disenchantment Bay.

Estimates of populations utilizing the North Gulf Coast and Prince William Sound: yearly, several 1,000's, probably 10,000's.

Lagopus leucurus – White-tailed Ptarmigan

The White-tailed Ptarmigan is an uncommon local resident of the mainland along the North Gulf Coast and Prince William Sound, occurring in the dry, windswept, alpine areas.

Shaffer annually has seen individuals and small flocks above Seward and at Lost Lake in upper Ressurrection Valley. Isleib has seen a few there and several in the vicinity of Thompson Pass. On 29 March 1969, he saw three above Flag Point, Mile 27 Copper River Highway. Gibson (unpubl. notes) found two birds at Thompson Pass on 6 May 1972: a male in changing plumage at about 3,200 ft (1,000 m) and an apparent winter-killed bird (UA 3245) at about 2,800 ft (850 m). George G. Cantwell (Gabrielson and Lincoln, 1959) collected specimens near Seward in 1913 and near Valdez in 1916. The White-tailed Ptarmigan undoubtedly occurs also where appropriate habitat is available along the Alsek River.

Estimates of populations utilizing the North Gulf Coast and Prince William Sound: yearly, several 100's, possibly a few 1,000's.

Grus canadensis — Sandhill Crane

The Sandhill Crane is a fairly common spring migrant and a common, occasionally abundant, fall migrant in the North Gulf Coast-Prince William Sound region.

Spring migrants begin arriving during the last half of April (earliest, a flock of 27 on 17 April 1969 at Cordova) and are present through May, the main passage being during the first week of May. Most flocks apparently move northwest along the North Gulf Coast to the Copper River Delta, thence west across Prince William Sound, over the Kenai Mountains, and into Cook Inlet — the same route utilized by most geese and ducks. Most spring migrants overfly the region, but a few stop on the marshes, especially those of the Copper River Delta (latest, one collected in Orca Inlet on 12 June 1908 [Grinnell, 1910a]).

There are several unverified reports of Sandhill Cranes summering on the marshes of the Copper River Delta, but the only specific record is of a pair seen by Julius Reynolds and Phillip D. Havens, Alaska Department of Fish and Game, (pers. comm.) in mid-July 1972 near Pete Dahl Slough. When flushed, these birds circled, calling, about the marsh, and realighted. In view of these observations, it seems likely that cranes may occasionally breed on the extensive marshes of the Copper River Delta.

Fall migrants occur from late August (earliest, flock of 70+ on 19 August 1970 at Egg Island, CRD) until early October (latest, flock of 110 on 8 October 1970 at Hartney Bay, Orca Inlet). Fall migration routes are a reverse of those in spring, but, in contrast to spring migrants, fall migrants may linger several days on the marshes of the Copper and Bering river deltas, especially if winds are easterly.

The numbers of fall migrants vary from year to year, ranging from a few 10,000's to several 100,000's. Steven R. Smith, local fisherman/photographer/biologist, (pers. comm.) witnessed an impressive migration of Sandhill Cranes during late September 1963; he estimated that more than 500,000 cranes passed over the eastern end of the Copper River Delta during the daylight hours over a 5-day period.

Estimates of populations utilizing the North Gulf Coast and Prince William Sound: migration-spring, several 1,000's — in some years, possibly 10,000's; migration-fall, a few 10,000's — in some years, several 100,000's (no estimates since 1963 have exceeded 100,000).

Fulica americana — American Coot

The American Coot has been recorded twice in the North Gulf Coast-Prince William Sound region, both times in the Cordova boat harbor. The first was seen on 3 June 1971 by Julius Reynolds, Alaska Department of Fish and Game, It remained for only one day, but Isleib saw a photograph of it obtained by Reynolds. The second coot was observed by Peter Fridgen, Alaska Department of Fish and Game, on 29 May 1973.

Haematopus bachmani — Black Oystercatcher

The Black Oytercatcher is a fairly common resident of the rocky shores and reefs of the North Gulf Coast-Prince William Sound region.

From April to September, Black Oystercatchers are scattered in pairs or family groups along the rocky shorelines, where they are common nesters immediately above the tide zone, especially on small islands. Nests and/or downy young have been found at numerous locations (Grinnell, 1910a; Shortt, 1939; Gabrielson and Lincoln, 1959; and pers. obs.).

Beginning in September and continuing throughout the winter, they occur in flocks, sometimes numbering over a hundred individuals. A flock of 120 birds was present in Constantine Harbor, Hinchinbrook Island, on 9 September 1971. Wintering flocks in Prince William Sound have been observed at Green, Montague, Knight, Hinchinbrook, and Latouche islands.

Estimates of populations utilizing the North Gulf Coast and Prince William Sound: yearly, several 100's, possibly a few 1,000's.

Charadrius semipalmatus — Semipalmated Plover

The Semipalmated Plover is a common migrant and breeder along the North Gulf Coast and in Prince William Sound.

Spring migrants arrive during the first week of May (earliest, two on 3 May 1969 at Hartney Bay, Orca Inlet) and are common during the second and third weeks of May.

Nesting pairs are on territory during the third week of May. Shortt (1939) saw these plovers commonly throughout the Yakutat area in 1936 and discovered several nests. The 1964 Alaska earthquake uplift created hundreds of acres of newly available gravelly beaches which have been a boon to the local nesting Semipalmated Plover population, although encroaching vegetation will eventually reduce the available habitat again. Solf reported that one pair nested in the east arm of Simpson Bay, PWS, pre-earthquake and that six or seven pairs were utilizing the additional earthquake-exposed habitat in June 1971.

Summer visitants, some of which may be unsuccessful nesters, occur regularly as scattered individuals on the tidal flats and beaches of the Copper River Delta through June and July.

Fall migrants begin arriving at the Copper River Delta in mid-July, and they are common (10 to 50 per day in proper habitat) during early August; a few are present during September (latest, one on 19 September 1969 at Hartney Bay, Orca Inlet).

Estimates of populations utilizing the North Gulf Coast and Prince William Sound: migration, several 1,000's; summer, a few 1,000's.

Charadrius vociferus — Killdeer

The Killdeer is a casual (perhaps rare) visitant to the North Gulf Coast-Prince William Sound region.

Shortt (1939) saw a single Killdeer on 27 July 1936 near the mouth of the Situk River. Isleib saw one at Cordova on 16 May and 22 May 1965 and another at Mile 7 Copper River Highway on 24 May 1972. Johnson (pers. field notes) saw one at Yakutat airport on 19 and 20 May 1966.

The Killdeer probably occurs more frequently than these observations would indicate; it may even occur annually or nearly annually as it does in adjacent Cook Inlet (Williamson et al., 1965; and pers. obs.).

Pluvialis dominica — American Golden Plover

The American Golden Plover is a common migrant and a casual summer visitant along the North Gulf Coast and in Prince William Sound.

Spring migrants normally appear in late April (earliest, one on 3 April 1972 over Valdez Arm, and two on 27 April 1969, Mile 22 Copper River Highway), often lingering for a few days, actively foraging in damp, open habitats. During the first two weeks of May, American Golden Plovers are common on portions of the Copper River Delta and along the outer beaches of Montague Island, and scattered individuals occur on the beaches and marshes at the heads of bays and fiords within Prince William Sound. Migrants are fairly common until the first week of June (latest, 33 on 10 June 1965 at Orca Inlet).

There are no observations to indicate breeding in the region, but during both 1964 and 1971, following cold, late springs, a few non-breeding, summer visitants were noted by Shaffer in June and July at Seward and along the Anchorage-Seward Highway.

Fall migrants are fairly common but scattered, often as singles, from mid-July (earliest, four on 12 July 1970 at Egg Island, CRD) until early September. After mid-September they are uncommon until mid-October (latest, 21 on 17 October 1969 on the tide flat near Canoe Pass, Hawkins Island).

Estimates of populations utilizing the North Gulf Coast and Prince William Sound: migration, several 1,000's, probably 10,000's; summer, in some years, a few individuals.

Squatarola squatarola — Black-bellied Plover

The Black-bellied Plover is a common migrant and uncommon summer visitant along the North Gulf Coast and in Prince William Sound.

Arriving spring migrants (earliest, four on 26 April 1969, Mile 21 Copper River Highway) are frequently associated with American Golden Plovers on the wet marshes of the Copper River Delta. They are common along the coast during the first half of May and fairly common during the last half of May, frequenting a wide variety of marsh and tidal habitats. Small flocks and occasional large, loose flocks (100+) are regular during spring migration on the Copper River Delta and the beaches of Montague Island.

Summer visitants are uncommon, occurring as scattered individuals and small flocks through June and July on beaches and tidal flats of the Copper River Delta and outer islands of Prince William Sound.

Fall migrants, appearing first in late July, are fairly common in August and until mid-September along the beaches and tidal flats and somewhat regular in lesser numbers until early October (latest, 10 on 14 October 1971 at Orca Inlet).

Estimates of populations utilizing the North Gulf Coast and Prince William Sound: migration, several 1,000's, possibly a few 10,000's; summer, a few, possibly several, 100's.

Aphriza virgata — Surfbird

The Surfbird is a resident along the North Gulf Coast and in Prince William Sound.

Spring migrants occur during the last half of April and first half of May, the earlier migrants usually associated with Black Turnstones and Rock Sandpipers. In late April they arrive in Prince William Sound in large flocks, and, during the first and second weeks of May (after the departure of most Black

Turnstones), they associate with the tremendous flocks of Ruddy Turnstones. On 7 May 1971, Isleib saw several thousand Surfbirds, mostly in flocks of several hundred each, in the Green and Montague island-Hinchinbrook Entrance area. Having entered Prince William Sound mainly via Hinchinbrook Entrance, large numbers apparently fly directly inland from the Prince William Sound area; they are abundant on the shores of some of the islands in Prince William Sound for several days in the first half of May and common in the bays and fiords of northern Prince William Sound, after which they largely disappear from the coast.

Some Surfbirds may breed in the coastal mountains, but there are no specific records. Scattered small flocks of non-breeders are fairly common through June and July in Prince William Sound.

Fall migrants are fairly common to common along the rocky shores and reefs after mid-July, are abundant in August and early September, and are locally common through mid-October. Surfbirds are uncommon after mid-October, although they winter regularly in small flocks (less than 100 individuals) on the outer islands and reefs of Prince William Sound.

Estimates of populations utilizing the North Gulf Coast and Prince William Sound: migration, a few, probably several, 10,000's; summer, several 100's; winter, several 100's, possibly a few 1,000's.

Arenaria interpres — Ruddy Turnstone

Ruddy Turnstones are abundant spring migrants, fairly common fall migrants, and uncommon summer visitants along the outer coasts of the North Gulf Coast-Prince William Sound region.

Spring migrants arrive along the North Gulf Coast during the first week of May (earliest, 19 on 4 May 1970 at Shag Rock, PWS) and are often mixed with the last of the Black Turnstone flocks or with Surfbirds. Throughout May, migrant Ruddy Turnstones are common as individuals or small flocks mixed with flocks of other migrant shorebirds. During the second week of May 1971, a few 100,000 Ruddy Turnstones moved through the region. They followed a migration pattern similar to that of the Black Turnstones two weeks previously: scores, possibly hundreds, of flocks, some with several thousand individuals, moved into Prince William Sound via Hinchinbrook Entrance or moved westward paralleling the outside of Montague Island. Those entering Prince William Sound concentrated on the shores of Montague and Green islands and nearby reefs and islets and departed from Prince William Sound via Montague Strait and Latouche Island. Those paralleling the outside of Montague Island stopped on the beaches of Montague and Wooded islands. The birds entering Prince William Sound were mixed with similar numbers of Surfbirds.

Summer visitants are regular but uncommon in small flocks, usually along the beaches of the outer coast.

Fall migrants are not present in the large numbers found in spring, but they are fairly common in small flocks from mid-July to early September. Infrequently, late small flocks remain until October (latest, six on 18 October 1971 at Cordova).

Estimates of populations utilizing the North Gulf Coast and Prince William Sound: migration-spring, several 10,000's — in some years, a few 100,000's; migration-fall, several 1,000's; summer, a few, possibly several, 100's.

Arenaria melanocephala — Black Turnstone

The Black Turnstone is a resident along the North Gulf Coast and in Prince William Sound.

Spring migrants are abundant along sections of the outer coasts during the last half of April and are common until mid-May. Solf saw several flocks of thousands in the Montague Island-Green Island area, PWS, during the last week of April 1971. Shortt (1939) saw "large numbers" in mid-May 1936 at Yakutat. Isleib saw several large flocks on 14 May 1963 near the Chugach Islands.

Black Turnstones are present as scattered singles and small flocks throughout the summer, both in Prince William Sound and along the outer coasts, but there is no evidence of nesting.

Fall migrants are fairly common in flocks along the outer coasts in mid-July and are common in large flocks in late July and early August on Montague Island (Solf and pers. obs.). They are uncommon in September and October.

Singles and small flocks are present in Prince William Sound and along the outer coast throughout the winter, sometimes associated with Surfbirds and Rock Sandpipers.

Estimates of populations utilizing the North Gulf Coast and Prince William Sound: migration, several 10,000's, possibly 100,000's; summer, a few, possibly several, 100's; winter, a few 100's.

Capella gallinago — Common Snipe

The Common Snipe is a resident of the North Gulf Coast-Prince William Sound region, occurring seasonally as a common migrant, a common breeder, and a rare winter visitant.

Migrants arrive during mid-April and by early May are common and widespread throughout the region. Migrants are still present in mid-May when local (Copper River Delta) breeders are incubating.

Shortt (1939) saw a few pairs that were evidently breeding near the coast between the Situk and Lost rivers in 1936. Snipes are common breeders over a large area of the upper Copper River Delta and breed locally elsewhere in many areas along the North Gulf Coast and in Prince William Sound. The earliest nest is one with four 1- or 2-day-old downy young, from which an adult was flushed on 26 May 1968 along the upper Grass Island Slough, CRD. Rausch (1958) thought this species was breeding on Middleton Island in early June 1956.

Fall migrants are regular from early August through late November. In September and early October, loose flocks are common on the marshes of the Copper River Delta (100+ per day in proper habitat); they are uncommon from mid-October until late November.

From November through the winter months, Common Snipes are rare and local, being most frequent during mild winters. O'Farrell and Sheets (1962) saw two snipes in an open marsh on Middleton Island on 25 February 1961.

Estimates of populations utilizing the North Gulf Coast and Prince William Sound: migration, a few, probably several, 10,000's; summer, a few, probably several, 1,000's; winter, a few individuals — in some years, 10's.

Numenius phaeopus — Whimbrel

The Whimbrel is a common migrant and uncommon summer visitant in the North Gulf Coast-Prince William Sound region.

Spring migrants move along the outer coasts during the first week of May (earliest, one on 4 May 1969 at Hartney Bay, Orca Inlet). During the second and third weeks of May, Whimbrels are common on portions of the Copper River Delta and on the beaches and tidal flats of the outer islands of Prince William Sound. On 7 May 1971 several hundred birds were present along the beaches of Montague Island.

Non-breeding summer visitants are uncommon in small flocks on the Copper River Delta and eastern Prince William Sound from late May through July. Rausch (1958) saw 2 on 11 and 13 June, respectively, 4 on 14 June, and 28 on 25 June 1956 on Middleton Island.

Fall migrants are fairly common by mid-July and are common from late July through August, usually as scattered small flocks along the outer beaches and tidal flats. Late fall migrants occur uncommonly until early October (latest, one on 9 October 1971 on Channel Isle off Green Island, PWS).

Estimates of populations utilizing the North Gulf Coast and Prince William Sound: migration, several 1,000's, possibly a few 10,000's; summer, a few, possibly several, 100's.

Numenius tahitiensis — Bristle-thighed Curlew

The Bristle-thighed Curlew is a casual (perhaps rare) migrant along the North Gulf Coast and in Prince William Sound.

Only a few sightings have been made in the region, although it may be an annual migrant in small numbers along the outer points of the North Gulf Coast:

1) A flock of nine Bristle-thighed Curlews was observed closely for nearly an hour on 8 August 1968 by Pete and Ruth Isleib on an open, sandy beach near Ocean Cape, Yakutat Bay.
2) A lone curlew was observed by West and Peyton (unpubl. notes) on 7 May 1970 at Hartney Bay, Orca Inlet. After considerable and lengthy observations, this bird was tentatively identified as a Bristle-thighed Curlew.
3) While participating in aerial surveys in Prince William Sound on 7 May 1971, Isleib saw a single Bristle-thighed Curlew near Cape Cleare, Montague Island, and a flock of seven on Latouche Island. These observations were from a light aircraft (PA-18) flying at 60 to 70 mph (96 to 113 kph) at 50 to 75 ft (15 to 25 m) elevation. The curlews were flushed from the beaches and flew parallel to the aircraft at a distance of 30 to 70 ft (10 to 20 m).

Actitis macularia — Spotted Sandpiper

The Spotted Sandpiper is a common migrant and common breeder along the North Gulf Coast and in Prince William Sound.

Spring migrants arrive during the second week of May (earliest, one on 9 May 1966 at Eyak Lake near Cordova) and are common during the latter half of May (10 to 50 per day in proper habitat).

Spotted Sandpipers breed throughout the drainages of the North Gulf Coast and Prince William Sound; Grinnell (1910a), Shortt (1939), and Gabrielson and Lincoln (1959) all reported them as common breeders within the region. Although most frequent on the banks and shores of gravelly streams and lakes, this sandpiper is fairly common about the shoreline of Prince William Sound.

Fall migrants are common in August (20 to 100 per day in proper habitat) and then are uncommon until mid-September (latest, one on 3 October 1970, Mile 15 Copper River Highway).

An unusual winter record has been reported by Shaffer, who told of a recently killed female he found on the road at Mile 11 Seward Highway, north of Seward, on 4 January 1971; unfortunately, the specimen was not saved.

Estimates of populations utilizing the North Gulf Coast and Prince William Sound: migration, several 1,000's; summer, a few, possibly several, 1,000's.

Tringa solitaria – Solitary Sandpiper

The Solitary Sandpiper is an uncommon spring migrant and a fairly common fall migrant along the North Gulf Coast and in Prince William Sound.

Spring migrants are uncommon during mid-May (earliest, one on 8 May 1966, Mile 13 Copper River Highway; latest, one on 28 May 1971 at Cordova); they occur as scattered individuals, occasionally associated with yellowlegs or dowitchers.

There are no observations of Solitary Sandpipers during the nesting season in the North Gulf Coast-Prince William Sound region, although they regularly breed in contiguous areas to the north and west.

Fall migrants are fairly common along the North Gulf Coast in August (earliest, one collected on 30 July 1908 at Hanning Bay, Montague Island [Grinnell, 1910a]). Shortt (1939) cited them as "numerous" along the Situk and Ahrnklin rivers in early August 1936. They are fairly common in August and early September on the Copper River Delta and in eastern Prince William Sound (5 to 20 per day in proper habitat) (latest, two on 13 September 1969, Mile 26 Copper River Highway).

Estimates of populations utilizing the North Gulf Coast and Prince William Sound: migration-spring, a few, probably several, 100's; migration-fall, several 100's, possibly a few 1,000's.

Heteroscelus incanum – Wandering Tattler

The Wandering Tattler is a common migrant and a locally common breeder along the North Gulf Coast and in Prince William Sound.

Spring migrants are common by the end of the first week in May (earliest, one on 29 April 1969 in Orca Inlet). Migrants are most frequent as singles or scattered individuals (10 to 50 per day in proper habitat) along rocky shores and reefs between 5 and 20 May.

Breeding was first reported within the region by the Alexander Expedition (Grinnell, 1910a), which collected a half-grown young on 28 July 1908 at Hanning Bay, Montague Island. Solf discovered a nest on a gravel bar in late June 1958 near Port Chalmers, Montague Island. Adults are common in June and July along the mountain streams flowing into the bays and fiords of the northern portion of Prince William Sound, and they probably breed there and locally elsewhere in the region.

Fall migration begins in late July (earliest, a female collected on 24 July 1936 at Khantaak Island, Yakutat Bay [Shortt, 1939]), and migrants are common in August and early September along the rocky shores and reefs (10 to 50 per day in proper habitat) (latest, one on 29 September 1969 at Hawkins Island, PWS).

Estimates of populations utilizing the North Gulf Coast and Prince William Sound: migration, a few, probably several, 1,000's; summer, several 100's, probably a few 1,000's.

Totanus melanoleucus – Greater Yellowlegs

The Greater Yellowlegs is a common migrant and a locally common breeder in the North Gulf Coast-Prince William Sound region.

Spring migrants are present from mid-April until mid-May (earliest, one on 15 April 1969, Mile 21 Copper River Highway), being common throughout most of the region in early May (20 to 100 per day in proper habitat).

Shortt (1939) reported "considerable numbers" breeding on "the muskeg and boggy" flats from Ocean Cape to the Ahrnklin River in 1936. Gabrielson (Gabrielson and Lincoln, 1959) secured downy young at the Situk River on 8 June 1940. Shaffer has found them nesting every year at the head of Resurrection Bay, where he found a nest with three eggs on 2 June 1971. They undoubtedly nest also on the upper Copper River Delta and in other areas of suitable habitat throughout the region.

Fall migrants begin departing in late July (earliest, several pairs observed on 24 July 1908 on Montague Island [Grinnell, 1910a]), and they are common during August and early September. Late migrants, consisting of individuals or small flocks, are uncommon until October (latest, one on 12 October 1969, Mile 9 Copper River Highway).

Estimates of populations utilizing the North Gulf Coast and Prince William Sound: migration, several 1,000's, probably a few 10,000's; summer, several 100's, probably a few 1,000's.

Totanus flavipes – Lesser Yellowlegs

The Lesser Yellowlegs is a fairly common migrant and a locally uncommon breeder along the North Gulf Coast and in Prince William Sound.

Spring migrants arrive on the Copper River Delta about the first of May (earliest, two on 26 April 1969, Mile 21 Copper River Highway). They are fairly common (10 to 50 per day in proper habitat) during the first half of May and uncommon in late May (latest probable migrant, two on 28 May 1971 at Cordova). During migration this species is regularly associated with, but usually outnumbered by, the Greater Yellowlegs.

The Lesser Yellowlegs breeds uncommonly and locally from the Copper River Delta eastward along the eastern North Gulf Coast. A vocal, aggressive pair was present on the upper portions of Grass Island Slough, CRD, on 7, 13, and 14 June 1968, behaving as if a nest or young were nearby. Shortt (1939:15) reported, "This species was not so common at Yakutat as the greater yellowlegs but was found breeding on the Situk River flats. A male collected on June 12 [1936] was evidently in breeding condition." Gabrielson (1944) found it in small numbers at Situk River on 8 June 1940.

Fall migrants are present in mid-July (earliest, three on 12 July 1954 in Portage Pass near Whittier [Lyon et al., unpubl. notes]), fairly common through August (10 to 50 per day in proper habitat), and uncommon in September (latest, three on 26 September 1970 at Copper Slough, CRD).

Estimates of populations utilizing the North Gulf Coast and Prince William Sound: migration, a few, probably several, 1,000's; summer, a few, probably several, 100's.

Calidris canutus — Knot

The Knot is an abundant spring migrant and a rare fall migrant in the North Gulf Coast-Prince William Sound region.

Knots have been recorded only from the Copper River Delta and eastern Prince William Sound. Spring migrants arrive during the first week in May (earliest, a flock of 70 on 4 May 1970 at Egg Island, CRD); during a 3- or 4-day period between 10 and 20 May, several thousand birds appear in a brief but spectacular movement (latest, 23 on 28 May 1966 at Copper Sands, CRD). What appears to be a large portion of the spring migrant Knots using the Pacific Coast of North America make landfall on the Copper River Delta's tidal flats during a brief period in May.

When leaving the Copper River Delta, these spring migrants execute one of two spectacular migration patterns: They either depart in hundreds of small flocks (a few to about 100 birds), flying in long lines or waves only a few feet above the tide flats and delta waters, or they form scores of large (a few hundred to well in excess of a thousand birds), compact, vocal (a mixture of raspy squeals and chattering, audible for distances in excess of 1 mile) flocks, flying directly WNW at 500 to 1000+ ft (150 to 300+ m) elevation.

Knots are rare during fall migration, suggesting that most southbound migrants either utilize another route or largely overfly the region (earliest, six on 10 August 1970 at Egg Island, CRD). The largest fall flock and latest fall migrants that have been recorded are approximately fifty birds on 8 September 1971 at Green Island, PWS.

Estimates of populations utilizing the North Gulf Coast and Prince William Sound: migration-spring, a few, possibly several, 10,000's; migration-fall, probably 100's.

Erolia ptilocnemis — Rock Sandpiper

The Rock Sandpiper is a common migrant and common winter visitant along the North Gulf Coast and in Prince William Sound.

Spring migration is difficult to document, because of large wintering populations, but Rock Sandpipers are probably migrating during April and early May (latest, three collected on 16 May 1936 at Yakutat Bay [Shortt, 1939]).

Fall migrants pass through the region beginning in mid-August (earliest, three on 17 August 1970 at Shag Rock, PWS) and are fairly common in September and October. After mid-October, the Rock Sandpiper is probably the most common shorebird within the region.

Wintering Rock Sandpipers are common in flocks of a few to several hundred birds on rocky shores and reefs, often in mixed flocks with Dunlins and other shorebirds. From mid-November to mid-March, during prolonged cold weather when the outer shores freeze with surf spray, flocks may move temporarily onto more protected beaches and tidal flats within the bays and inlets. Under these circumstances, flocks in excess of 5,000 birds may forage the tidal flats along the Cordova waterfront.

Estimates of populations utilizing the North Gulf Coast and Prince William Sound: migration, probably several 1,000's, possibly 10,000's; winter, several 1,000's, possibly 10,000's.

Erolia acuminata — Sharp-tailed Sandpiper

The Sharp-tailed Sandpiper is a casual (perhaps rare) migrant in the North Gulf Coast-Prince William Sound region.

Sharp-tailed Sandpipers have been observed twice within the region. Two females were collected at Valdez Narrows on 18 September 1908 (Grinnell, 1910a), and Isleib saw one on the tidal flats at Canoe Pass on the eastern shore of Hawkins Island, PWS, on 9 September 1969.

The Sharp-tailed Sandpiper is probably a regular migrant in limited numbers, but, because of the abundance of other shorebirds, large areas of suitable habitat, its similarity to the Pectoral Sandpiper, and a lack of experienced observers, it has passed unnoticed.

Erolia melanotos — Pectoral Sandpiper

The Pectoral Sandpiper is a fairly common migrant along the North Gulf Coast and in Prince William Sound.

Spring migrants arrive during the first week of May (earliest, two on 3 May 1971, Mile 21 Copper River Highway), becoming fairly common in the marshes from 10 to 25 May (latest, three on 28 May 1971 at Cordova). Spring migrant Pectoral Sandpipers usually occur as singles, scattered individuals, or small flocks, often associated with Greater Yellowlegs, Lesser Yellowlegs, and Least Sandpipers.

Fall migrants are fairly common in mid-August (earliest, seven on 2 August 1969 at Cordova), becoming common in late August and early September. Fall migrants are common in small flocks (10-30 individuals) in the marshes and along the upper edges of the tidal flats of the Copper River Delta. They are uncommon in late September and rare in October (latest, one on 7 October 1969, Mile 17 Copper River Highway, and three on 13 October 1972, Mile 8 Copper River Highway).

Estimates of populations utilizing the North Gulf Coast and Prince William Sound: migration, several 1,000's, possibly 10,000's.

Erolia bairdii — Baird's Sandpiper

The Baird's Sandpiper is an uncommon migrant along the North Gulf Coast and in Prince William Sound.

Spring migrants arrive in early May (earliest, nine on 2 May 1973 at Hartney Bay, Orca Inlet), and they occur uncommonly during the second and third weeks of May, usually as singles or a few individuals associated with other shorebirds (latest, two on 26 May 1971 at Cordova).

Most fall migrants pass through the region in August (earliest, four on 2 August 1969 at Cordova). They are usually associated with Western Sandpipers and Pectoral Sandpipers on the saltwater marshes and tidal flats (latest, one with Pectoral Sandpipers on 7 September 1968 at Grass Island Slough, CRD).

Estimates of populations utilizing the North Gulf Coast and Prince William Sound: migration, several 100's, possibly a few 1,000's.

Erolia minutilla — Least Sandpiper

The Least Sandpiper is an abundant migrant and common breeder along the North Gulf Coast and in Prince William Sound.

Spring migrants arrive during the last week of April (earliest, two on 26 April 1969, Mile 21 Copper River Highway) but do not become common until the first week in May. The species is an abundant migrant during the second and third weeks of May and is common until early June.

The Least Sandpiper is a common breeder on the Copper River Delta and eastward along the North Gulf Coast in tidal and freshwater marshes. Shortt (1939) found it breeding in "some numbers" in 1936 along the coastal plain east of Ocean Cape. Isleib found 12 nests (2-4 eggs) on the marshes near Grass Island Slough, CRD, between 3 and 10 June 1967, 1968, and 1969. Rausch (1958) found it the most abundant shorebird at Middleton Island during June 1956 and, although no nests were found, the birds' behavior indicated nesting. Least Sandpipers also are common on the outer beaches and tidal flats through June and July; at least some of these are non-breeding birds and/or unsuccessful nesters.

Fall migrants are common in late July and abundant in August on the Copper River Delta, and they are fairly common during this period elsewhere in the region at water margins, both freshwater and saltwater. After early September, they are uncommon (latest, two on 20 September 1969 at Grass Island Slough, CRD).

Estimates of populations utilizing the North Gulf Coast and Prince William Sound: migration, several 10,000's, probably 100,000's; summer, several 1,000's, probably 10,000's.

Erolia alpina — Dunlin

The Dunlin is a resident of the North Gulf Coast-Prince William Sound region; it is an abundant migrant and a locally common visitant in both summer and winter.

Spring migrants arrive about the first of May (earliest, flock of 40+ on 30 April 1971 at Hartney Bay, Orca Inlet) and become abundant by the end of the first week of May. Dunlins are the second most abundant shorebird (after Western Sandpiper) on the Copper River Delta from 5 to 20 May, with millions moving through during this period.

Summer visitants are common locally through June and July on the beaches and tidal flats; however, there have been no observations that would indicate breeding.

Fall migrants are abundant in late July and the first half of August, common until early September, and rare and local from mid-September until mid-October.

From October until April, winter visitants are common locally and are mixed with the large flocks of wintering Rock Sandpipers.

Estimates of populations utilizing the North Gulf Coast and Prince William Sound: migration, 1,000,000's; summer, several 100's, possibly a few 1,000's; winter, a few 1,000's.

Limnodromus griseus — Short-billed Dowitcher

The Short-billed Dowitcher is an abundant migrant and a locally common breeder in the North Gulf Coast-Prince William Sound region.

Spring migrants arrive in late April (earliest, one on 26 April 1969 at Hartney Bay, Orca Inlet) and become common during the first week of May. They are abundant during the second and third weeks of May and common into early June.

Breeders are common on territories on the marshes of the Copper River Delta by late May. Shortt (1939) found this dowitcher a common nester on the coastal plains near the Situk River in 1936. Hudson (1956) observed six at Pete

Dahl Slough, CRD, on 25 June 1955; behavior of the adults indicated the presence of young, and John Walker, U. S. Fish and Wildlife Service, showed him a nest that had had eggs on 10 June. Shepherd (pers. field notes) found a nest with four eggs at Pete Dahl Cutoff, CRD, on 19 May 1959, and he flushed a male (collected) from a nest of four eggs at Copper Slough, CRD, on 25 May 1959. Isleib watched a half-grown young being harassed and eventually killed by a Parasitic Jaeger on 27 June 1968 at Grass Island Slough, CRD. Small flocks, presumably non-breeders, are present through June on the mud flats of Orca Inlet.

Fall migrants are common through July and August and uncommon in September (latest, three on 21 September 1968, Copper River Delta).

Estimates of populations utilizing the North Gulf Coast and Prince William Sound: migration, several 10,000's; summer, a few 1,000's.

Limnodromus scolopaceus — Long-billed Dowitcher

The Long-billed Dowitcher is a common migrant along the North Gulf Coast and in Prince William Sound.

Spring migrants arrive during the first week of May, generally a few days later than the first Short-billed Dowitchers (earliest, 12 on 3 May 1970 at Hartney Bay, Orca Inlet; latest, nine on 5 June 1970 at Point Whitshed, CRD). The Long-billed Dowitcher is normally not as numerous as the Short-billed, but on the Copper River Delta and in eastern Prince William Sound during the second week of May 1964, 1970, and 1971 it was common and its numbers comparable to those of Short-billed Dowitchers.

Fall migrants occur in early August (earliest, four on 2 August 1968 at Yakutat Bay) and are fairly common during the last half of August and early September; thereafter, they are uncommon until October (latest, six lingering 7-12 October 1969 at Alaganik Slough, CRD).

Estimates of populations utilizing the North Gulf Coast and Prince William Sound: migration, a few 1,000's — in some years, probably a few 10,000's, possibly several 10,000's.

Ereunetes pusillus — Semipalmated Sandpiper

The Semipalmated Sandpiper is an uncommon migrant and rare summer visitant along the North Gulf Coast and in Prince William Sound.

Spring migrants arrive during the first week of May (earliest, 30 on 3 May 1970, Mile 21 Copper River Highway [West and Peyton, unpubl. notes]). Semipalmated Sandpipers are uncommon in May, normally occurring as scattered individuals or small flocks, either mixed with the masses of Western Sandpipers on the beaches and tidal flats or loosely associated with Least Sandpipers and Pectoral Sandpipers on the marshes of the Copper River Delta.

Semipalmated Sandpipers are rare in June, and those present are probably non-breeders and/or unsuccessful nesters. Isleib saw one with Western Sandpipers at Egg Island, CRD, on 13 June 1965; three at the same location on 24 June 1970; and four with Western Sandpipers at Orca Inlet on 5 June 1970. Rausch (1958) saw this species on Middleton Island in company with Western Sandpipers on 25 June 1956; he collected a female which had a refeathering brood patch.

Fall migrants are uncommon during July and early August and rare thereafter until they disappear in late August (latest, one on 27 August 1964 at Copper Sands, CRD, and three on 27 August 1966 at Egg Island, CRD). During their fall movement, Semipalmated Sandpipers usually are associated with other small shorebirds and occur in a variety of habitats.

Estimates of the populations utilizing the North Gulf Coast and Prince William Sound: migration, several 100's, probably a few 1,000's; summer, possibly a few 100's.

Ereunetes mauri — Western Sandpiper

The Western Sandpiper is a conspicuously abundant migrant and a common summer visitant along the North Gulf Coast and in Prince William Sound.

Spring migrants arrive about the first of May (earliest, several flocks totaling 500+ birds on 28 April 1972 at Pt. Whitshed, CRD, and 35 on 29 April 1969 at Hartney Bay, Orca Inlet) and are abundant before the end of the first week of May. Between 5 and 20 May several millions utilize the beaches and tidal flats of the Copper River Delta and Prince William Sound; during this period they are the most abundant shorebird on the Copper River Delta. More than 250,000 individuals fed in a 1-square-mile (2.59 km^2) area on the tidal flats east of Copper Sands, CRD, on 16 May 1964; and over 6.5 million utilized a 6-mile (10-km) stretch of tidal flats in Orca Inlet between 28 April and 31 May 1973. During spring migration, Western Sandpipers are often associated with the second most abundant migrating shorebird, the Dunlin. Combined, these two sandpipers outnumber all other shorebirds on the beaches and tidal flats of the Copper River Delta during the second and third weeks of May, when dense concentrations of 50,000 to 100,000 birds (mixed flocks) occur regularly at many locations at high tide. Late migrants, non-breeders, and unsuccessful nesters are common on the outer beaches throughout June.

Occasional observations of single individuals on the marshes of the Copper River Delta during June suggest possible breeding, but no nests have been found.

Fall migrants are returning by late June. Rausch (1958) found them numerous on 25 June 1956 at Middleton Island; on that date he collected seven birds, all with refeathering brood patches. Western Sandpipers are abundant along the outer beaches and tidal flats during July and August and are fairly common into early September (latest, 20 on 19 September 1970 at Copper Sands, CRD).

Estimates of populations utilizing the North Gulf Coast and Prince William Sound: migration, several 1,000,000's; summer, a few 1,000's.

Limosa lapponica — Bar-tailed Godwit

The Bar-tailed Godwit is a casual migrant in the North Gulf Coast-Prince William Sound region.

The only record is of one watched by Isleib and others on tidal flats near the Cordova boat harbor 30 and 31 May 1973. Primarily a winter-plumaged bird, it kept company with a score of Whimbrels.

Limosa haemastica — Hudsonian Godwit

The Hudsonian Godwit is an uncommon spring migrant and probably an uncommon fall migrant in the North Gulf Coast-Prince William Sound region.

Spring migrants arrive during the first week of May (earliest, two on 3 May 1969, Mile 21 Copper River Highway) and are regular during the second week of May. West and Peyton (unpubl. notes) saw 3 on 6 May, 13 on 7 May, and 26 on 8 May 1970 along the Copper River Highway and road system near Cordova. During the second week of May 1971, Isleib saw three at Valdez; one at Coghill

River flats, PWS; seven at Hartney Bay, Orca Inlet; and four at Mile 21 Copper River Highway (latest, four on 18 May 1966 at Copper Sands, CRD).

A Hudsonian Godwit was collected by George G. Cantwell at Valdez on 10 May 1907 (Gabrielson and Lincoln, 1959). Shepherd (pers. comm.) was the first to report it in recent years, a flock of 12 on 1 July 1959 at Pete Dahl Slough, CRD. The marshes of the Copper River Delta would appear to provide attractive breeding habitat for this species, but Shepherd's is the only summer observation in the region.

The only fall record is of one with a flock of 20 Whimbrels in Orca Inlet on 9 August 1972. Further field work in proper habitat in mid-August, however, will undoubtedly show this godwit to be an annual fall migrant through the region.

Estimates of the populations utilizing the North Gulf Coast and Prince William Sound: migration, several 10's, possibly a few 100's.

Crocethia alba — Sanderling

The Sanderling is a common migrant, a fairly common summer visitant, and a rare winter visitant along the North Gulf Coast and in Prince William Sound.

A few spring migrants arrive in early May, scattered amid flocks of other shorebirds (earliest, one on 4 May 1970 at Egg Island, CRD); they become common during the third and fourth weeks of May. The bulk of the spring migrants apparently migrate later than other small shorebirds; and, during late May and early June, Sanderlings outnumber all other migrant shorebirds on tidal flats and sand beaches on the Copper River Delta and in eastern Prince William Sound.

Non-breeding summer visitants are fairly common on the beaches and tidal flats of the Copper River Delta during June and July.

Fall migrants arrive sometime in July and are common throughout August, becoming rare in September (latest, six on 9 September 1970 at Egg Island, CRD).

The only winter record is of 17 Sanderlings at MacLeod Harbor, Montague Island, on 18 March 1973, but it seems probable that a few may overwinter regularly on protected, sandy beaches of the region, since they winter in the Aleutians, on the Alaska Peninsula, and as far north in southeastern Alaska as Glacier Bay (Univ. Alaska unpubl. records).

Estimates of populations utilizing the North Gulf Coast and Prince William Sound: migration, 10,000's; summer, a few, probably several, 100's; winter, a few, probably several, 10's.

Phalaropus fulicarius — Red Phalarope

The Red Phalarope is an abundant migrant and an uncommon summer visitant in the North Gulf Coast-Prince William Sound region.

Spring migrants move through the inshore waters from mid-May (earliest, five on 14 May 1963 near the Chugach Islands) until mid-June. Several hundred small flocks, totaling several thousand birds, were present along the barrier islands of the Copper River Delta between 29 May and 3 June 1971, following a series of storms in the northern Gulf of Alaska. Considering the lateness of the dates, these birds were probably laggards and not the main population of migrants, which utilizes the offshore waters of the Gulf of Alaska (latest, about 50 some 100 miles east of Kodiak on 10 June 1946 [Gabrielson and Lincoln, 1959]).

Summer visitants in inshore waters are rare. Rausch (1958) collected a male on 26 June 1956 at Middleton Island. Joseph Dixon (Grinnell, 1910a) collected a female on 1 July 1908 at Hinchinbrook Island. Isleib saw six in the middle of Prince William Sound on 12 July 1964, and he has seen singles on several occasions in late June and early July in the inshore waters off the Copper River Delta.

Information on fall migration is sparse because of the pelagic habits of the species. Red Phalaropes are regular in small numbers each fall between late August and mid-September on Resurrection Bay, where Shaffer has seen up to 20 birds per trip on numerous occasions. Isleib saw three Red Phalaropes in Hinchinbrook Entrance on 5 August 1969. Gabrielson and Lincoln (1959) reported the latest fall record, four on 2 October 1944 some 75 miles (120 km) offshore, east of Kodiak.

Estimates of populations utilizing the North Gulf Coast and Prince William Sound: migration, probably 100,000's; summer, probably several 100's.

Lobipes lobatus — Northern Phalarope

The Northern Phalarope is a conspicuously abundant migrant, a common summer visitant, and an abundant breeder in the North Gulf Coast-Prince William Sound region.

Spring migrants arrive during the first week of May (earliest, two on 3 May 1969, Mile 17 Copper River Highway); immense numbers pass through the region during the second and third weeks of May; and migrants continue to be common until early June. A huge raft of tens of thousands of phalaropes was present in Hinchinbrook Entrance on 8 May 1971.

The Northern Phalarope is a common summer visitant throughout inshore and offshore waters in June and July. It is an abundant breeder on the Copper River Delta and a locally common breeder on marshes elsewhere in the region. Grinnell (1910a), Shortt (1939), Rausch (1958), Gabrielson and Lincoln (1959), and Yocom (1963) all referred to the Northern Phalarope as a common breeder; they found several nests and eggs and collected specimens. Isleib found six nests in less than 2 hours on 10 June 1968 at Grass Island Slough, CRD. Shepherd (pers. field notes) recorded newly hatched chicks on 25 June 1959 from eggs that hatched after being incubated for 19 days.

Fall migrants are abundant from late July until September, common through September, rare during October, and usually absent by 1 November (latest, one on 1 December 1969 on a small pond near Mile 12 Seward Highway by Shaffer).

Estimates of populations utilizing the North Gulf Coast and Prince William Sound: migration, a few 1,000,000's; summer, a few 10,000's.

Stercorarius pomarinus — Pomarine Jaeger

The Pomarine Jaeger is a fairly common migrant and a rare summer visitant along the North Gulf Coast and in Prince William Sound.

Spring migrants occur from mid-April to mid-June (earliest, one on 17 April 1970 in Hinchinbrook Entrance); they are fairly common off the Copper River Delta from mid-May until the second week of June (10 to 50 per day, generally between Pete Dahl Bar and Softuk Bar; 1 in 20 in dark-phase plumage). The Pomarine Jaeger is more common as a spring migrant in inshore waters than the other jaegers. While on a boat trip from the Chugach Islands to Cordova 13 through 18 May 1963, Isleib counted seven Pomarine Jaegers, three Long-tails, and one Parasitic.

Summer visitants (mid-June to mid-July) are rare but regular in the waters off the Copper River Delta and Yakutat Bay and probably elsewhere in the region.

Fall migrants are common in late July and early August; they are uncommon after mid-August, and numbers continue to decline through October (latest, one on 4 November 1968 at Middleground Shoal, Orca Bay). The U. S. Fish and Wildlife Service survey 21 July-4 August 1972 estimated over 1600 jaegers in Prince William Sound, most of which were migrating Pomarine Jaegers. On 26 July 1968, 2 miles off Ocean Cape, Yakutat Bay, Pete and Ruth Isleib saw over 40 Pomarine Jaegers, 3 Long-tailed Jaegers, 14 Parasitic Jaegers, and 1 Skua – all four stercorariids together.

Estimates of populations utilizing the North Gulf Coast and Prince William Sound: migration, several 1,000's, probably 10,000's; summer, a few, possibly several, 100's.

Stercorarius parasiticus – Parasitic Jaeger

The Parasitic Jaeger is an uncommon spring migrant, a common fall migrant, and a locally common breeder along the North Gulf Coast and in Prince William Sound.

Spring migrants move through the region between late April (earliest, one on 23 April 1969 at Strawberry Bar, CRD) and mid-May.

Breeders become common during the second week of May on the Copper River Delta. Isleib saw a pair copulating and other pairs on territory on 23 May 1963 at Little Glacier Slough; Shepherd (pers. comm.) saw two half-grown young with an adult on 19 July 1959 on the delta; and Yocom (1963) saw a juvenal barely able to fly on 24 July 1962 on the delta.

The Copper River Delta population during May-June 1963 was approximately 250 individuals (all dark-phase, except two light- and three intermediate-phase birds). In May-July 1970 approximately 160 to 170 breeding pairs were utilizing the Copper River Delta area, as well as 70 or more non-territorial individuals. Shortt (1939) found Parasitic Jaegers "fairly common" in the Yakutat area in 1936, particularly about the Malaspina Glacier, and reported that about 65% were dark-phase birds. A dark-phase bird, apparently one of a breeding pair, was collected by the Alexander Expedition on Hawkins Island, PWS, on 23 June 1908 (Grinnell, 1910a).

Non-breeders and/or unsuccessful nesters are uncommon but regular in inshore and offshore waters during the summer.

Fall migrants are common along the coast from late July until mid-September, uncommon until mid-October (a few linger on the Copper River Delta until early October), and rare in November (latest, one on 18 November 1968 in Orca Bay).

Estimates of populations utilizing the North Gulf Coast and Prince William Sound: migration, several 1,000's, probably 10,000's; summer, a few 1,000's.

Stercorarius longicaudus – Long-tailed Jaeger

The Long-tailed Jaeger is a rare migrant along the North Gulf Coast and in Prince William Sound.

Spring migrants move through the region without lingering. They probably begin passing through in early May, although the earliest observation is of two on 14 May 1963 between the Chugach Islands and Gore Point. They are regular (2 to 5 per spring migration) through late May (latest, one on 31 May 1963 off the Copper River Delta).

Although Long-tails probably nest on the mainland alpine tundra, there are no breeding records for the region. Closely adjacent to the region, however, 40 miles (64 km) northwest of Seward in the Kenai Mountains, an adult at a nest with two young was photographed in July 1960 by Gerry Atwell, Alaska Department of Fish and Game (Steven R. Smith, pers. comm.). Gabrielson (1944) saw one flying along the Fairweather Range near Yakutat on 7 June 1940, and Shortt (1939) saw an individual in Disenchantment Bay on 7 July 1936 that may not have been the transient he assumed.

While observed more frequently than in spring, Long-tailed Jaegers are rare fall migrants, occurring from late July until early September (3 to 5 per fall migration) (latest, one on 7 September 1967 at Grass Island Bar, CRD). Gabrielson (Gabrielson and Lincoln, 1959) saw one off Cape Fairweather on 30 July 1943, and Isleib saw three with other jaegers 2 miles off Ocean Cape on 26 July 1968. Shaffer saw an adult coursing the bay and flats off the Seward docks in mid-December 1963 — an incredibly late date for a species which should by then be at southern latitudes.

Estimates of populations utilizing the North Gulf Coast and Prince William Sound: migration, a few, probably several, 100's, possibly 1,000's.

Catharacta skua — Skua

The Skua appears to be a casual summer visitant to the North Gulf Coast-Prince William Sound region.

Isleib has seen this wanderer from southern latitudes on two occasions along the North Gulf Coast, both times under conditions of good visibility: one in Montague Straits, PWS, on 25 July 1965, and another with numerous jaegers, gulls, and terns 2 miles off Ocean Cape on 26 July 1968.

Local fishermen and LeRoy W. Sowl, U. S. Fish and Wildlife Service, have reported large, dark-brown, gull-like birds that were stockier and swifter than gulls, and some of these birds may have been Skuas. Extensive field work in the Gulf of Alaska may reveal the Skua as a rare annual visitant into offshore waters.

Larus hyperboreus — Glaucous Gull

The Glaucous Gull is an uncommon resident along the North Gulf Coast and in Prince William Sound.

Glaucous Gulls occur regularly (20 to 100 per year) in inshore and offshore waters, mostly immatures and subadults. Of approximately 40 age determinations made in the Copper River Delta-Prince William Sound area in 1971, two were adults (present 20 December 1971-18 January 1972 at Cordova), three were second-year birds, and the rest were first-year birds. Small numbers (up to 20 birds) occur annually in Resurrection Bay (Shaffer, pers. comm.); the highest one-day count within the entire region is 17, counted in the Resurrection Bay area by Isleib on 20 December 1961.

If food sources are abundant, many of these individuals linger in one area from several weeks to several months. Five first-year birds fed in a 30 sq mile (80 km^2) area about Middleground Shoal, Orca Bay, from mid-January through March 1970. Other Glaucous Gulls are scattered throughout the year about fish processing plants, city waterfronts, dumps, at salmon spawning streams, etc.

Estimates of populations utilizing the North Gulf Coast and Prince William Sound: yearly, a few, possibly several, 100's.

Larus glaucescens — Glaucous-winged Gull

The Glaucous-winged Gull is an abundant resident of the North Gulf Coast-Prince William Sound region.

This gull is the region's principal scavenger and the "sea gull" best known to the people living in the region. It is abundant about the waterfronts of Yakutat, Cordova, and Seward, especially during any seafood processing activities, and it occurs commonly at sea, considerable distances from the coast, at all seasons. Approximately 10,000 gulls are attracted by the salmon offal from the Cordova canneries during July and August, some from breeding colonies 20 miles (32 km) away on the Copper River Delta.

Although Glaucous-winged Gulls are present in numbers throughout the year, spring and fall migratory movements are evident, mainly between mid-April and mid-May and between mid-September and mid-October.

Large Glaucous-winged Gull colonies exist at Yakutat Bay, on the barrier islands off the Copper River Delta, and on islands at the mouth of Resurrection Bay; smaller colonies, too numerous to list, are scattered along the entire length of the North Gulf Coast and in Prince William Sound. Egg-laying usually begins during the second week of May. U. S. Fish and Wildlife Service surveys estimated more than 40,000 of these gulls in Prince William Sound 24 March-4 April 1972 and more than 60,000, 21 July-4 August 1972.

During August and September, much of the Glaucous-winged Gull population occurs along the numerous salmon spawning streams, feeding on dead and dying, spawned-out salmon. During the first week of October 1971, several thousand gulls were present at a stream containing a large, late salmon run in Sheep Bay, PWS.

Although a portion of the population shifts southward along the coast during the winter, considerable numbers remain in the region. About 400 Glaucous-winged Gulls were present at the head of Resurrection Bay on 22 December 1962, and 896 were present along the Cordova waterfront on 27 December 1969.

Estimates of populations utilizing the North Gulf Coast and Prince William Sound: summer, a few, possibly several, 100,000's; winter, several 10,000's, possibly 100,000's; total annual utilization, several 100,000's.

Larus argentatus — Herring Gull

The Herring Gull is a resident along the North Gulf Coast and in Prince William Sound, occurring seasonally as a common spring and fall migrant (20 to 100 per day in proper habitat), an uncommon summer visitant and possible local breeder (0 to 10 per day in proper habitat), and a fairly common winter visitant (10 to 50 per day in proper habitat).

Migration occurs mainly between mid-April and early May and between mid-September and mid-October.

A few colonies may exist within the region. Gabrielson (1944) reported a small nesting colony mixed with Mew Gulls on the Copper River Delta on 10 June 1940, but no evidence of this colony now exists.

In winter, Herring Gulls are outnumbered by Glaucous-winged Gulls by at least twenty to one. Twenty-two Herring Gulls were present at Seward on 22 December 1962, and 59 were present at Cordova on 27 December 1969.

Small numbers of "Thayer's Gulls" (*L. a. thayeri*) are present at all seasons, but most frequently from October through April (1 to 10 per day in proper habitat). Shortt (1939) reported *L. a. thayeri* as "not uncommon" about Yakutat in 1936 and obtained a specimen on 21 August; Willett (1923) and Webster (1941) reported it a common wintering bird in southeastern Alaska.

L. glaucescens x *L. argentatus* intergrades occur regularly in numbers similar to *L. a. thayeri* and are also most frequent during the winter months. (See Williamson and Peyton [1963] for discussion of interbreeding among these gulls in the Cook Inlet region.)

Estimates of populations utilizing the North Gulf Coast and Prince William Sound: migration, a few, probably several, 1,000's; summer, a few, possibly several, 100's; winter, several 100's, possibly a few 1,000's. Sixty to 80% are "typical" Herring Gulls.

Larus canus — Mew Gull

The Mew Gull is an abundant resident of the North Gulf Coast and Prince William Sound.

This medium-sized gull is an abundant migrant, abundant breeder, and a common winter resident in the region. Several hundreds may be observed daily along the coasts from April through November, dozens from December through March.

Mew Gulls migrate from mid-March through May and from August through November.

These gulls breed throughout the region as scattered pairs and loose aggregations on marshes and beaches and barrier islands above tide level. Locally, at the heads of fiords and bays in Prince William Sound, they nest in conifers. Shortt (1939) found Mew Gulls very commonly throughout the Yakutat area in 1936 and took eggs from a small colony at Icy Bay near the Malaspina Glacier. Shepherd (pers. field notes) recorded a nest with two eggs on 14 May 1959 on the Copper River Delta.

Mew Gulls commonly join other gulls at sources of food abundance, e.g., at seafood processing plants and at salmon spawning streams. At such sites they may occur in aggregations of several hundred birds.

Although Mew Gulls are common in winter, in both inshore and offshore waters, most of the population moves to more southern latitudes. Sixty-five Mew Gulls were present at Seward on 22 December 1962 and 403 were at Cordova on 27 December 1969.

Estimates of populations utilizing the North Gulf Coast and Prince William Sound: migration, several 10,000's, possibly 100,000's; summer, several 1,000's, probably 10,000's; winter, a few, possibly several, 1,000's.

Larus philadelphia — Bonaparte's Gull

The Bonaparte's Gull is a common migrant and a locally common breeder along the North Gulf Coast and in Prince William Sound.

Spring migrants arrive during the last week of April and the first half of May (earliest, seven on 23 April 1969 at Strawberry Bar, CRD). These migrants normally occur in small flocks (3 to 30 individuals), but whenever food is abundant, concentrations of a few hundred to several thousand occur. Several thousand congregate in the vicinity of Tatitlek Narrows, PWS, each spring (late April-early May) to feed on Pacific Herring spawn.

Breeding Bonaparte's Gulls are common at the heads of several of the bays and fiords of the region, where they nest in conifers, often in association with Mew Gulls; young in early flight stages are common in mid-July. Shortt (1939) found the Bonaparte's Gull a "plentiful summer bird" of the Yakutat area in 1936 and collected a juvenal just able to fly on 14 July 1936 at the Malaspina Glacier.

Fall migrants are common from late July through mid-October. Several hundreds fed in inshore waters off Ocean Cape in the last week of July 1968, and flocks of 100 to 500 birds (occasionally thousands) gather annually about alluvial outwash at the mouths of salmon spawning streams during late summer and early fall. Bonaparte's Gulls are rare after mid-October (latest observation and possible overwintering, six on 20 December 1961 at the head of Resurrection Bay).

Estimates of populations utilizing the North Gulf Coast and Prince William Sound: migration, a few, possibly several, 10,000's; summer, several 1,000's, possibly a few 10,000's.

Rissa tridactyla — Black-legged Kittiwake

The Black-legged Kittiwake is a resident of the North Gulf Coast-Prince William Sound region, occurring as an abundant migrant, an abundant breeder, and an uncommon winter visitant.

The Black-legged Kittiwake is the most numerous gull within the region, being abundant throughout most of the inshore and offshore waters from early April through October. This gull is highly pelagic during the non-breeding season and is common far out at sea in the Gulf of Alaska.

Kittiwakes breed in numerous colonies throughout the region, but especially in Prince William Sound and along the western North Gulf Coast. These colonies vary in size from a few pairs on some islets to tens of thousands of birds on the coastal bluffs, islands, and sea stacks. U. S. Fish and Wildlife Service surveys 21 July - 4 August 1972 found 22 colonies in Prince William Sound; the largest were at Pinnacle Rocks and Boswell Bay (5,636 nests), Passage Canal (2,780 nests), Blackstone Bay (990 nests), Icy Bay and Nassau Fiord (3,000 nests), and Porpoise Rocks (975 nests). The easternmost colony known in the region today is one of several hundred pairs in the Martin Islands near Katalla, although a small colony has been reported adjacent to the region at Glacier Bay (Wik and Streveler, 1968), and Shortt (1939) thought that they bred somewhere in the vicinity of Yakutat. Shortt based his assumption on the presence of immature and adult birds showing up in numbers in late July; this date, however, is too early for birds-of-the-year, and Shortt may have been seeing non-breeders and unsuccessful nesters.

Birds begin arriving at colony sites in mid- or late March, and all breeders apparently are present by early May; nesting, however, usually does not begin until early June. The peak of hatch is generally in mid-July. Birds leave the colonies between mid-August and mid-September, and numbers in the region have declined to winter levels by November.

Wintering Black-legged Kittiwakes are uncommon; most are first- and second-year birds (subadults) and occur mostly in the inshore waters along the outer coasts and in offshore waters. Five kittiwakes were present at Seward on 22 December 1962, and four were at Cordova on 27 December 1969.

Estimates of populations utilizing the North Gulf Coast and Prince William Sound: migration, 1,000,000's; summer, a few, possibly several, 100,000's;winter, a few, probably several, 1,000's.

Xema sabini — Sabine's Gull

The Sabine's Gull is a rare spring migrant and an uncommon fall migrant in the North Gulf Coast-Prince William Sound region.

Spring migrants occur regularly in offshore waters from early May until early June. Inshore observations by Isleib include two Sabine's Gulls on 7 May 1971 along the outer coast of Montague Island; one on 17 May 1963 flying westward some 2 miles (3 km) off Cape Junken, Kenai Peninsula; and occasional individuals in late May off the Copper River Delta. Shaffer saw three at the head of Resurrection Bay on 30 May 1971 (latest, one on 8 June 1946 in the Gulf of Alaska by Gabrielson [Gabrielson and Lincoln, 1959]).

Fall migrants occur from mid-July through early October. Inshore records include a flock of six on 25 July 1965 in Montague Straits, a flock of over 100 individuals that lingered for several days during late July 1968 near Ocean Cape, and scattered individuals occurring uncommonly during August and early September off the Copper River Delta and in Prince William Sound (latest, one on 5 October 1969 in Orca Inlet).

Estimates of populations utilizing the North Gulf Coast and Prince William Sound: migration, a few, possibly several, 1,000's.

Sterna paradisaea — Arctic Tern

The Arctic Tern is an abundant migrant and abundant breeder in the North Gulf Coast-Prince William Sound region.

Spring migrants occur from late April through mid-May (earliest, two on 26 April 1969, Mile 17 Copper River Highway); they become common during the first week of May and are abundant thereafter. Over 20,000 Arctic Terns, mostly migrants, were present in Prince William Sound waters between 4 and 9 May 1971 (U. S. Fish and Wildlife Service survey); most of these were migrants in numerous small flocks flying northwestward across eastern Prince William Sound on 8 and 9 May.

An abundant breeder throughout the region, the Arctic Tern nests as numerous, scattered pairs throughout a wide variety of habitats. Shepherd (pers. field notes) located six nests, each containing one or two eggs, on 13 May 1959 at Pete Dahl Slough, CRD. Locally, especially on islands, Arctic Terns nest in colonies of up to a few hundred pairs. U. S. Fish and Wildlife Service surveys 21 July-4 August 1972 estimated over 45,000 of these terns in Prince William Sound.

Fall migrants are abundant from late July through mid-August, common through late August, and uncommon during the first two weeks of September. A concentration of over 10,000 Arctic Terns remained for several days during the last week of July 1968 on the east side of Yakutat Bay. After late August, most migrants are immatures wandering southeastward along the outer coasts and islands (latest, three on 18 September 1971 at Egg Island, CRD).

Estimates of populations utilizing the North Gulf Coast and Prince William Sound: migration, a few, probably several, 100,000's, possibly 1,000,000's; summer, several 10,000's.

Sterna aleutica — Aleutian Tern

The Aleutian Tern is an uncommon local breeder in the North Gulf Coast-Prince William Sound region.

Spring arrivals appear on the Copper River Delta during the first two weeks of May, and the population is established by mid-May. Because they apparently arrive directly from the Gulf of Alaska/Pacific Ocean as high seas migrants, there are only two observations of spring migrants. On 4 May 1970, two Aleutian Terns flew over Egg Island and entered the Copper River Delta area from the southwest. On 7 May 1971, three Aleutian Terns flew northeast along the seaward side of Hinchinbrook Island toward the Copper River Delta, approximately 12 miles (19 km) away.

Nesting on the Copper River Delta is confined to a 1- to 2-mile-wide strip of the outer marshes between the entrance of Eyak River and Mirror Slough, a distance of approximately 40 miles (65 km). Nesting pairs are scattered throughout this area. Isleib estimated the population at a few hundred birds on the Copper River Delta in late May 1963 and 300-500 birds in early June 1970.

Aleutian Terns also occur more or less regularly near Controller Bay, on the Bering River Delta, off the Situk River, and rarely in eastern Prince William Sound. Walker (1920) reported this tern on the Situk River flats and at Dry Bay in July 1916 and 1917 and again on the Situk River flats, where he found it nesting, on 12 June 1922 (Walker, 1923). Shortt (1939) was unable to find it at the Situk River in 1936, nor did Gabrielson (Gabrielson and Lincoln, 1959) mention it, although he visited the Situk River on several occasions.

Breeders on the Copper River Delta depart soon after the young are flying in late July, and they are rare on the delta after early August (latest, three on 12 August 1970 at Egg Island, CRD). Aleutian Terns generally leave the North Gulf Coast in late July and early August. Over 100 Aleutian Terns congregated for several days during the last week of July 1968 in Yakutat Bay; these birds may have come from the nearby Situk River or Dry Bay areas.

Estimates of populations utilizing the North Gulf Coast and Prince William Sound: summer, several 100's.

Uria aalge — Common Murre

The Common Murre is a fairly common resident in the North Gulf Coast-Prince William Sound region; it is locally abundant at sites along the outer coast.

Little is known about population movements of the Common Murre within the region, but recent reports from local commercial fishermen (William F. Webber and others) indicate that substantial numbers of murres migrate through the offshore waters. Over a 3-day period during the last week of April 1972, these fishermen reported seeing many tens of thousands of murres streaming westward over offshore waters off Hinchinbrook and Montague islands — constantly moving birds visible over a 20-mile (32-km) front.

Seven or more colonies of these murres are present during the summer on coastal bluffs, islands, and sea stacks along the open coasts from the Martin to the Chugach islands. The largest breeding colony is at Barwell Island, where many thousands spend the summer. A few thousand Common Murres frequent the bluffs and adjacent waters of Porpoise Rocks in Hinchinbrook Entrance and the Martin Islands, but most of these are non-breeders. Rausch (1958) reported both species of murres breeding on Middleton Island in 1956; the largest colony numbered about 200 birds. Isleib found Common Murres fairly common in the Yakutat Bay area in July and August 1968, over 100 miles (160 km) from the nearest known colony.

From early September until April, murres are common (several 1,000's, irregularly probably 10,000's) in the more sheltered waters of Prince William Sound, most notably in Montague Straits and Orca Bay. Alcids form the bulk of the wintering birds in the offshore waters of the North Gulf Coast, but little is known about their offshore wintering densities. Kenneth Mitchell, U. S. Forest Service, (pers. comm.) saw hundreds of storm-killed murres and murrelets on the outer beaches of Montague Island in January 1970, suggesting that offshore wintering populations are substantial.

Estimates of populations utilizing the North Gulf Coast and Prince William Sound: migration, largely unknown (see above); summer, several 10,000's, probably 100,000's; winter, 10,000's, probably 100,000's.

Uria lomvia — Thick-billed Murre

The Thick-billed Murre is a rare resident of the North Gulf Coast-Prince William Sound region.

Only Rausch (1958:237) has reported breeding Thick-billed Murres from the North Gulf Coast region; on Middleton Island in June-July 1956, he observed some 400 murres and found that "Thick-billed Murres were several times more abundant than Common Murres." Shaffer has seen several Thick-billed Murres in Resurrection Bay on scattered dates throughout the year, and the species is casual in Prince William Sound—one at Porpoise Rocks 22 July 1972, two in Port Gravina in January 1970, and several in Orca Bay in February 1970.

Further ornithological work in the region probably will reveal occasional breeding Thick-billed Murres amid the Common Murre colonies along the western North Gulf Coast and probably will show it to be somewhat more common than currently realized.

Estimates of populations utilizing the North Gulf Coast and Prince William Sound: yearly, a few 100's, probably 1,000's.

Cepphus columba — Pigeon Guillemot

The Pigeon Guillemot is a common resident throughout the North Gulf Coast-Prince William Sound region.

Pigeon Guillemots are abundant locally from April to October, breeding especially throughout the rocky coastal portions of the North Gulf Coast and Prince William Sound. Several pairs nest in the rock bluffs of Spike Island, only 100 yards (90 m) from the Cordova boat harbor. Shortt (1939) found this species a "very common" breeder about the islands in Yakutat Bay in 1936. Grinnell (1910a) reported that it bred commonly along the seacoasts of Prince William Sound in 1908. Shaffer has seen numerous nesting pairs along the shores of Resurrection Bay. U. S. Fish and Wildlife Service surveys 21 July - 4 August 1972 estimated 15,000 guillemots in Prince William Sound. They remain common during the winter and are dispersed throughout the inshore and offshore waters.

Estimates of populations utilizing the North Gulf Coast and Prince William Sound: yearly, a few, possibly several, 10,000's.

Brachyramphus marmoratum — Marbled Murrelet

The Marbled Murrelet is an abundant resident of the North Gulf Coast and Prince William Sound region.

During the summer the Marbled Murrelet, occurring mostly as numerous, scattered pairs and individuals, is an abundant and conspicuous bird, composing probably the greatest avian biomass in Prince William Sound. U. S. Fish and Wildlife Service surveys 21 July-4 August 1972 estimated about 250,000 Marbled Murrelets on the waters of Prince William Sound.

Almost nothing is known about the nesting habits of Marbled Murrelets. Recent reports indicate tree nesting (Kuziakin, 1963; Harris, 1971; Savile, 1972), but in the North Gulf Coast-Prince William Sound region, they appear also to be nesting above timberline in the mountains, probably in screes. Relatively dense populations of murrelets occur in the fiords of Prince William Sound during the breeding season; and, although the birds are most active at night, Isleib and Solf on numerous occasions have watched murrelets descending from the mountains to the fiord waters and have watched them ascend to at least 1,000 ft (300 m), carrying small fish in their bills, and fly out of sight toward the upper mountain slopes. Young birds begin to appear on the inshore waters after mid-July, at which time they appear to be independent and capable of flight.

Marbled Murrelets show no evidence of migratory movements, although they disperse throughout inshore and offshore waters in the fall and are less common during the winter at the heads of the bays and fiords.

Estimates of populations utilizing the North Gulf Coast and Prince William Sound: yearly, several 100,000's, probably 1,000,000's.

Brachyramphus brevirostre — Kittlitz's Murrelet

The Kittlitz's Murrelet is a common resident of the North Gulf Coast-Prince William Sound region.

Apparently preferring glacial moraines for nesting, these murrelets are abundant locally in inshore waters during the summer, especially near glaciated coastal areas; they are most abundant in the waters of upper Unakwik Inlet, upper College Fiord, and in waters abutting the Malaspina-Bering icefields, outnumbering all other alcids in these waters. U. S. Fish and Wildlife Service surveys 21 July-4 August 1972 estimated approximately 57,000 Kittlitz's Murrelets in Prince William Sound, almost all in the fiords and bays on the northern and western periphery of the sound. On 30 July 1972, there were more than 10,000 Kittlitz's Murrelets above Unakwik Reef in Unakwik Inlet, about 2,500 birds in a single, loose flock; Kittlitz's outnumbered the Marbled Murrelet in this area, whereas the reverse was true just below Unakwik Reef.

Although there are no specific breeding records for the region, these birds apparently nest above timberline and/or on unvegetated coastal glacial moraines.

During the winter, Kittlitz's Murrelets apparently disperse throughout inshore and offshore waters, becoming rare at the heads of the fiords. Several hundred Kittlitz's Murrelets were present in Prince William Sound during U. S. Fish and Wildlife Service surveys 17 March-1 April 1973. Laing (1925) reported six at Yakutat Bay on 12 March 1924.

Estimates of populations utilizing the North Gulf Coast and Prince William Sound: yearly, several 10,000's, probably a few 100,000's.

Synthliboramphus antiquum — Ancient Murrelet

The Ancient Murrelet is an uncommon resident of the North Gulf Coast-Prince William Sound region.

This murrelet is uncommon but regular and widely distributed throughout the summer as individuals and small groups in the inshore waters along the outer coasts. Ancient Murrelets probably breed in the region, since they breed both in southeastern Alaska (Gabrielson and Lincoln, 1959) and on Kodiak Island (Friedmann, 1935), but, other than recurrent summer observations, there are no substantiating data. Their nocturnal habits and early (at about 4 days of age and mostly prior to mid-June [Willett, 1915]) departure from nesting sites are responsible, in part, for our dearth of knowledge on breeding.

U. S. Fish and Wildlife Service surveys estimated 965 Ancient Murrelets (most in non-breeding plumage) along the outer periphery of Montague Island 22-23 July 1972. Rausch (1958) saw a few off Middleton Island in late June 1956 and collected a female on 27 June. During July and August 1968, Pete and Ruth Isleib saw 400-500 widely-distributed Ancient Murrelets at the mouth of Yakutat Bay. Gabrielson (Gabrielson and Lincoln, 1959) collected an Ancient Murrelet at Cordova on 27 September 1941 and another at Chiswell Islands on 31 July 1945. Within Prince William Sound, they occur only during the fall, when they are regular in small numbers from August through October (Solf, and pers. obs.).

Shaffer has made the only winter observations of this murrelet in the region; he saw one in late November 1965 and two in mid-January 1966 at the head of Resurrection Bay. It is probably rare but regular in winter, mostly in the offshore waters of the region.

Estimates of populations utilizing the North Gulf Coast and Prince William Sound: yearly, a few, probably several, 1,000's, possibly 10,000's.

Ptychoramphus aleutica — Cassin's Auklet

The Cassin's Auklet is a casual visitant in the North Gulf Coast-Prince William Sound region.

The only record of this auklet between Kodiak Island and Cape Spencer is of a few birds seen by Gabrielson (Gabrielson and Lincoln, 1959) on 31 July 1945 at the Chiswell Islands. The Cassin's Auklet is probably more frequent than this single observation would indicate, however, since it has been recorded breeding in southeastern Alaska (Willett, 1915) and on Kodiak Island (Friedmann, 1935).

Cyclorrhynchus psittacula — Parakeet Auklet

The Parakeet Auklet is an uncommon local breeder in the North Gulf Coast-Prince William Sound region.

Little is known about arrival and departure dates because of a lack of field work near colony sites. Earliest records, however, include one on 31 March 1973 near Storey Island, PWS, and several on 17 May 1963 near Montague Island, PWS; the latest record is of 16 on 27 August 1908 near Knight Island, PWS (Grinnell, 1910a).

This auklet occurs primarily at colonies in coastal bluffs, especially on the small islands of Prince William Sound and off the western North Gulf Coast; there are no observations from the eastern North Gulf Coast. U. S. Fish and Wildlife Service surveys 21 July-4 August 1972 estimated approximately 3,000 of these auklets in Prince William Sound; most of these birds were located in the vicinity of six colonies: Wooded, Little Smith, Smith, Naked, Storey, and Fool islands. Gabrielson (Gabrielson and Lincoln, 1959) saw one at the Chiswell Islands on 31 July 1945, and Roseneau (unpubl. notes) in 1965 found this auklet breeding on closely adjacent East Amatuli Island, Barren Islands (100's present).

Estimates of populations utilizing the North Gulf Coast and Prince William Sound: summer, a few, probably several, 1,000's.

Aethia cristatella — Crested Auklet

The Crested Auklet is probably a rare visitant to the North Gulf Coast-Prince William Sound region.

There are only three observations of this auklet in the region, all by Isleib during the winter of 1972-73. He saw two birds at sea about 25 miles (40 km) east of Hinchinbrook Entrance on 27 December 1972; three near Porpoise Rocks, Hinchinbrook Entrance, on 29 December 1972; and one near Seal Island, PWS, on 24 March 1973.

Closely adjacent to the region, Roseneau (unpubl. notes) identified four Crested Auklets in Amatuli Cove, Barren Islands, and possibly two others at the mouth of the cove, on 4 June 1965. These observations, plus the fact that the species reportedly breeds on Kodiak Island (Friedmann, 1935), makes it likely that it occurs with some regularity, at least in winter, in the waters along the outer points of the western North Gulf Coast.

Cerorhinca monocerata — Rhinoceros Auklet

The Rhinoceros Auklet is a rare visitant and probable breeder in the North Gulf Coast-Prince William Sound region.

During U. S. Fish and Wildlife Service surveys 21 July-4 August 1972, breeding-plumaged Rhinoceros Auklets were observed at the following colonies in the Prince William Sound area: Wooded Islands (30+ birds), Storey Island (1 bird), and Channel Island in Montague Strait (1, probably 2, birds). These auklets appeared to be nesting in the area, particularly the individuals about Wooded Islands, where they were among several thousand nesting Tufted Puffins.

Prior to these 1972 observations, there were only three records of the Rhinoceros Auklet from the region: Shortt (1939) saw one in Yakutat Bay on 8 June 1936, and Isleib saw two in Hinchinbrook Entrance on 22 July 1964 and two on open water in the middle of Prince William Sound on 22 June 1972.

Closely adjacent to the region, Roseneau (unpubl. notes) saw two at the Barren Islands on 14 and 15 June 1965. On the basis of these records, it seems likely that the Rhinoceros Auklet is a rare, local breeder in the North Gulf Coast-Prince William Sound region.

Estimates of populations utilizing the North Gulf Coast and Prince William Sound: summer, a few, probably several, 10's, possibly 100's.

Fratercula corniculata — Horned Puffin

The Horned Puffin is a fairly common local resident in the North Gulf Coast-Prince William Sound region.

During the summer these puffins are found largely at colonies from Cape St. Elias westward through Prince William Sound and along the western North Gulf Coast; they have not been seen east of Cape St. Elias. U. S. Fish and Wildlife Service surveys 21 July-4 August 1972 located 21 Horned Puffin breeding colonies, ranging from 5 to 140 pairs, within Prince William Sound. Shaffer saw approximately 10 pairs, undoubtedly breeders, at Rugged Island and a like number at Caines Head in Resurrection Bay in early June 1969. Sowl (pers. comm.) saw Horned Puffins commonly amid the masses of Tufted Puffins at seabird colonies between Resurrection Bay and the Chugach Islands during an aerial survey of the area in August 1971.

There are no winter records for the region, but Horned Puffins probably disperse into the offshore waters in the Gulf of Alaska adjacent to their breeding areas.

Estimates of populations utilizing the North Gulf Coast and Prince William Sound: yearly, several 1,000's, possibly a few 10,000's.

Lunda cirrhata – Tufted Puffin

The Tufted Puffin is a resident of the North Gulf Coast-Prince William Sound region.

From May to October, this puffin is an uncommon visitant between Cape Fairweather and Cape St. Elias. Shortt (1939) saw small numbers during May 1936 in Yakutat Bay but did not observe any during the summer. Pete and Ruth Isleib saw scattered individuals in inshore and offshore waters between the Situk River and Cape St. Elias during July and August 1968 but did not see suitable nesting habitat along that coastline.

The Tufted Puffin is a common breeder (abundant locally) from Cape St. Elias westward. Between Cape St. Elias and Cape Resurrection, the more than one hundred breeding colonies vary in size from a few pairs to several thousand pairs. Most of these colonies are along the outer coasts and in the main body of Prince William Sound; no colonies are known from the northern fiords of Prince William Sound. The largest colony in this area is one of 7,000 pairs on the Wooded Islands. Rausch (1958) reported Tufted Puffins as fairly common breeders on the southern end of Middleton Island in June 1956.

Between Cape Resurrection and the Chugach Islands, colonies are larger and more numerous than they are to the eastward. The largest colony, with an estimated 38,000 pairs, is on the Chiswell Islands (Sowl, pers. comm.).

From November to April, Tufted Puffins are rare in the inshore waters, although they may be locally uncommon in some areas, e.g., the Green Island-Montague Strait area. They apparently disperse mainly into the offshore waters, occurring with increasing abundance with increasing distances at sea.

Estimates of populations utilizing the North Gulf Coast and Prince William Sound: yearly, several 10,000's, probably 100,000's.

Zenaidura macroura – Mourning Dove

The Mourning Dove is a casual fall visitant to the North Gulf Coast-Prince William Sound region.

There are only five reports from the region: 1) A Mourning Dove was shot during fall duck-hunting season some years ago (late 1950's) on the marshes of the Copper River Delta by local hunter Les Maxwell (pers. comm.). 2) Cordova resident Cliff Collins (pers. comm.) watched one feed along a roadside in Cordova for over an hour early in October 1962. 3) The fresh remains of a Mourning Dove were found on the beach at Constantine Harbor, Hinchinbrook Island, on 12 October 1964 by Ed Klinkhart, Alaska Department of Fish and Game; the wing was deposited at the University of Alaska Museum (UA 3230). 4) One was shot at Boswell Bay, Hinchinbrook Island, on 15 October 1968 by Les Maxwell (UA 3236). And 5) one was seen in Cordova on 28 October 1968 by Ray Gutowski (Johnson, pers. field notes).

The October appearances of Mourning Doves suggest a post-breeding dispersal. Although no definite breeding records have been reported in Alaska, there have been numerous sightings of Mourning Doves in southeastern Alaska, some 20 records from southcentral and interior Alaska (Williamson, et al., 1965; Univ. Alaska unpubl. records), and other records from western Yukon Territory (Godfrey, 1966; Isleib and Kessel, unpubl. data). Also, Cliff Collins (pers. comm.) reported seeing them annually in September-October near Long Lake in the Chitina River area, about 80 miles (130 km) inland from the Copper River Delta.

Otus asio – Screech Owl

Only Shortt (1939) has reported this species in the North Gulf Coast-Prince William Sound region. He heard three calling in deep woods near the headwaters of the Situk River on 5 and 6 August 1936 and collected a male on 6 August (ROM 36, 9, 18, 52). The Screech Owl is probably resident at least as far north as Yakutat Bay, but ornithologists have not visited the appropriate habitats along the eastern North Gulf Coast in recent years.

Bubo virginianus – Great Horned Owl

The Great Horned Owl is a fairly common resident of the North Gulf Coast-Prince William Sound region.

This species is the most conspicuous nocturnal owl of the region and occurs regularly throughout the forest and woodland areas of the Copper River Delta, Prince William Sound, and Resurrection Valley (20 to 100 per year in proper habitat). Five individuals were heard calling simultaneously at Mile 19 Copper River Highway by Cordova trapper/fisherman Larry Kritchen (pers. comm.) on 21 January 1971.

At least four nests have been found in the vicinity of Cordova, and Shaffer has reported that Great Horned Owls often utilize old Goshawk nests in Resurrection Valley.

Estimates of populations utilizing the North Gulf Coast and Prince William Sound: yearly, a few, probably several, 100's.

Nyctea scandiaca – Snowy Owl

The Snowy Owl is a rare winter visitant in the North Gulf Coast-Prince William Sound region.

Many Cordova residents remember an invasion of Snowy Owls on the Copper River Delta during the winter of 1957-58: "White Owls on every other stump and stub." The barrier islands and the marshes of the Copper and Bering river deltas reportedly (via local trappers and bush pilots) are visited by a few "white owls" at least one or two winters out of five. One of the few spring observations is one seen by Isleib on a reef near Knight Island, PWS, on 27 March 1972.

O'Farrell and Sheets (1962:441) reported that "Snowy Owls were first reported on Middleton Island in November of 1957, and four to six individuals have remained on the island, probably because of the abundance of rabbits." These are feral domestic rabbits (*Oryctolagus cuniculus*) introduced in 1952 (Rausch, 1958). According to local hearsay, a few Snowy Owls visit Middleton Island every winter, and occasionally individuals spend the summer there, but there have been no indications of nesting.

Estimates of populations utilizing the North Gulf Coast and Prince William Sound: winter, a few individuals – in some years 10's, possibly 100's.

Surnia ulula – Hawk Owl

The Hawk Owl is an uncommon resident of the North Gulf Coast-Prince William Sound region.

This owl is present throughout the year in the forests and woodlands of the region, including those of the islands of Prince William Sound. It is most conspicuous in winter and occurs regularly along the Seward and Copper River highways. On the Copper River Highway, from Mile 5 to Mile 27, 1 to 10 Hawk Owls per day are present from October to March, 0 to 3 per day from March through September. Local abundance is affected by winter weather conditions and rodent numbers. During May and June 1972, at a rodent "high," Shaffer reported seeing "hundreds" of Hawk Owls, apparently non-breeders, each day on the Kenai Peninsula between Seward and Cooper Landing.

There are no substantiated nesting observations for the region, but a pair of Hawk Owls was resident from April through July, 1969 and 1970, in a large cottonwood stand at Mile 25-26 Copper River Highway, presumably nesting.

Estimates of populations utilizing the North Gulf Coast and Prince William Sound: yearly, a few 100's.

Glaucidium gnoma – Pygmy Owl

The Pygmy Owl may be a rare resident along the eastern North Gulf Coast as far west as Prince William Sound.

Only Shortt (1939) has reported the Pygmy Owl within the North Gulf Coast-Prince William Sound region. He collected a male on 12 August 1936 (ROM 36, 9, 18, 53) in the "dense evergreen forests" at the foot of Mount Tebenkof near Yakutat.

Robert Ingebo, Cordova resident, (pers. comm.) heard and closely observed a small, dark-brown owl at Indian Creek, Galena Bay, PWS, during July 1953. His description of the bird and its whistled call, "a hoo or hoot every 2 or 3 seconds," were diagnostic of this species.

Strix nebulosa – Great Gray Owl

The Great Gray Owl is a rare resident of the North Gulf Coast-Prince William Sound region.

Shortt (1939) observed it at Lost River, near Yakutat, on 28 July 1936. Frank Erb, a long-time resident of Prince William Sound, saw "two very large gray earless owls" at the north end of Esther Passage, Port Wells, during the 1920's (Solf, pers. comm.). J. Ed King, a Cordova trapper and guide, (pers. comm.) saw "large gray owls without eartufts in the Martin River Valley east of the Copper River in March of 1968 and 1969"; he saw and heard four or five pairs within a small portion of the heavily timbered parts of the valley, and no Great Horned Owls, with which he is more familiar.

Shaffer and Isleib examined two immatures in February 1962 that had been shot recently near Seward. Since then, Shaffer has reported that more than ten Great Gray Owls have been shot in the Nash Road area near Seward. On 16 August 1971 Shaffer saw two young-of-the-year calling for food along Nash Road.

Estimates of populations utilizing the North Gulf Coast and Prince William Sound: yearly, several 10's, possibly a few 100's.

Asio flammeus – Short-eared Owl

The Short-eared Owl is a resident of the North Gulf Coast-Prince William Sound region, occurring seasonally as a fairly common migrant, an uncommon local breeder, and a rare winter visitant.

Spring migrants are present from late April (earliest, one on 19 April 1964, Copper River Delta) to early June (latest, one on 6 June 1972 at sea off the Copper River Delta), with most occurring during mid-May (10 to 50 per spring migration in proper habitat).

Short-eared Owls are present nearly every summer near the old airport at the head of Resurrection Bay, and Shaffer found a nest with five young at this location during late July 1970. On the Copper River Delta, the breeding population of Short-eared Owls fluctuates with the rodent populations. During the "high" rodent years 1968-1970, approximately 10 pairs nested on the western portion of the Copper River Delta marshes. One nest at Grass Island Slough contained eight eggs on 9 June 1969. During the rodent "low," 1965-67, only three or four pairs were present and no nests were found. Only an occasional Short-eared Owl was present on the Copper River Delta during June and July 1971, another rodent "low."

Fall migration is from mid-August through October, with greatest intensity in late August and early September (10 to 50 per fall migration in proper habitat). On 19 August 1969, 29 Short-eared Owls were present between Mile 10 and Mile 19 Copper River Highway, including 14 at one location. Isleib has seen this diurnal owl on several occasions several miles offshore during migration, and Gray (1945) reported two Short-eared Owls following a ship 70 miles (113 km) southeast of Kodiak (57°24'N, 150°10'W) on 13 October 1943.

Short-eared Owls winter on the Copper River Delta 2 or 3 years out of 5, their occurrence and abundance related to weather conditions and the availability of rodents.

Estimates of populations utilizing the North Gulf Coast and Prince William Sound: migration, several 100's, possibly a few 1,000's; summer, a few 10's; winter, in some years, a few individuals.

Aegolius funereus — Boreal Owl

The Boreal Owl is a rare resident of the North Gulf Coast-Prince William Sound region.

Shaffer has seen this owl regularly during the winter months along the Seward Highway just north of Seward; he found a kill, eaten by another raptor, along the Seward Highway in late December 1970. A Boreal Owl was collected in Prince William Sound in May 1778 on Captain Cook's last voyage (Stresemann, 1949). Larry Kritchen and James Webber, Cordova trappers/fishermen, (pers. comm.) have reported that "eight to ten very small gray owls" were caught in steel traps during the winter of 1957-58, apparently attracted to small mammals under or near the traps. These birds were either Boreal or Saw-whet owls, "gray" coloring more closely fitting Boreals.

Solf saw briefly a small owl, which he identified as either a Boreal or a Saw-whet, in the dense coniferous forest near Eshamy Bay, PWS, in October 1958.

Estimates of populations utilizing the North Gulf Coast and Prince William Sound: yearly, 10's, possibly a few 100's.

Aegolius acadicus — Saw-whet Owl

The Saw-whet Owl is a rare resident in the North Gulf Coast-Prince William Sound region.

There are only two reports of the Saw-whet Owl in the region, unless some of those listed under Boreal Owl refer to this species. In late March 1965, Steven R. Smith, local fisherman/photographer/biologist, (pers. comm.) heard one calling at night near Seal River (between Icy Bay and Cape Suckling); and an adult female was caught in a steel trap on the Copper River Delta 14 miles (23 km) east of Cordova by local resident Mark King in late November 1970 (Wash. State Univ. 71-3).

Closely adjacent to the region, Shaffer has found Saw-whet Owls resident in the Granite Creek area, about 63 miles (101 km) north of Seward on the Seward Highway; and Williamson et al. (1965) reported it as an "uncommon breeding bird" in Cook Inlet.

Estimates of populations utilizing the North Gulf Coast and Prince William Sound: yearly, 10's, possibly a few 100's.

Chordeiles minor — Common Nighthawk

The Common Nighthawk is casual in the North Gulf Coast-Prince William Sound region.

There are only two reports for the region. Shortt (1939:21) reported that "on Aug. 8 [1936] at about 7 p.m. a nighthawk passed over our camp on the Situk river, flying high and travelling in a southeasterly direction. The unmistakable call note was uttered three times within our hearing." Ruth Isleib (pers. comm.) saw a nighthawk and heard it calling over Cordova on 1 August 1972.

Calypte anna — Anna's Hummingbird

The only known record of the Anna's Hummingbird in the North Gulf Coast-Prince William Sound region is of a male that appeared at a hummingbird feeder in Cordova on 13 November 1971; identifiable photographs were obtained and are on file at the University of Alaska. This hummingbird remained until 19 December 1971, disappearing during a period of 0°F (-18°C) temperatures and gale-force winds. During the few weeks prior to 13 November 1971, there were several unverified reports of hummingbirds about Cordova, but it is not known if this Anna's Hummingbird arrived at an earlier date or if more than one bird was present. It is of interest to note that fall departure dates for Rufous Hummingbirds were unusually late in 1971, one remaining at a Cordova feeder until 26 October.

This occurrence at Cordova is exceptional, although Anna's Hummingbirds have been occurring with increasing frequency in British Columbia (see recent issues of *American Birds*), and there have been several observed since 1967 at Juneau (Richard J. Gordon, in litt., 1967 and 1968).

Selasphorus rufus — Rufous Hummingbird

The Rufous Hummingbird is a common migrant and common breeder along the North Gulf Coast and in Prince William Sound, occurring commonly along the eastern North Gulf Coast and in Prince William Sound and rarely and locally along the western North Gulf Coast.

The earliest spring migrants, mostly males, arrive during the first half of May (earliest, two on 3 May 1973 at Cordova); most birds, however, arrive during the latter half of May. During the height of migration, Rufous Hummingbirds occur regularly over the open waters of Prince William Sound and, paralleling the eastern North Gulf Coast, out to 4 miles (6 km) at sea. In 1971, cold weather and heavy snow-cover prevailed until late May; between 22 May and 24 May 1971, about 3,000 Rufous Hummingbirds concentrated in and about Cordova. More than 50 birds were present in one 2-block area, 15 fighting over one feeder.

During June, Rufous Hummingbirds are common, conspicuous, and widely dispersed throughout the forests and woodlands. Grinnell (1910a) reported numerous observations of this species about the islands in Prince William Sound in 1908. Shortt (1939) found it conspicuous in the Yakutat area in the early summer of 1936.

The Rufous Hummingbird is inconspicuous after early July, and fall migration apparently begins in late July. Only a few birds linger beyond mid-September (latest, one unidentified hummingbird [probably Rufous] seen by Solf as it appeared briefly aboard ship in Hinchinbrook Entrance on 13 October 1971, and an adult male at a feeder in Cordova until 26 October 1971).

Estimates of populations utilizing the North Gulf Coast and Prince William Sound: migration and summer, several 1,000's.

Megaceryle alcyon – Belted Kingfisher

The Belted Kingfisher is a resident of the North Gulf Coast-Prince William Sound region, occurring seasonally as an uncommon migrant, a fairly common breeder, and an uncommon winter resident.

Kingfishers are widely distributed along the coast and in the river systems, wherever proper habitat occurs. Usually no more than one or two pairs occur in any particular locality.

Migrants occur along the coasts from mid-April to mid-May and again from mid-August to early October.

Nesting begins early; a pair was excavating a burrow on 12 May 1971 at Eyak Lake near Cordova. Grinnell (1910a) reported numerous observations of Belted Kingfishers throughout the Prince William Sound area during the summer of 1908, and Shortt (1939) found them nesting fairly commonly about Yakutat, Situk River, and Lost River during 1936.

Wintering birds are uncommon, but regular, in sheltered lagoons, inlets, and bays, and about the open freshwater streams of the region.

Estimates of populations utilizing the North Gulf Coast and Prince William Sound: migration, 100's, probably a few 1,000's; summer, several 100's, probably a few 1,000's; winter, a few 100's.

Colaptes auratus – Yellow-shafted Flicker

The Yellow-shafted Flicker is a rare summer visitant and rare fall migrant in the North Gulf Coast-Prince William Sound region.

There are relatively few observations of this woodpecker in the region; it can be expected irregularly at Yakutat, Cordova, Valdez, and Seward. Isleib saw one at Yakutat on 18 July 1968, and, during August and September 1964, 1965, and 1969, he saw several migrants between Cordova and Mile 27 Copper River Highway. Shaffer has seen a few Yellow-shafted Flickers nearly every summer or fall in Resurrection Valley. Shortt (1939) did not see them during his excellent coverage of the Yakutat area in 1936, although he was given a specimen taken in June 1935 by Hardy Trefzegar, Commissioner of the Yakutat district, who reported it was the only one he had seen in the vicinity. Gabrielson (1944) saw one at Yakutat on 8 June 1940.

There has been no evidence of breeding in the region, although there are recurrent summer observations of the species. Earliest and latest observations, respectively, are Gabrielson's (ibid.) at Yakutat on 8 June 1940 and one seen by Isleib at Cordova on 5 October 1972.

Estimates of populations utilizing the North Gulf Coast and Prince William Sound: migration-fall and summer, a few, probably several, 10's.

Colaptes cafer – Red-shafted Flicker

The Red-shafted Flicker is a casual visitant in the North Gulf Coast-Prince William Sound region.

The only record within the region is one seen by Isleib at the Seward airport on 28 October 1962 (Williamson et al., 1965). Adjacent to the region, however, in lower Cook Inlet, near Homer, another one was seen in early May 1963 by Anchorage resident George Velikanje (pers. comm.).

Dendrocopos villosus – Hairy Woodpecker

The Hairy Woodpecker is an uncommon resident of the North Gulf Coast-Prince William Sound region.

These woodpeckers are rare throughout most of the region but are uncommon in the coastal woodlands east of Yakutat and in Resurrection Valley. Shortt (1939:22) collected two specimens in the Yakutat area in 1936 and listed it as "not uncommon in the wooded districts east of Yakutat and on Khantaak Island." Shaffer has seen it regularly throughout the year in Resurrection Valley. In the Prince William Sound-Copper River Delta areas, however, Isleib has recorded fewer than ten individuals a year, usually in the spring and fall.

Hairy Woodpeckers breed in Resurrection Valley and undoubtedly also in the Yakutat area. In June 1970, Shaffer watched about four pairs near Seward and located two nests.

Estimates of populations utilizing the North Gulf Coast and Prince William Sound: yearly, a few, possibly several, 100's.

Dendrocopos pubescens – Downy Woodpecker

The Downy Woodpecker is an uncommon resident of the North Gulf Coast-Prince William Sound region.

The Downy Woodpecker is probably the most numerous woodpecker in the region, being found in forests, woodlands, and thickets from shore to timberline (10 to 50 per year in proper habitat). In Resurrection Valley, numbers equal those of the Hairy Woodpecker; it is the only woodpecker occurring regularly throughout the year in the Prince William Sound-Copper River Delta area; and it is apparently less numerous than the Hairy Woodpecker along the eastern North Gulf Coast-Yakutat area, as Shortt (1939) did not list it there in 1936 and Isleig saw only one in that area in 1968 (one at Ocean Cape on 8 August 1968).

Shaffer found a nest at Mile 5 Seward Highway in June 1971.

Estimates of populations utilizing the North Gulf Coast-Prince William Sound region: yearly, a few, probably several, 100's.

Picoides arcticus – Black-backed Three-toed Woodpecker

The Black-backed Three-toed Woodpecker appears to be only a casual visitant in the North Gulf Coast-Prince William Sound region.

The only record of this boreal forest bird in the region is of one seen by Isleib at the forest edge near the entrance of Mosquito Creek, Barry Arm, Port Wells, on 23 March 1973.

Picoides tridactylus – Northern Three-toed Woodpecker

The Northern Three-toed Woodpecker is a rare local resident of the North Gulf Coast-Prince William Sound region.

A small population is present throughout the year in the mixed deciduous-spruce woodlands of the Resurrection Valley area, apparently an extension of the main Kenai Peninsula population. Shaffer has estimated that there are about ten pairs in this area, and he saw adults feeding newly fledged young in July 1970.

Elsewhere in the region, the Northern Three-toed Woodpecker is only casual. Solf saw one near Eshamy Lake, PWS, in December 1958, and Cordova resident Robert Ingebo and Solf watched one for 2 days in early November 1969 at Cordova.

Estimates of populations utilizing the North Gulf Coast-Prince William Sound region: yearly, a few 10's.

Sayornis saya – Say's Phoebe

The Say's Phoebe is probably casual (perhaps rare) in the North Gulf Coast-Prince William Sound region, although the only known record is of one collected by Gabrielson (Gabrielson and Lincoln, 1959:578) on 9 August 1940 "north of Valdez along the Richardson Highway."

This flycatcher is a rare spring and fall migrant throughout southeastern Alaska and nests regularly just north of the region in Cook Inlet and in the upper Copper River basin. Hence it probably occurs in the North Gulf Coast-Prince William Sound region more frequently than the single observation to date would indicate, and it should be looked for where appropriate habitat exists, especially near the Keystone Canyon and Thompson Pass areas north of Valdez, above the delta of the Copper River, and along the Alsek River.

Empidonax traillii – Traill's Flycatcher

The Traill's Flycatcher is an uncommon migrant and a fairly common local breeder in the North Gulf Coast-Prince William Sound region.

Migrants appear in late May-early June (earliest, one on 25 May 1971 at Eyak Lake near Cordova), and they are fairly common on breeding territories along the Copper River Highway by the second week of June.

Joseph Dixon (Grinnell, 1910a) collected a male, possibly a migrant, on 10 June 1908 in an alder thicket at the head of Orca Inlet. Gabrielson (Gabrielson and Lincoln, 1959) saw two Traill's Flycatchers at Seward on 2 July 1950. Shaffer has seen a few annually during June and July in riparian shrub thickets in Resurrection Valley near Seward, but he has found them more numerous in the adjacent Cook Inlet drainages of the Kenai Peninsula.

Fall migrants are retiring and inconspicuous and apparently leave the region before the end of August (latest, one on 22 August 1969, Mile 19 Copper River Highway).

Estimates of populations utilizing the North Gulf Coast and Prince William Sound: migration and summer, several 100's, possibly 1,000's.

Empidonax difficilis – Western Flycatcher

The only known record of the Western Flycatcher in the North Gulf Coast-Prince William Sound region is of two (an adult and juvenal it was feeding; ROM 36, 9, 18, 61 and ROM 36, 9, 18, 60) collected in a "low, swampy, mixed woods" on 12 August 1936 at Situk Lake, east of Yakutat, by Shortt (1939).

The Western Flycatcher is the most abundant *Empidonax* flycatcher of southeastern Alaska, where it is a common breeder, and it probably breeds regularly but locally within the coastal forest belt between southeastern Alaska and Yakutat.

Contopus sordidulus – Western Wood Pewee

The Western Wood Pewee is a casual visitant in the North Gulf Coast-Prince William Sound region.

Shaffer is the only person to report this flycatcher from the region. On several occasions, spanning different years, he has heard pewees calling during mid- and late August in the vicinity of Mile 10-11 Seward Highway, and he saw one near Seward on 21 August 1969.

The Western Wood Pewee is widely distributed in the adjacent upper Cook Inlet-Kenai Peninsula region and in the upper Copper River Valley, suggesting that it occurs more widely in the North Gulf Coast-Prince William Sound region than is now recognized.

Nuttallornis borealis — Olive-sided Flycatcher

The Olive-sided Flycatcher is probably rare in the North Gulf Coast-Prince William Sound region.

Rausch (1958) collected a male with enlarged testes on 26 June 1956 on Middleton Island. On 15 May 1971, Isleib saw one which subsequently lingered several days on the Cordova waterfront and was last seen on 22 May. Pete and Ruth Isleib saw three Olive-sided Flycatchers along the shores of Eyak Lake near Cordova on 16 May 1971.

The Olive-sided Flycatcher occurs in all the mainland areas surrounding the region, and it probably occurs annually in the North Gulf Coast-Prince William Sound region and may breed.

Eremophila alpestris — Horned Lark

The Horned Lark is probably a rare migrant and a local breeder in the North Gulf Coast-Prince William Sound region.

Rausch (1958) was the first to report this species from the North Gulf Coast, collecting a female on 9 June 1956 on Middleton Island. Johnson (pers. field notes) found a Horned Lark dead on the runway of the Cordova airport (Mile 13, Copper River Highway) on 19 May 1966 and showed it to Isleib. Another was present at Cordova on 20 May 1973.

In spite of the paucity of records, the Horned Lark probably occurs annually in the dry, alpine areas of the Chugach and Kenai mountains. It is an uncommon summer resident in the upper Cook Inlet region; Gibson (unpubl. field notes) recorded it during the breeding season on Dumpling Mountain in Katmai National Monument in both 1966 and 1967; Dufresne found it in the Kenai Mountains in June and July 1933 (Gabrielson and Lincoln, 1959); and Roseneau (unpubl. notes) saw two pairs, which he thought were breeding, on East Amatuli Island, Barren Islands, on 20 June 1965.

Tachycineta thalassina — Violet-green Swallow

The Violet-green Swallow is a fairly common migrant and locally abundant breeder along the North Gulf Coast and in Prince William Sound.

Spring migrants arrive about 1 May (earliest, two on 29 April 1969 at Cordova), and they are fairly common through the Copper River Delta-Prince William Sound area in mid- and late May. Freely mixing in migrant flocks with the more numerous Tree Swallow, at least a few thousand occur annually in this area between 6 May and 25 May. Lyon et al. (unpubl. notes) reported many about Whittier on 22 May 1954.

Violet-green Swallows nest abundantly in the cliffs of the Resurrection Bay drainage and less commonly about Seward and in the coastal bluffs of Resurrection Bay, where Isleib watched a pair feeding nestlings in a coastal bluff on 4 July 1962.

They nest fairly commonly, though locally, in the Copper River Delta-Prince William Sound area, nesting in crevices in cliffs and sometimes in old buildings or in bird houses about Valdez and Cordova. The Alexander Expedition (Grinnell, 1910a) reported several about Cordova and in Orca Inlet during the first half of June 1908, and Shortt (1939) reported 15 Violet-green Swallows in company with Tree Swallows on 30 June 1936 along the Situk River. Young swallows are usually flying by mid-July.

Fall migrants leave earlier than most other passerines, soon after the young are out of the nest. Most depart during the last half of July (latest, one on 9 August 1970 over Eyak Lake near Cordova, and three with Tree Swallows on 12 August 1970 on the Copper River Delta).

Estimates of populations utilizing the North Gulf Coast and Prince William Sound: migration, several 1,000's, possibly 10,000's; summer, a few, probably several, 1,000's.

Iridoprocne bicolor — Tree Swallow

The Tree Swallow is a common migrant and common breeder along the North Gulf Coast and in Prince William Sound.

Spring migrants begin arriving in late April (earliest, one on 27 April 1964 at Cordova, two on 27 April 1970 at Cordova, and one on 27 April 1971 at Double Bay, Hinchinbrook Island), but they do not become common until the second or third week of May. A flock of about 2,000 Tree and Violet-green swallows was present over Eyak Lake near Cordova from 13 to 17 May 1971, and another flock of about 500 Tree Swallows sat on the shore ice at Hartney Bay, Orca Inlet, on 16 May 1971.

Tree Swallows breed commonly on the upper Copper River Delta and eastward along the North Gulf Coast's coastal lowlands, and less commonly, locally, in Prince William Sound and along the western North Gulf Coast. About 12 to 15 pairs nest in old buildings and bird houses in Cordova. Nesting begins soon after they arrive, with some beginning as early as 12 May; some young are out of the nest by early July.

Shortt (1939) found Tree Swallows nesting fairly commonly in tree cavities along the Situk River in 1936. Rausch (1958) reported Tree Swallows nesting in old buildings in 1956 on Middleton Island. Yocom (1963) reported hundreds of Tree Swallows, including many young birds, on 11 and 12 July 1962 along the Copper River Highway east of Cordova.

Most fall migrants leave or pass through the region between mid-July and mid-August, although a few stragglers may be seen until early September (latest, two on 4 September 1969 at Grass Island Slough, CRD, and one on 16 September 1969 which came aboard ship some 55 miles [90 km] off Cape Fairweather [Humberg, pers. comm.]).

Estimates of populations utilizing the North Gulf Coast and Prince William Sound: migration, a few 10,000's; summer, several 1,000's.

Riparia riparia — Bank Swallow

The Bank Swallow is a rare migrant and an uncommon local breeder in the North Gulf Coast-Prince William Sound region.

A few spring migrants usually are among the flocks of Tree and Violet-green swallows in mid- and late May (earliest, three on 14 May 1969 at Eyak Lake near Cordova, and two on 16 May 1971 at Hartney Bay, Orca Inlet).

Birds begin excavating burrows along the cutbanks of the Copper River in the Copper River Delta area as early as 27 May, and total populations appear to be present by 1 June. Scattered small colonies of Bank Swallows occur along the cutbanks of the upper portions of the Copper River Delta from Cottonwood Point and upper Grass Island Slough to Miles Glacier, on the Copper River. Gabrielson (Gabrielson and Lincoln, 1959) saw a few pairs near Seward on 2 July 1950. Shaffer saw several pairs with burrows in cutbanks at the Seward dump in June 1968, but they did not nest there in 1969. Rausch (1958) found a few pairs of Bank Swallows at burrows in a small gravel pit on Middleton Island in 1956. Isleib and Sowl found a small colony on the Wooded Islands on 23 July 1972.

Fall migration begins soon after the young are able to fly. One colony on the upper Copper River Delta had already been vacated by 19 July 1970. Yocom (1963) saw several Bank Swallows at Mile 20 Copper River Highway on 11 July 1962, apparently birds that had recently left their colonies and were preparing to move south. The lack of observations of Bank Swallows in migration along the coast suggests that these birds enter and leave the region via river valleys and passes into the interior of Alaska (latest, one with Tree Swallows on 2 August 1970 at Eyak Lake near Cordova, and several on 9 August 1972 flying eastward across Orca Inlet).

Estimates of populations utilizing the North Gulf Coast and Prince William Sound: migration and summer, several 100's, possibly a few 1,000's.

Hirundo rustica — Barn Swallow

The Barn Swallow is an uncommon migrant and an uncommon local breeder in the North Gulf Coast-Prince William Sound region.

Spring migrants arrive in the Copper River Delta-Prince William Sound area in mid-May (earliest, two on 14 May 1969 at Cordova, and two on 16 May 1971 at Hartney Bay, Orca Inlet).

Barn Swallow nests have been found about buildings and bridges in Prince William Sound, the Cordova area, throughout the Copper River Delta, and at Yakutat and Seward. They probably breed as scattered pairs throughout most of the coastal areas, wherever suitable habitat exists. Shortt (1939) found Barn Swallows nesting fairly commonly in 1936 about the cannery buildings at the Situk River and in Yakutat, and Shaffer found a pair nesting near Seward during June and July 1972, the only known record of the species in that area. Numbers are subject to fluctuations: from 1962 to 1964 none nested in Cordova, but between 1965 and 1970 the population built up to 10 or 12 pairs, simular to the 10 pairs reported by Grinnell (1910a) at Cordova and at the head of Orca Inlet during early June 1908.

Nest building usually takes place from 27 May to 12 June. Young, however, have been observed in the nest as late as 12 August.

Some Barn Swallows have lingered into September (latest, 3 on 12 September 1967 at Softuck Bar, CRD; and 10 on 17 September 1972, 6 on 18 September 1972, and 3 on 20 September 1972, all at Cordova).

Estimates of populations utilizing the North Gulf Coast and Prince William Sound: migration and summer, a few 100's.

Petrochelidon pyrrhonota — Cliff Swallow

The Cliff Swallow is a rare migrant and a local breeder along the North Gulf Coast and in Prince William Sound.

This swallow is generally the latest swallow to arrive, first appearing in late May or early June (earliest, one on 28 May 1971 at Cordova); in some years they have not been observed in the Cordova area until the second week in June. Rausch (1958) saw a few Cliff Swallows, probably migrants, feeding over the ponds on Middleton Island on 12 June 1956.

The only known nesting colonies of Cliff Swallows are on buildings at Yakutat and Cordova. Most nest-building takes place during the last half of June, but some sites are under construction as late as the first week of July. The first young usually fledge in early August, but some remain in the nest as late as 18 August.

Little is known about fall migration. Latest observations are of an adult feeding a fledged young on 27 August 1964 at Cordova and one with six Barn Swallows on 3 September 1969 over the Copper River Delta.

Estimates of populations utilizing the North Gulf Coast and Prince William Sound: migration and summer, several 10's, probably a few 100's.

Progne subis — Purple Martin

The Purple Martin is accidental in the North Gulf Coast-Prince William Sound region.

Shaffer watched a pair of Purple Martins with Tree and Violet-green swallows for several days during the last week of May 1961 at the Bear Lake sawmill, some 5 miles (8 km) north of Seward. Shaffer, who is familiar with this species in more southern latitudes, closely observed this pair sitting on a utility wire and flying over the lake and open area nearby.

Perisoreus canadensis — Gray Jay

The Gray Jay is an uncommon local resident along the North Gulf Coast and in Prince William Sound.

An inhabitant of the boreal coniferous forests to the north, the Gray Jay is an uncommon resident of upper Resurrection Valley, near Thompson Pass, and along the Copper River above the Copper River Delta. Over the years, Shaffer has seen 0-5 jays per day in proper habitat in upper Resurrection Valley. Local trappers have reported that Gray Jays are uncommon and local along the Copper River above the Copper River Delta throughout the year, especially in the Martin River area. A few occur between Keystone Canyon and Thompson Pass, above Valdez.

An invasion of Gray Jays occurred in the Prince William Sound-Copper River Delta area during the fall of 1969. Beginning in August 1969, this invasion, which involved thousands of birds, continued until October. Cordova residents who had been acquainted with the Gray Jay in the interior of Alaska remarked at never having seen Gray Jays previously along the coast, in some cases referring to 40 years of experience in the region. Twenty-five birds could be seen easily in one day in the Cordova area; they appeared everywhere — on the beaches, islands, and in town. The number of Gray Jays observed daily began to decline in November 1969, but several were still present along the Copper River Highway east of Cordova in May 1970. Larry Kritchen, Cordova trapper/fisherman, (pers. comm.) reported that he inadvertently caught 24 Gray Jays between 15 November and 1 December 1969 in his traps on the Copper River Delta.

A less extensive invasion of Gray Jays occurred also in 1969 in southeastern Alaska (Richard J. Gordon, in litt., 1970), but Shaffer did not observe such movements on the Kenai Peninsula. As an aside, it is of interest to note that the fall of

1969 also brought tremendous invasions of Red-breasted Nuthatches and White-winged Crossbills into the North Gulf Coast-Prince William Sound region.

Estimates of populations utilizing the North Gulf Coast and Prince William Sound: yearly, a few 100's — in some years, possibly a few 1,000's.

Cyanocitta stelleri — Steller's Jay

The Steller's Jay is a common resident along the North Gulf Coast and in Prince William Sound.

The Steller's Jay is a resident throughout the moist hemlock-Sitka Spruce forests of the region. It is numerous on the forested islands and somewhat less common on the mainland. It is a conspicuous bird during the warmer months, but in winter it seems quite shy, retiring to the densest portions of the forest, although it occasionally forages along the upper portions of the beaches and tidal flats. Grinnell (1910a) reported this jay as one of the most abundant forest birds throughout Prince William Sound in 1908. Shortt (1939) saw them commonly throughout the coniferous forest in the Yakutat area and on 14 July 1936 found a nest, from which the young had recently flown, in a timbered tract on the Malaspina Glacier moraine.

Estimates of populations utilizing the North Gulf Coast and Prince William Sound: yearly, several 1,000's, probably 10,000's.

Pica pica — Black-billed Magpie

The Black-billed Magpie is a fairly common resident along the North Gulf Coast and in Prince William Sound.

Magpies are well-distributed throughout the region during the non-breeding season. During the breeding season, however, they occur primarily in areas of shrub thicket, especially in the valleys away from the coast and near timberline, both on the mainland and on the larger islands. Grinnell (1910a) reported five juvenals collected in mid- and late August 1908 on Montague Island and other magpies seen at various locations in Prince William Sound. Shortt (1939) did not find them common in 1936 in the Yakutat area, but he collected a young female from a family group in Russell Fiord on 6 August. Gabrielson (Gabrielson and Lincoln, 1959) saw magpies during the summer months at Yakutat, Valdez, and Seward.

Family groups appear to stay together in the late summer and fall, dispersing by winter. During fall and winter, magpies are frequent foragers of the beaches and tidal flats, often competing with other corvids and gulls.

Estimates of populations utilizing the North Gulf Coast and Prince William Sound: yearly, several 1,000's.

Corvus corax — Common Raven

The Common Raven is an abundant resident along the North Gulf Coast and in Prince William Sound.

The raven is a numerous and conspicuous bird throughout the region, from high on the mountain slopes to the beaches of the islands. From 100 to over 300 ravens occupy a winter roost on the forested slope north of Eyak Lake near Cordova, the size of the roost varying from year to year; many of these ravens feed about the Cordova dump and adjacent waterfront. Grinnell (1910a) reported the Common Raven from nearly all locations in Prince William Sound in July 1908 and reported several families at Zaikof Bay, Montague Island. Shortt (1939) found ravens abundant throughout the Yakutat area in 1936. He found a late, newly constructed nest without eggs on a cliff on 24 May 1936 and one with a young bird in a large spruce on 5 June 1936. Isleib found a nest on a bluff at Martin River Slough, CRD, on 29 May 1963 that contained three young that were within a week of fledging.

Estimates of populations utilizing the North Gulf Coast and Prince William Sound: yearly, several 1,000's, possibly a few 10,000's.

Corvus caurinus — Northwestern Crow

The Northwestern Crow is an abundant resident of the North Gulf Coast-Prince William Sound region.

This corvid is especially noticeable as a gregarious resident of the shoreline, rarely venturing inland more than a few hundred yards. It occurs throughout most of the coastal areas and is especially numerous in protected bays and inlets and about the port cities of Yakutat, Cordova, Valdez, and Seward. Grinnell (1910a) reported flocks at nearly every locality visited in Prince William Sound in 1908 and noted young recently out of the nest on 26 June at Hinchinbrook Island. Shortt (1939) found crows numerous in the Yakutat Bay area in 1936 and remarked on their tameness and their habits as principal scavengers of the beaches. A U. S. Fish and Wildlife Service survey by boat 24 March-4 April 1972 estimated about 9,000 crows in Prince William Sound; the crows were mostly in small flocks of 20 to 50 birds.

Winter aggregations of up to 500 individuals of this garrulous bird may occur in the fiords of Prince William Sound. Censuses taken along the Cordova waterfront produced counts of 332 on 27 December 1969 and 235 on 29 December 1971.

Estimates of populations utilizing the North Gulf Coast and Prince William Sound: yearly, a few 10,000's.

Parus atricapillus — Black-capped Chickadee

The Black-capped Chickadee is an uncommon resident and rare migrant in the North Gulf Coast-Prince William Sound region.

This chickadee is an uncommon resident of the mixed deciduous-spruce woodlands of Resurrection Valley near Seward, the Lowe River Valley near Valdez, the upper portions of the Copper River Delta, the Malaspina Glacier end moraine, and probably other areas of similar habitat in the region. Grinnell (1910a) reported it in 1908 from the Lowe River Valley near Valdez. Shortt (1939) collected a male on 6 July 1936 and saw others at the moraine of the Malaspina Glacier. Gabrielson (Gabrielson and Lincoln, 1959) saw one on 19 July 1945 in hemlock-Sitka Spruce forest on Evans Island, PWS.

A few chickadees, presumably fall migrants, occur regularly with migrating warblers and kinglets from late August until mid-October on the Copper River Delta. A "wave" of Black-capped Chickadees, composed of singles and small flocks, moved eastward through the eastern Prince William Sound-Copper River Delta area in September and October 1971; the largest flock, seen on 11 October 1971 at Mile 8 Copper River Highway, contained over 30 Black-capped Chickadees and several kinglets of both species.

Estimates of populations utilizing the North Gulf Coast and Prince William Sound: yearly, a few, probably several, 100's; migration, a few 100's — in some years, several 100's.

Parus hudsonicus — Boreal Chickadee

The Boreal Chickadee is a fairly common resident in Resurrection Valley and appears to be a locally rare or casual visitant elsewhere in the North Gulf Coast-Prince William Sound region.

A boreal forest bird, this chickadee occurs regularly only in the Resurrection Valley (10 to 20 per day in proper habitat [Shaffer, pers. comm.]). It has been observed occasionally, also, in the Lowe River Valley near Valdez and on the upper Copper River Delta—natural corridors into the interior boreal forests. Isleib saw two Boreal Chickadees on 26 November 1962 along the Richardson Highway between Thompson Pass and Valdez, three on 15 October 1969 at Mile 25 Copper River Highway, and one at Mile 27 Copper River Highway on 27 March 1969.

Estimates of populations utilizing the North Gulf Coast and Prince William Sound: yearly, a few 100's.

Parus rufescens — Chestnut-backed Chickadee

The Chestnut-backed Chickadee is a common resident of the North Gulf Coast-Prince William Sound region.

This chickadee is common in the hemlock-Sitka Spruce forests from Cape Fairweather to Seward. The Alexander Expedition in 1908 recorded it as "several seen" to "very abundant" at various locations in Prince William Sound (Grinnell, 1910a). Shortt (1939) found it "very common" in the coniferous forests east of Yakutat and north of Situk Lake in 1936 and found a nest of four young in a hole 20 ft (6 m) up in a Sitka Spruce on 30 June. Although no previous records exist west of Prince William Sound, Isleib has seen it on several occasions in the coniferous forests at the head of Resurrection Bay, and it is probably an uncommon resident even farther westward along the North Gulf Coast.

Outside of the breeding season, Chestnut-backed Chickadees are generally found in small flocks, often foraging through the upper foliage of the forest and often accompanied by other small passerines.

Estimates of populations utilizing the North Gulf Coast and Prince William Sound: yearly, several 1,000's, possibly 10,000's.

Sitta canadensis — Red-breasted Nuthatch

The Red-breasted Nuthatch is a rare resident of the North Gulf Coast-Prince William Sound region.

The Red-breasted Nuthatch was first reported in the North Gulf Coast-Prince William Sound region 13-22 May 1964, when up to three individuals frequented Cliff Collins' feeding station near Cordova (Hemming, 1966); three birds overwintered at this same feeder in 1964-65 (Cliff Collins, pers. comm.). Shaffer first noted Red-breasted Nuthatches in the Resurrection Valley in 1964, where it continues to be a rare annual visitant.

In the fall of 1969, an invasion of Red-breasted Nuthatches spread into the Prince William Sound-Copper River Delta area, with numbers totaling in the thousands. The first nuthatch appeared on 22 August 1969 at Mile 19 Copper River Highway. From mid-September until early November, they were abundant in the coniferous forests of the area and were fairly common in Cordova, where they climbed on buildings, utility poles, rosebushes, etc. Numbers began to decline in November, and by late December fewer than 10 nuthatches could be seen per day. Several birds overwintered in the Copper River Delta-Prince William Sound area, the last being noted in April 1970. Subsequently, a few to several individuals have been recorded every fall during migration; and, during the winters of 1970-71, 1971-72, and 1972-73, respectively, three, one, and eight Red-breasted Nuthatches frequented feeders in Cordova.

Estimates of populations utilizing the North Gulf Coast and Prince William Sound: yearly, a few 100's – in some years, 1,000's.

Certhia familiaris – Brown Creeper

The Brown Creeper is an uncommon resident in the North Gulf Coast-Prince William Sound region.

The Alexander Expedition collected eight specimens and heard a few other birds at various points in Prince William Sound during 1908 (Grinnell, 1910a). Clarke P. Streator collected a small series of Brown Creepers and considered them rather common in 1895 at Yakutat Bay (Gabrielson and Lincoln, 1959). Shortt (1939), however, did not list them from the Yakutat area in 1936. According to Solf, the Brown Creeper is an uncommon resident in Prince William Sound; he has found three nests during his 18 years in the region (two at Port Chalmers, Montague Island, and one at Eshamy Bay, PWS).

Brown Creepers occur more commonly in the fall, indicating some movement at this time, either a population shift or some migration. Isleib has noticed increased numbers in fall in the Copper River Delta-Prince William Sound area, as has Shaffer in the Resurrection Bay area.

Estimates of populations utilizing the North Gulf Coast and Prince William Sound: yearly, a few, probably several, 100's.

Cinclus mexicanus – Dipper

The Dipper is a fairly common resident of the North Gulf Coast-Prince William Sound region.

Most of the mountain streams and their outlets into lakes and coastal inlets in Prince William Sound and along the entire North Gulf Coast have resident Dippers. The Alexander Expedition collected eight specimens, finding Dippers at various localities throughout Prince William Sound in 1908 (Grinnell, 1910a). Shortt (1939) saw one in 1936 at the mouth of a stream in Yakutat Bay. Lyon et al. (unpubl. notes) noted several in Port Wells and Passage Canal during the summer of 1954. Solf has located a number of nests and has banded young over the years in Prince William Sound.

Estimates of populations utilizing the North Gulf Coast and Prince William Sound: yearly, several 1,000's.

Troglodytes troglodytes – Winter Wren

The Winter Wren is an uncommon resident of the North Gulf Coast and in Prince William Sound.

Middleton Island is the only location within the region where the Winter Wren occurs in any abundance; Rausch (1958) reported it as a common resident of the high shrub zone of Middleton Island during 1956. No nests were found on Middleton Island, but all of the several females collected during June and July showed well-developed brood patches. Isleib has seen Winter Wrens at Seward, Cordova, and in the Prince William Sound area, where it seems more numerous on the islands than on the mainland. The Alexander Expedition (Grinnell, 1910a) collected 13 specimens in 1908 and regarded this wren as sparsely distributed through the forests of the islands and adjacent mainland of Prince William Sound. Shortt (1939) found the Winter Wren uncommon in the Yakutat area in 1936. Willett (1928) saw three or four at Seward in late November 1926 and collected a male there on 19 November 1926. Gabrielson saw this species at Yakutat on 8 June 1940, a single bird at Valdez on 28 July 1945, one on Evans Island on 29 July 1945, and a single bird at Port Dick Creek on the Kenai Peninsula on 31 July 1945 (Gabrielson and Lincoln, 1959).

Estimates of populations utilizing the North Gulf Coast and Prince William Sound: yearly, a few, possibly several, 1,000's.

Turdus migratorius – Robin

The Robin is a resident along the North Gulf Coast and in Prince William Sound, occurring seasonally as a fairly common migrant, a fairly common breeder, and a rare winter visitant.

Fairly common migrants from the coast to above timberline, Robins arrive from mid-April to mid-May (earliest, seven on 16 April 1964 and eight on 19 April 1969, all at Cordova); they are most numerous during early May.

Breeding Robins are widely distributed throughout the region. Shortt (1939) found them "very common" at Yakutat, on the Malaspina Glacier moraine, and at Situk River in 1936, where a nest with four eggs was found on 9 June. Rausch (1958) saw a Robin on 5 June 1956 in some willows on Middleton Island.

Fall migration begins in August, and the majority of Robins has departed by early October. A few late migrants regularly linger into November, feeding on High-bush Cranberry and Mountain Ash berries; some remain throughout the winter. Single birds overwinter almost every year at Seward (Shaffer, pers. comm.; Williamson et al., 1965), and one to three birds overwintered in Cordova during both 1971-72 and 1972-73.

Estimates of populations utilizing the North Gulf Coast and Prince William Sound: migration, several 1,000's, probably 10,000's; summer, several 1,000's, possibly 10,000's; winter, a few individuals.

Ixoreus naevius – Varied Thrush

The Varied Thrush is a resident of the North Gulf Coast-Prince William Sound region, occurring seasonally as an abundant migrant, an abundant breeder, and a rare winter visitant.

Spring migrants begin arriving between late March and early April (earliest, six on 27 March 1973 and one on 7 April 1969, all at Cordova) and are abundant by early May.

During the summer the Varied Thrush is conspicuous and widely distributed throughout the region, from timberline to tidal flats. Gabrielson (Gabrielson and Lincoln, 1959) saw newly fledged young as early as 8 June 1940 at Yakutat. Shortt (1939) recorded about-to-fledge young in the same area on 26 June 1936.

Fall migration begins in mid-August, but the rush and volume of birds is during September. These thrushes are still fairly common through October, with the last of the migrants departing by mid-November.

Wintering Varied Thrushes are rare but regular at Cordova, as singles or small flocks; and, according to Shaffer, a few winter in and near Seward. Occasional birds or small flocks winter in Prince William Sound, generally near open freshwater areas in sheltered inlets.

Estimates of populations utilizing the North Gulf Coast and Prince William Sound: migration, a few, probably several, 100,000's; summer, a few, possibly several, 100,000's; winter, 10's, probably a few 100's.

Hylocichla guttata — Hermit Thrush

The Hermit Thrush is an abundant migrant and an abundant breeder in the North Gulf Coast-Prince William Sound region.

Spring migrants begin arriving in April (earliest, one on 19 April 1969 near Cordova) and are abundant by mid-May. During migration they occur from the beaches to above timberline and occasionally land aboard ships a few miles off the coast.

Hermit Thrushes breed abundantly in forests, woodlands, and thickets throughout the region. Grinnell (1910a) reported them as abundant throughout the islands and mainland of Prince William Sound in 1908. Shortt (1939) regarded them as common birds in almost every part of the Yakutat area in 1936 and found nests at four separate localities. Gabrielson (Gabrielson and Lincoln, 1959) reported Hermit Thrushes at various points from Yakutat to Seward.

Fall migration begins in mid-August, with migrants being especially numerous in late August and September; some regularly linger until 10 October, and occasional stragglers may remain until late October (latest, one on 21 October 1969, Mile 23 Copper River Highway).

Estimates of populations utilizing the North Gulf Coast and Prince William Sound: migration, 100,000's, probably 1,000,000's; summer, 100,000's, possibly 1,000,000's.

Hylocichla ustulata — Swainson's Thrush

The Swainson's Thrush is a rare migrant and probably a local breeder in the North Gulf Coast-Prince William Sound region.

This thrush is a rare spring migrant in the eastern Prince William Sound-Copper River Delta area (earliest, one on 17 May 1971, Mile 6 Copper River Highway; latest, several until 14 June 1972 about Cordova [a late spring]). Gabrielson (Gabrielson and Lincoln, 1959) reported the Swainson's Thrush at Seward on 2 and 3 July 1950, and Shaffer and Isleib have seen it in Resurrection Valley frequently enough to believe it is probably an uncommon breeder in that area.

Several factors seem to account for the limited occurrence of Swainson's Thrushes in the region and make it unlikely that they breed elsewhere than in Resurrection Valley. First, this species is abundant in areas adjacent to the north and west of the North Gulf Coast-Prince William Sound region, even though it is only a rare migrant through the region; apparently, migrants reach Resurrection Valley via the interior of Alaska. Second, their preferred breeding habitat of mixed deciduous-spruce woodlands is limited and localized in the region and, except for Resurrection Valley, is isolated from similar habitats of the interior.

The Swainson's Thrush is a rare fall migrant in the eastern Prince William Sound-Copper River Delta area (earliest, one on 22 August 1969, Mile 19 Copper River Highway; latest, two on 29 August 1966 at Cordova).

Estimates of populations utilizing the North Gulf Coast and Prince William Sound: migration, 10's, probably 100's; summer, probably a few 100's.

Hylocichla minima — Gray-cheeked Thrush

The Gray-cheeked Thrush is a rare migrant and a local breeder in the North Gulf Coast-Prince William Sound region.

A few migrants usually pass through the Copper River Delta-eastern Prince William Sound area each spring and fall (5 to 20 per migration season in proper habitat), but apparently most of the Gray-cheeked Thrushes that breed in western Alaska utilize the interior valleys during migration. Spring migrants arrive in May (earliest, one on 6 May 1970 near Cordova [West and Peyton, unpubl. notes]; latest, one on 25 May 1971 at Cordova).

Only Shortt (1939:25) has previously recorded this thrush within the region; he reported that the Gray-cheeked Thrush was "not uncommon in the mixed woods on the terminal moraine of the Malaspina Glacier. Anxious parent birds, carrying food were observed on July 7 [1936] near Black glacier"; he collected a male carrying food at this location on 7 July 1936 (ROM 36, 9, 18, 78).

Fall migrants appear in the Copper River Delta-eastern Prince William Sound area during the latter part of August, passing through somewhat later than Swainson's Thrushes (earliest, two on 22 August 1969, Mile 15 Copper River Highway; latest, one on 13 September 1969, Mile 23 Copper River Highway).

Estimates of populations utilizing the North Gulf Coast and Prince William Sound: migration, probably 100's; summer, probably a few 100's.

Oenanthe oenanthe — Wheatear

The Wheatear is probably a rare breeder and rare migrant in the North Gulf Coast-Prince William Sound region.

The Wheatear has been reported only twice within the region. Shaffer watched a pair during early July 1969 that appeared to be breeding in the tundra pass (elev. 2,600 ft or 790 m) between Nelly Juan River and Paradise Lakes. Roseneau (unpubl. notes) identified a Wheatear that came aboard a boat anchored in Nuka Bay along the southern side of the Kenai Peninsula on 2 December 1969. This species is probably more common in the region than records to date would indicate, since, in addition to these two records, Isleib has seen them during both migration and breeding seasons in closely adjacent areas of the Kenai and Chugach mountains.

Estimates of populations utilizing the North Gulf Coast and Prince William Sound: migration and summer, a few individuals, probably 10's.

Regulus satrapa — Golden-crowned Kinglet

The Golden-crowned Kinglet is a resident along the North Gulf Coast and in Prince William Sound, occurring seasonally as a fairly common migrant, an uncommon breeder, and an uncommon winter visitant.

This kinglet is found throughout the year in most of the hemlock-Sitka Spruce forests of the region. Migrants are fairly common in small mixed passerine flocks during April and May and again from mid-August until mid-October

Grinnell (1910a) reported that Golden-crowned Kinglets were not very numerous in Prince William Sound in 1908, but six specimens were collected and others were seen at various localities. Shortt (1939) recorded this kinglet only "sparingly" in the Yakutat area in 1936.

Wintering birds are uncommon and are frequently found in company with small flocks of chickadees.

Estimates of populations utilizing the North Gulf Coast and Prince William Sound: migration, a few, probably several, 1,000's; summer, a few, possibly several, 1,000's; winter, several 100's, probably a few 1000's.

Regulus calendula — Ruby-crowned Kinglet

The Ruby-crowned Kinglet is an abundant migrant and an abundant breeder along the North Gulf Coast and in Prince William Sound.

This kinglet is one of the most abundant birds in the forests and woodlands, particularly in the hemlock-Sitka Spruce forests along the eastern North Gulf Coast east of Prince William Sound.

Spring migration occurs between mid-April and mid-May (earliest, several on 14 April 1969, Mile 13 Copper River Highway).

Shortt (1939) regarded the Ruby-crowned Kinglet as probably the commonest bird of the coniferous forests of the Yakutat area during the summer of 1936. The Alexander Expedition (Grinnell, 1910a) collected ten specimens and reported it as common throughout Prince William Sound during the summer of 1908.

Fall migrants become noticeable in early August, are abundant from mid-August until early September, and then remain fairly common until early October (latest, one on 17 November 1970, Mile 23 Copper River Highway).

An occasional bird may overwinter. Shaffer observed one at Seward on 12 December 1962, and George Velikanje (Hemming, 1966) had a group of five at his feeder at Anchorage on adjacent Cook Inlet from 20 December 1964 to 8 January 1965.

Estimates of populations utilizing the North Gulf Coast and Prince William Sound: migration and summer, several 10,000's, probably 100,000's; winter, in some years, a few individuals.

Anthus spinoletta — Water Pipit

The Water Pipit is a common migrant and common breeder in the North Gulf Coast-Prince William Sound region.

Spring migrants begin arriving in mid-April (earliest, seven on 12 April 1970 at Hartney Bay, Orca Inlet) and are common in numerous flocks in early and mid-May on the beaches, marshes, and other open areas.

During the summer, the Water Pipit is one of the commonest birds of the alpine tundra habitat. Grinnell (1910a) reported evidence of breeding throughout the alpine areas on both the mainland and islands of Prince William Sound in 1908, reporting a female collected with a shelled egg in the oviduct on 13 June at the head of Orca Inlet and a nest containing three small young on Montague Island on 7 July. Shortt (1939) found what he believed were locally breeding Water Pipits common at Disenchantment Bay in late May 1936.

Fall migrants are common in flocks along the beaches and tidal flats from mid-August until early October. Occasional late migrants or stragglers remain on the beaches until November (latest, three on 8 November 1964 at Fish Bay, Hinchinbrook Island).

Estimates of populations utilizing the North Gulf Coast and Prince William Sound: migration, several 10,000's, possibly 100,000's; summer, several 10,000's.

Bombycilla garrulus — Bohemian Waxwing

The Bohemian Waxwing is a resident of the North Gulf Coast-Prince William Sound region, occurring as an uncommon resident in Resurrection Valley and a rare visitant in the Prince William Sound-Copper River Delta area.

Shaffer has seen Bohemian Waxwings every summer in upper Resurrection Valley and occasionally in Seward. He found a nest with young in a spruce at Seward during July 1965, and Gabrielson (Gabrielson and Lincoln, 1959) saw a pair there on 2 July 1950 which he thought was nesting. Small, summering flocks have been seen in Prince William Sound: Gabrielson (Gabrielson and Lincoln, 1959) saw three in College Fiord, Port Wells, on 13 August 1945; and Isleib saw small flocks, apparently non-breeders, during July-August 1972 at Port Wells, Valdez Arm, Hawkins Island, and Cordova.

Small flocks of waxwings occur nearly every fall (August-November) in the Copper River Delta-Prince William Sound area, and occasional birds overwinter. Such flocks have occurred in the Valdez-Thompson Pass area; a small flock was present at Mile 19 Copper River Highway on 2 January 1967 (Johnson, pers. field notes); and a single bird remained in Cordova through December 1972. Small flocks are present almost every winter at Seward (Shaffer, pers. comm.).

Estimates of populations utilizing the North Gulf Coast and Prince William Sound: yearly, a few 100's.

Lanius excubitor — Northern Shrike

The Northern Shrike is an uncommon resident of the North Gulf Coast-Prince William Sound region.

A few shrikes are resident and probably breed throughout the region, but the only positive breeding records come from 1 mile north of Seward, where Shaffer reported that a pair nested in a spruce during June 1969 and where, in July 1972, he saw an adult and three fledglings near their nest.

From September to April, the shrike is regular in the shrub thickets of the upper Copper River Delta, its habit of sitting atop a snag or tree in an otherwise barren-appearing landscape making it unusually conspicuous. Usually these wintering birds are not numerous (1 to 5 per day in proper habitat), but during some winters they are fairly common (5 to 20 per day in proper habitat), probably due to winter shifts by populations from the interior of Alaska.

Estimates of populations utilizing the North Gulf Coast and Prince William Sound: yearly, several 100's.

Sturnus vulgaris — Starling

The Starling is a rare visitant in the North Gulf Coast - Prince William Sound region.

The first Starling reported in the region was a single bird observed by Isleib at Seward on 13 November 1962 (Williamson et al., 1965). Since 1964, Shaffer has seen two to five Starlings every spring and fall in and about Seward. Pete and Ruth Isleib saw one foraging briefly on the beach with a flock of Northwestern Crows at Cordova on 13 November 1970.

In view of the continuing spread of Starlings through southeastern, southcentral, and interior Alaska, they will undoubtedly increase in numbers in future years in the North Gulf Coast-Prince William Sound region and perhaps become residents and breeders.

Estimates of populations utilizing the North Gulf Coast and Prince William Sound: migration, several individuals, possibly 10's.

Vireo olivaceus — Red-eyed Vireo

The Red-eyed Vireo is accidental in the North Gulf Coast-Prince William Sound region. Rausch (1958) collected a female on 26 June 1956 at Middleton Island.

Vermivora celata — Orange-crowned Warbler

The Orange-crowned Warbler is an abundant migrant and abundant breeder in the North Gulf Coast-Prince William Sound region.

The Orange-crowned Warbler is the most abundant warbler in the region. It occurs in a wide variety of localities and habitats, from timberline to shoreline, during the nesting season and, even commonly, along the shoreline and aboard ship several miles out at sea during migration.

Spring migrants begin arriving in early May (earliest, one on 4 May 1969 at Cordova) and are abundant during the latter half of May.

The Orange-crowned Warbler breeds throughout the region. Grinnell (1910a) reported it as the most numerous breeding warbler in 1908 in the Prince William Sound area, where both young and adults were found in a wide variety of localities. Shortt (1939) found it nesting commonly in the Yakutat area in 1936; he collected a female with a nest and four eggs on 2 June and reported that fledged young became conspicuous about 1 July. Gabrielson (Gabrielson and Lincoln, 1959) considered it common about Seward on 2 and 3 July 1950.

Fall migration for the Orange-crowned Warbler begins in early August and continues until early October, migrants being abundant from mid-August until mid-September (latest, one on 7 October 1969 at Cordova).

Estimates of populations utilizing the North Gulf Coast and Prince William Sound: migration, a few, probably several, 100,000's; summer, several 100,000's.

Dendroica petechia — Yellow Warbler

The Yellow Warbler is a fairly common migrant and fairly common breeder along the North Gulf Coast and in Prince William Sound.

Spring migrants arrive in late May and early June (earliest, one on 24 May 1965 that came aboard ship off the Copper River Delta), becoming fairly common around 1 June (latest, several on 14 June 1972 at Cordova). Lyon et al. (unpubl. notes) reported that this warbler arrived at Whittier in fairly large numbers in late May 1954.

Breeding Yellow Warblers are fairly common in the willow shrub thickets on the Copper River Delta and elsewhere in the region. Solf flushed a Yellow Warbler from a nest with four eggs at Eshamy Bay, PWS, in June 1969. Rausch (1958) reported it as an abundant breeding bird of the shrub formation on Middleton Island in 1956. Shortt (1939) reported that it was "not common" near Yakutat during the breeding season in 1936. Gabrielson (Gabrielson and Lincoln, 1959) saw them during summers between 1940 and 1950 at Seward, Valdez, Cordova, Yakutat, and Situk River.

Fall migration begins in late July, with migrants being fairly common in mid-August; a few linger until late August and early September (latest, one on 3 September 1969, Copper River Delta, and an adult female on 21 September 1972 at Cordova).

Estimates of populations utilizing the North Gulf Coast and Prince William Sound: migration and summer, several 1,000's.

Dendroica coronata — Myrtle Warbler

The Myrtle Warbler is a rare migrant and locally common breeder in the North Gulf Coast-Prince William Sound region.

Spring migrants are rare along the coast; they usually occur in mid- and late May (earliest, one on 12 May 1966 at Cordova; latest, one on 27 May 1971 at Eyak Lake near Cordova).

During the summer, Myrtle Warblers are common in Resurrection Valley, especially in the mixed deciduous-spruce woodlands where they undoubtedly breed. They may breed also in other areas in the region, specifically in the Valdez area (Gabrielson[Gabrielson and Lincoln, 1959] reported a few near Valdez on 1 August 1945) and along the Copper River above the Copper River Delta (Shepherd [pers. comm.] found it breeding in the adjacent Bremner River region on 27 June 1958).

A few fall migrants occur annually between mid-August and mid-September in the eastern Prince William Sound-Copper River Delta area, usually as single birds associating with other passerine migrants (latest, one on 14 September 1969 at Cordova). Grinnell (1910a) reported three birds, which were probably migrants, collected at the head of Port Nellie Juan on 18 and 19 August 1908.

Estimates of populations utilizing the North Gulf Coast and Prince William Sound: migration, a few, possibly several, 100's; summer, several 100's.

Dendroica townsendi — Townsend's Warbler

The Townsend's Warbler is an uncommon migrant and a fairly common breeder in the North Gulf Coast-Prince William Sound region.

Spring migrants arrive between mid-May and early June (earliest, one on 16 May 1971 at Eyak Lake near Cordova). Rausch (1958) reported an apparent late stray migrant at Middleton Island on 11 June 1956.

The Townsend's Warbler probably breeds, at least locally, in much of the hemlock-Sitka Spruce forest of the region. At the present time, however, it has been reported in summer only in Resurrection Valley and in the eastern Prince William Sound-western Copper River Delta area. Shaffer and Isleib have found it a fairly common bird, apparently breeding, in Resurrection Valley; and Gabrielson (Gabrielson and Lincoln, 1959) found it "rather common and paired" near Seward on 2 July 1950. In the Cordova-upper Copper River Delta area, Isleib has found it fairly common and apparently breeding in most years. Grinnell (1910a) reported that three Townsend's Warblers were collected in the Cordova-Orca Inlet area by the Alexander Expedition on 7 and 9 June 1908. Shortt (1939) did not report this warbler in the Yakutat Bay area in 1936.

There is some indication that breeding numbers in a given locality fluctuate from year to year. Townsend's Warblers were one of the most common nesting birds on the forested slopes above Eyak Lake near Cordova in 1966, but there were only a few individuals there in 1970. Gabrielson (ibid.) experienced a similar situation on the Kenai Peninsula in 1950 when he found these warblers common and paired in locations where he had failed to find them in 1940 and 1945.

Fall migration is mostly in August, and Grinnell (1910a) reported the collection of eight Townsend's Warblers from mixed flocks of warblers, chickadees, and kinglets between 13 and 18 August 1908 at the head of Port Nellie Juan, PWS. Rarely, individuals remain into September (latest, two on 7 September 1969 at Eyak Lake near Cordova).

Estimates of populations utilizing the North Gulf Coast and Prince William Sound: migration, a few 1,000's; summer, several 100's, probably 1,000's.

Dendroica striata — Blackpoll Warbler

The Blackpoll Warbler is a rare local breeder in the North Gulf Coast-Prince William Sound region.

Upper Resurrection Valley is the only locality within the region where the Blackpoll Warbler is known to occur; this population is undoubtedly an extension of the population from the boreal forests of the adjacent portions of the Kenai Peninsula. During the first week of July 1963, a few apparently territorial Blackpoll Warblers were present along the Lost Lake Trail near Mile 7 Seward Highway, and Shaffer has seen a few every summer, apparently breeding, along the railroad grade near Mile 12 Seward Highway.

Estimates of populations utilizing the North Gulf Coast and Prince William Sound: summer, a few 10's.

Seiurus noveboracensis — Northern Waterthrush

The Northern Waterthrush is a rare migrant and an uncommon local breeder in the North Gulf Coast-Prince William Sound region; it has been recorded only from Resurrection Valley and the Copper River Delta areas.

Spring migrants have been observed only in the Copper River Delta-Cordova area, where they occur rarely in late May and early June.

This warbler is widespread throughout the interior of Alaska and the western Kenai Peninsula during the breeding season, and it apparently extends from there into Resurrection Valley, where it is uncommon but probably breeds. Waterthrushes seen by Solf in early July 1954 along Martin River Slough on the eastern Copper River Delta were apparently also from adjacent interior populations, extending into the region via the Copper River Valley. In the closely adjacent Bremner River area, Shepherd (pers. comm.) saw several Northern Waterthrushes on 27 July 1958.

A few fall migrants pass through the eastern Prince William Sound-Copper River Delta area (earliest, one on 12 August 1964 at Galena Bay, PWS; latest, three on 3 September 1972 at Cordova). The greatest number counted on a single day has been three seen and several others heard on 22 August 1969 at Mile 19 Copper River Highway.

Estimates of populations utilizing the North Gulf Coast and Prince William Sound: migration, probably 100's; summer, probably a few 100's.

Geothlypis trichas — Yellowthroat

The Yellowthroat is accidental in the North Gulf Coast-Prince William Sound region. A male was closely observed by Pete and Ruth Isleib on 7 October 1969 in Cordova. This bird appeared the morning following a full day of 100 to 120 mph (160-190 kph) winds and was seen in the same shrubbery as a male Wilson's Warbler and an Orange-crowned Warbler, the latest fall records of these latter two species.

Wilsonia pusilla — Wilson's Warbler

The Wilson's Warbler is a common migrant and common breeder (locally abundant) along the North Gulf Coast and in Prince William Sound.

Spring migrants begin arriving in early May but are not common until late May (earliest, one on 7 May 1966 at Cordova). During migration, the Wilson's Warbler occurs regularly on coastal rocks, reefs, and islets, and on boats at sea.

During the summer, this warbler is conspicuous throughout most of the region, becoming locally abundant in most areas of extensive shrub thickets. The Alexander Expedition (Grinnell, 1910a) found this warbler throughout Prince William Sound in 1908 and reported it as one of the commonest breeding birds locally. Shortt (1939) found the Wilson's Warbler "very common" in the Yakutat area in 1936 and found it breeding in numbers near the Situk River, where a nest with six young was discovered on 27 June. Rausch (1958) collected a single male on 26 June 1956 on Middleton Island.

Fall migrants depart from early August until late September, being most common in late August (latest, a male on 7 October 1969 at Cordova).

Estimates of populations utilizing the North Gulf Coast and Prince William Sound: migration, several 10,000's, possibly 100,000's; summer, several 10,000's.

Agelaius phoeniceus — Red-winged Blackbird

The Red-winged Blackbird is casual (perhaps rare) in the North Gulf Coast-Prince William Sound region.

Shepherd (1962) reported breeding Red-winged Blackbirds in the adjacent Bremner River region in 1957 and 1958; however, there have been only three reports of this blackbird in the North Gulf Coast-Prince William Sound region. In May 1964 a singing male lingered several days at Mile 7 Copper River Highway and was seen by several Cordova residents (J. Ed King and others, pers. comm.). Johnson (pers. field notes) observed an adult male on 25 March 1968 at Tawah Creek near the Yakutat airport. Isleib watched a conspicuously alarmed adult female in a marshy thicket on the shore of Bering Lake on 9 August 1972.

The Red-winged Blackbird is probably more frequent in the region than observations to date indicate and is probably a rare, local breeder, but large areas of coastal marshes east of Prince William Sound have never been examined more than superficially.

Euphagus carolinus — Rusty Blackbird

The Rusty Blackbird is a resident of the North Gulf Coast-Prince William Sound region, occurring seasonally as an uncommon spring migrant, a rare local breeder, a fairly common fall migrant, and a rare winter visitant.

Spring migrants, usually in small flocks, appear in April and May; they are uncommon and are probably birds that overwintered along adjacent coastal areas to the southeast.

A few Rusty Blackbirds occur in Resurrection Valley nearly every summer, but the only definite nesting record for the region is of a female feeding young in a nest along Nash Road near Seward in late June-early July 1969 (Shaffer, pers. comm.). Scattered individuals and pairs are present nearly every summer on the upper portions of the Copper River Delta, indicating that a few probably breed in this area too. In fact, it is likely that future observers will locate the Rusty Blackbird as a breeder in other areas of appropriate habitat within the region.

Fall migrants are fairly common from mid-August until late October, especially on the marshes of the Copper River Delta. Numerous small flocks, totaling several hundred blackbirds, moved eastward across the upper marshes of the Copper River Delta during the first days of September 1969.

Small flocks of overwintering Rusty Blackbirds are rare but regular in the Copper River Delta-Prince William Sound area and probably throughout the North Gulf Coast, especially if any freshwater marshes remain unfrozen. Williamson et al. (1965) reported similar overwintering in adjacent upper Cook Inlet.

Estimates of populations utilizing the North Gulf Coast and Prince William Sound: migration-spring, 100's; migration-fall, a few, probably several, 1,000's; summer, 10's, possibly a few 100's; winter, a few 100's.

Quiscalus quiscula – Common Grackle

The Common Grackle is accidental in the North Gulf Coast-Prince William Sound region. A single male was observed closely and positively identified on 28 and 29 August 1966 at the Yakutat airport by Johnson (Johnson, 1968 and pers. field notes), who was well-acquainted with the species.

Pinicola enucleator – Pine Grosbeak

The Pine Grosbeak is a fairly common resident along the North Gulf Coast and in Prince William Sound.

The Pine Grosbeak is fairly common and widely distributed throughout the region all year. The Alexander Expedition (Grinnell, 1910a) found a family of adults and young on Latouche Island on 5 August 1908 and saw others from sea level to above timberline throughout Prince William Sound; Shortt (1939) saw Pine Grosbeaks throughout the Yakutat area during the summer of 1936; and Gabrielson (Gabrielson and Lincoln, 1959) saw or collected this species during his visits within the region at Seward, Yakutat, and in Prince William Sound.

Some migratory movement is apparent in the area, especially during October, when small flocks are common flying eastward across the upper forested portion of the Copper River Delta. During mid-October 1969 a regular stream of flocks, totaling at least a few thousand birds, occurred in this area, a movement which coincided with several ten thousand migrating White-winged Crossbills.

Pine Grosbeaks winter regularly in the region (1 to 5 small flocks per day in proper habitat).

Estimates of populations utilizing the North Gulf Coast and Prince William Sound: migration-fall, several 100's, probably a few 1,000's – in some years, probably several 1,000's; summer, several 1,000's; winter, a few, probably several, 1,000's.

Leucosticte tephrocotis – Gray-crowned Rosy Finch

The Gray-crowned Rosy Finch is probably a fairly common migrant, a fairly common breeder, and an uncommon local winter resident in the North Gulf Coast-Prince William Sound region.

Spring migrants pass through the region in March and April. The first rosy finch ever recorded at Cordova, a male, lingered several days at a feeder in early March 1970. In 1971, a year in which a tremendous accumulation of snow at both high and low elevations persisted unusually late, a flock of 18 rosy finches was first noted at Cordova on 11 April, and by 24 April numbers had increased to approximately 3,000 birds.

Gray-crowned Rosy Finches probably nest regularly throughout suitable alpine areas of the region, but most of these areas are not visited by ornithologists. The Alexander Expedition (Grinnell, 1910a) saw four birds during the summer of 1908 between 2,000 and 2,200 ft (600 and 700 m) elevation in the high alpine zones on Hinchinbrook and Montague islands. Isleib saw several pairs of Gray-crowned Rosy Finches during late June-early July 1962 and 1963 in what were probably breeding areas between 3,500 and 4,500 ft (1100 and 1400 m) in the Kenai Mountains, north of Seward. Grinnell (1910b) reported a specimen taken near Yakutat on 10 June 1908. Unusual nesting occurred at Cordova in 1971, due undoubtedly to the above-mentioned late persistence of snow; two pairs raised eight young and remained in the area until early August (Harry Curran, Cordova resident, pers. comm.). A pair apparently nested at the same locality in 1972 (ibid.), and two pairs were carrying nesting material there on 20 May 1973.

Wintering flocks have been reported only from Seward, where Shaffer has seen them annually in flocks varying from a dozen to more than a hundred birds.

Estimates of populations utilizing the North Gulf Coast and Prince William Sound: migration and summer, several 1,000's; winter, several 10's, possibly 100's.

Acanthis hornemanni — Hoary Redpoll

The Hoary Redpoll is a rare winter visitant in the North Gulf Coast-Prince William Sound region.

A few birds visit the region each winter. During "invasion years," this redpoll is fairly common on the Copper River Delta and occurs, at least sparingly, throughout the entire region (earliest, one with Common Redpolls on 9 November 1968 at Hartney Bay, Orca Inlet; latest, three on 17 April 1969, Mile 11 Copper River Highway).

During the winter of 1968-69, the Hoary Redpoll was fairly common in mixed flocks of Common Redpolls and in small, separate flocks; a few, probably several, hundred were present on the upper Copper River Delta during February and March 1969.

Estimates of populations utilizing the North Gulf Coast and Prince William Sound: winter, 10's, possibly 100's — in some years, 100's, probably a few 1,000's.

Acanthis flammea — Common Redpoll

The Common Redpoll is a fairly common resident in the North Gulf Coast-Prince William Sound region.

Breeding Common Redpolls are distributed sparsely throughout most of the timberline areas of the region, and a few summer occurrences at or near the coast suggest that it breeds occasionally in some coastal areas. Rausch (1958) saw a few Common Redpolls on Middleton Island in June 1956 and thought that they may have nested there. Grinnell (1910a) reported six specimens collected between 9 July and 25 August 1908 from elevations of 1,000 to 2,000 ft (300 to 600 m) on the islands and mainland of Prince William Sound. Shortt (1939) saw a few redpolls in the Disenchantment Bay area in late May and again in July 1936. Lyon et al. (unpubl. notes) reported seeing single birds several times in July and August 1954 at Whittier. Shaffer has found the Common Redpoll a fairly common breeder along the Lost Lake Trail, Resurrection Valley, where he has located nests.

Some migratory movement is apparent in the fall and early spring when the Common Redpoll becomes fairly common at lower elevations and along the coast. Normally, several hundred are seen in each of these seasons in the Copper River Delta, but in some years in the Copper River Delta-Prince William Sound area several thousand birds occur in numerous flocks.

Winter numbers fluctuate on the Copper River Delta from a high of a few thousand in some years to only a few small flocks between late November and early March in other years.

Estimates of populations utilizing the North Gulf Coast and Prince William Sound: migration, a few 1,000's — in some years, 10,000's; summer, probably a few 1,000's; winter, a few 100's — in some years, several 1,000's.

Spinus pinus — Pine Siskin

The Pine Siskin is a resident of the North Gulf Coast-Prince William Sound region, generally common during the spring and fall, fairly common during the summer, and uncommon or rare during the winter.

The Pine Siskin, a gregarious species, occurs throughout the forest and woodland habitats of the region. In some years it is locally common or abundant throughout the year on both the mainland and the islands, appearing in numerous flocks of up to several hundreds of birds. During winters of low abundance, it is present only as occasional, small flocks.

The siskin undoubtedly breeds annually in the region, but the only positive breeding reports are from Yakutat, where Eliot Blackwelder took eggs in June 1906 (Gabrielson and Lincoln, 1959) and where Shortt (1939) found it locally common and breeding in 1936, collecting a female on 18 June that had recently laid eggs and collecting a young bird on 22 July.

Estimates of populations utilizing the North Gulf Coast and Prince William Sound: yearly, varies from periodic highs of several 10,000's, especially in fall, to some winter lows of probably 100's.

Loxia curvirostra — Red Crossbill

The Red Crossbill is a rare resident of the North Gulf Coast-Prince William Sound region.

In recent years, these crossbills have been reported in the North Gulf Coast-Prince William Sound region during 1955, 1964-65, 1967, 1969-70, and 1972-73, although they probably occur more frequently than these observations would indicate. When present, they occur in the hemlock-Sitka Spruce forests, mostly in small flocks.

Red Crossbills occur most frequently during the spring, summer, and fall, suggesting probable breeding, but there are no substantiated nesting records. George E. Hudson (in litt., 1973) collected a subadult male (Wash. State Univ. 55-306) at Martin River Slough, CRD, on 1 July 1955. Isleib saw several Red Crossbills on Esther Island, PWS, in early July 1965, and Solf saw a small, mixed flock of both species of crossbills at Pigot Bay, PWS, in early July 1967. Shaffer saw a few near Seward during the fall of 1964.

Red Crossbills overwintered in the region in 1969-70: Shaffer saw several flocks near Seward in the late summer and fall of 1969; Isleib saw several small flocks and a few in flocks mixed with White-winged Crossbills in the Copper River Delta-Prince William Sound area in the fall of 1969 and during the winter and spring of 1970; and West and Peyton (unpubl. notes) collected an immature male and an adult male (both with only 2 mm testes) from a flock of 20 near Cordova on 1 May 1970.

These crossbills were in the region again in 1972-73, from late summer through winter in Resurrection Valley and adjacent portions of the Kenai Peninsula. They were fairly common (comprising about 5% of the total crossbill population — Red and White-winged — which totaled at least several thousand in Resurrection Valley) and were displaying territorial behavior in January 1973.

Estimates of populations utilizing the North Gulf Coast and Prince William Sound: probably yearly, varies from periodic highs of a few 1,000's to perhaps none.

Loxia leucoptera — White-winged Crossbill

The White-winged Crossbill is an uncommon resident of the North Gulf Coast-Prince William Sound region.

A few flocks occur every year and, in 1964, 1969, and 1972-73, these crossbills were common throughout the year and were well-distributed throughout the forests and woodlands of the area. Most ornithologists who have worked in the region have reported White-winged Crossbills (Gabrielson and Lincoln, 1959; Grinnell, 1910a; Shortt, 1939); the species undoubtedly breeds, at least irregularly, within the coastal region, although no nests have been reported.

During mid-October 1969 a spectacular "wave" of White-winged Crossbills funneled eastward along an isolated, 1-mile-wide belt of forest between Mile 17 and Mile 27 Copper River Highway. On 10 October only three small flocks of White-winged Crossbills were present in the forest belt, but between 13 and 17 October scores of flocks, totaling thousands of White-winged Crossbills, continually flew eastward along the belt. Probably between 50,000 and 100,000 birds funneled through here during this brief period. After 17 October 1969 the numbers declined to only a few flocks per day, and during the winter of 1969-70 one to five flocks per day could be observed in proper habitat throughout most of the Copper River Delta-Prince William Sound area. This movement of White-winged Crossbills coincided in 1969 with smaller "waves" of Pine Siskins and Pine Grosbeaks, with invasions of Red-breasted Nuthatches and Gray Jays, and with the periodic presence of Red Crossbills.

From late summer through winter 1972-73, another dramatic invasion occurred in Resurrection Valley and adjacent areas of the Kenai Peninsula. White-winged Crossbills were abundant in the hemlock-Sitka Spruce forests, where they seemed to saturate available niches, with territorial males singing vigorously throughout January 1973. There were probably at least several thousand of these crossbills in Resurrection Valley, maybe ten thousand.

White-winged Crossbills not infrequently are reported in Alaska flying out over the oceans. Two such instances have been reported along the North Gulf Coast: Clarke P. Streator (Gabrielson and Lincoln, 1959) reported a pair that came aboard ship some 50 miles (80 km) off Yakutat in July 1895, and Humberg (pers. comm.) reported a male that came aboard some 15 miles (25 km) off Cape St. Elias in mid-October 1969.

Estimates of populations utilizing the North Gulf Coast and Prince William Sound: yearly, varies from periodic highs of 100,000's to lows of 100's.

Passerculus sandwichensis — Savannah Sparrow

The Savannah Sparrow is an abundant migrant and abundant breeder along the North Gulf Coast and in Prince William Sound.

Spring migrants arrive as early as late April (earliest, several on 26 April 1969 at Hartney Bay, Orca Inlet), but the majority arrive in mid-May. During migration the Savannah Sparrow is one of the most common passerines along the outer coasts, on reefs, on coastal rocks, and even on boats miles from shore. In these areas, weary migrants sometimes fall prey to gulls and jaegers.

The Savannah Sparrow is an abundant breeder in sedge-grass areas throughout the region. Grinnell (1910a) reported that the Alexander Expedition collected 38 specimens throughout Prince William Sound during 1908 and that individuals were numerous in various habitats from shoreline to above timberline; a nest with five eggs was found on Hinchinbrook Island on 27 July 1908. Shortt (1939) found it one of the commonest species in the Yakutat area in 1936 and reported four nests with eggs during June; several ornithologists over the years have also reported it breeding at Yakutat (Gabrielson and Lincoln, 1959). Rausch (1958) regarded Savannah Sparrows as numerous on Middleton Island, reporting a nest with eggs on 11 June 1956 and fledged young of another nest on 25 June 1956.

Fall migrants first occur in early August, becoming abundant along the coasts in late August and early September. They are fairly common until late October, and a few stragglers may remain until early winter (latest, one on 21 November 1968 at Hartney Bay, Orca Inlet).

Estimates of populations utilizing the North Gulf Coast and Prince William Sound: migration, 100,000's, possibly 1,000,000's; summer, a few, possibly several, 100,000's.

Junco hyemalis – Slate-colored Junco

The Slate-colored Junco is an uncommon resident of the North Gulf Coast-Prince William Sound region.

Spring migrants arrive in mid-April and are present until late May, being most numerous, yet uncommon, in early May.

During the summer Slate-colored Juncos are sparingly distributed throughout most of the region, breeding from the Kenai Peninsula eastward through the Prince William Sound drainages. Shortt (1939) did not record this junco in the Yakutat area in 1936, and the eastern limit of its summer range is unknown. Shaffer has found the Slate-colored Junco a locally fairly common breeder in the Resurrection Valley-Seward area, especially along the Lost Lake Trail. Isleib has found this junco uncommon, but probably breeding, on the slopes near Cordova in the eastern Prince William Sound-Copper River Delta area, where it is accompanied by the Oregon Junco. The Alexander Expedition in 1908 (Grinnell, 1910a) collected a female from a pair of Slate-colored Juncos near Orca Inlet on 10 June and saw or collected others in the western and northern portions of Prince William Sound between 16 August and 4 September. Gabrielson (Gabrielson and Lincoln, 1959) saw Slate-colored Juncos fairly commonly at College Fiord, Port Wells, on 13 August 1945.

Fall migration becomes evident by mid-August and continues to late October, with small numbers overwintering with some regularity. Shaffer has seen Slate-colored Juncos almost every winter at Seward, as has Isleib in the Cordova area, and they probably winter locally elsewhere in the region.

The Slate-colored Junco and Oregon Junco, probably conspecific, have overlapping breeding ranges in the eastern Prince William Sound-Copper River Delta area, and a few juncos in the vicinity of Cordova appear to be intergrades.

Estimates of populations utilizing the North Gulf Coast and Prince William Sound: migration, several 1,000's; summer, a few 1,000's; winter, a few 100's.

Junco oreganus — Oregon Junco

The Oregon Junco is an uncommon resident of the North Gulf Coast-Prince William Sound region.

During the spring and summer months, it is well-distributed, although uncommon, in the Copper River Delta-eastern Prince William Sound area, where it probably breeds. Isleib saw this junco in the Bering River-Kayak Island area in late June-early July 1967 and at Yakutat in July and August 1968, where it had been reported previously by Clarke P. Streator as breeding in 1895 (Gabrielson and Lincoln, 1959) and by Shortt (1939) as uncommon and breeding in 1936. In western Prince William Sound, Isleib saw one at Pigot Bay on 4 May 1971.

Wintering birds are rare in the Copper River Delta-Prince William Sound area and usually occur in small, mixed junco flocks. At Seward, Shaffer has found winter visitants irregularly among the Slate-colored Junco flocks.

Apparently, the Oregon Junco has been extending its range westward in recent years, since it was not recorded during the extensive survey of Prince William Sound by the Alexander Expedition in 1908 (Grinnell, 1910a). In fact, it has only been recorded in the central and western portions of the North Gulf Coast-Prince William Sound region since the early 1960's.

Estimates of populations utilizing the North Gulf Coast and Prince William Sound: summer, a few 1,000's; winter, 10's, possibly a few 100's.

Spizella arborea — Tree Sparrow

The Tree Sparrow is a rare local resident in the North Gulf Coast-Prince William Sound region.

The only summer record of this sparrow is one by Rausch (1958) from Middleton Island, where he collected two males in breeding condition on 28 June 1956 and thought the species might be breeding, although it was uncommon. It is possibly a local breeder in other portions of the region, however, and should be looked for in the drainages leading into the interior, e.g., Resurrection, Copper River, and Alsek River valleys.

Tree Sparrows are rare but regular fall and winter visitors (late September-early April) in the coastal areas of the region, especially in marsh and open shrub thicket habitats. Shaffer has reported them as irregular winter visitants at Seward; Isleib has recorded them in small numbers every fall and winter at Cordova; and Grinnell (1910b) reported two specimens collected at Yakutat on 13 and 14 October 1908.

Estimates of populations utilizing the North Gulf Coast and Prince William Sound: migration-fall, a few 100's; summer, probably 10's; winter, 10's, probably a few 100's.

Zonotrichia leucophrys — White-crowned Sparrow

The White-crowned Sparrow is a resident in the North Gulf Coast-Prince William Sound region, occurring seasonally as an uncommon migrant, a rare local breeder, and a casual winter visitant.

In the Copper River Delta-Prince William Sound area, spring migrants are uncommon among the masses of other migrant sparrows during May (earliest, one on 5 May 1969 at Cordova; latest, four with Golden-crowned Sparrows on 28 May

1971 at Cordova). In Resurrection Valley, spring migrants are fairly common (Shaffer, pers. comm.).

The White-crowned Sparrow is a common or abundant breeder in the adjacent upper Copper River Valley and the Cook Inlet drainages of the Kenai Peninsula, and extensions of these populations are found locally during the summer, apparently breeding, in the upper Resurrection Valley, the Lowe River Valley near Valdez, and along the Copper River above the delta. The only summer observation other than in these areas is one by Yocom (1963) of two White-crowned Sparrows seen some 20 miles (32 km) east of Cordova on 20 July 1962.

Fall migrants are uncommon, usually occurring in flocks of a few indiviuals to 50 birds. They are found along the coast from late August (earliest, one with migrating Golden-crowned Sparrows on 22 August 1969 at Cordova) until early November.

Wintering White-crowned Sparrows were present at Cordova in 1968-69 and again in 1969-70: 12 to 15 birds lingered into December 1968, with three still present in late January 1969; and during 1969-70 an immature White-crowned Sparrow fed throughout the winter at a feeder, being last noted in late April 1970.

Estimates of populations utilizing the North Gulf Coast and Prince William Sound: migration, several 100's; summer, a few, possibly several, 100's; winter, in some years, a few individuals.

Zonotrichia atricapilla — Golden-crowned Sparrow

The Golden-crowned Sparrow is an abundant migrant, an abundant local breeder, and a casual winter visitant along the North Gulf Coast and in Prince William Sound.

Spring migrants begin arriving in late April (earliest, several on 28 April 1969 at Cordova) and, in most years, are abundant between 10 and 25 May. During migration, the Golden-crowned Sparrow is one of the most numerous passerines along the outer coasts, on reefs and coastal rocks, and it regularly lands on boats miles from shore.

The Golden-crowned Sparrow breeds abundantly in scattered localities throughout most of the region. In Disenchantment Bay and on the wooded moraine of the Malaspina Glacier, Shortt (1939) found it a common nester in 1936, finding a nest with two young on 6 July. It is also a locally common or abundant breeder in shrub thickets in the upper Copper River Delta, in Prince William Sound, and at Seward. It is interesting to note that the Alexander Expedition to Prince William Sound did not find summering birds in 1908, reporting only fall migrants between 28 August and 2 September (Grinnell, 1910a). At least a partial answer to this recent extension of breeding range into the Prince William Sound area probably lies in the effect that logging operations have had on the habitat; Golden-crowned Sparrows are now locally abundant where logging operations have left second-growth slashes in lieu of formerly continuous, mature forests.

Fall migrants appear along the outer coasts in mid-August and are abundant in late August-early September; they usually disappear about 1 October (latest, three with juncos on 15 October 1969, Mile 23 Copper River Highway).

There are two winter records from the region, both of immatures: one along a brushy roadside near Seward in company with Tree Sparrows on 22 December 1962 (Williamson et al., 1965) and another at a feeder for several days in late December 1969 at Cordova.

Estimates of populations utilizing the North Gulf Coast and Prince William Sound: migration, 100,000's; summer, a few, possibly several, 10,000's.

Zonotrichia albicollis — White-throated Sparrow

The White-throated Sparrow is accidental in the North Gulf Coast-Prince William Sound region.

The only record of this species in the region is of an adult closely observed by Pete and Ruth Isleib 7-9 October 1972 in their yard at Cordova. The bird associated with a loose, mixed flock of 10 to 15 sparrows that was present for the same time period, a flock containing White-crowned, Golden-crowned, and Fox sparrows.

White-throated Sparrows have been recorded three times previously in Alaska, all from the interior (Univ. Alaska unpubl. records).

Passerella iliaca — Fox Sparrow

The Fox Sparrow is an abundant migrant and abundant breeder along the North Gulf Coast and in Prince William Sound.

Spring migrants begin arriving in April (earliest*, one on 21 April 1969 at Cordova) and are abundant along the coastal areas during the first half of May.

The Fox Sparrow is abundant and widely distributed throughout the region's shrub thickets, from the borders of the beaches to timberline. The Alexander Expedition in 1908 (Grinnell, 1910a) found it breeding throughout Prince William Sound and reported that it was "superabundant" on Hinchinbrook, Montague, and Latouche islands. Shortt (1939) found the Fox Sparrow one of the commonest nesting species throughout the Yakutat area in 1936. Rausch (1958) reported that it was the second most numerous passerine on Middleton Island in 1956 (after Savannah Sparrow).

Fall migration takes place between early August and mid-October, with most of the Fox Sparrows migrating between late August and late September (latest, six on 7 October 1969, four on 10 October 1971, and three on 19 October 1972, all at Cordova).

Estimates of populations utilizing the North Gulf Coast and Prince William Sound: migration, 100,000's; summer, 100,000's.

Melospiza lincolnii — Lincoln's Sparrow

The Lincoln's Sparrow is a fairly common migrant and a locally common breeder in the North Gulf Coast-Prince William Sound region.

Spring migrants arrive in May, somewhat later than most other sparrows (earliest, two on 10 May 1969 at Cordova).

Lincoln's Sparrows are locally common breeders in the coastal, marshy, shrub thickets of the region. Shortt (1939) saw Lincoln's Sparrows at various locations in the Yakutat area in 1936, where he collected four nests, each containing five eggs, between 7 and 12 June; he considered them the commonest breeding bird in the vicinity of his Situk River camp. Annie M. Alexander (Grinnell, 1910a) collected five specimens and a nest with eggs at Orca Inlet between 10 and 13 June 1908. Gabrielson (Gabrielson and Lincoln, 1959) found Lincoln's Sparrows "fairly numerous" at Valdez on 1 August 1943 and saw or collected them at Valdez,

*A rufous-tailed Fox Sparrow, probably *P. i. zaboria,* was observed by Solf on 29 March 1969 at Cordova — the only such sighting for the region.

Port Ashton, Hawkins Island, Sheep Bay, Seward, and on the Situk River in July and August 1945.

Lincoln's Sparrows migrate from mid-August until mid-September. They apparently leave the region earlier than most other sparrows (latest, one caught in a trap on 18 September 1908 in Valdez Narrows [Grinnell, 1910a]).

Estimates of populations utilizing the North Gulf Coast and Prince William Sound: migration, 1,000's; summer, several 1,000's, possibly 10,000's.

Melospiza melodia — Song Sparrow

The Song Sparrow is a resident of the North Gulf Coast-Prince William Sound region, occurring seasonally as an uncommon migrant, a locally fairly common breeder, and an uncommon winter resident.

Migrants arrive between mid-April (earliest, one on 16 April 1969 at Alaganik Slough, CRD) and early May.

The Song Sparrow is a fairly common breeder throughout most of the coastal areas of the region, frequenting areas of Beach Rye, marshes, and shrub thickets at or near shorelines, sloughs, and waterways. Shortt (1939) considered it "not uncommon" in the Yakutat area in 1936. Grinnell (1910a) reported it generally well-distributed at shore locations throughout Prince William Sound in 1908. Gabrielson (Gabrielson and Lincoln, 1959) saw it commonly during his visits to Yakutat and noted it regularly at Seward and in Prince William Sound. Rausch (1958) found Song Sparrows absent from Middleton Island in 1956.

Fall migrants have not been detected as such, but migration is presumed to be in September and early October because Song Sparrows are uncommon and of local distribution after mid-October and through the winter.

Wintering birds are fairly common visitants about docks, wharves, and harbors. They are uncommon at other localities, but occur regularly throughout the region, especially along the shores of sheltered inlets and bays.

Estimates of populations utilizing the North Gulf Coast and Prince William Sound: migration, 1,000's; summer, several 1,000's; winter ,several 100's, probably a few 1,000's.

Calcarius lapponicus — Lapland Longspur

The Lapland Longspur is an uncommon migrant and probably a local breeder in the North Gulf Coast-Prince William Sound region.

Spring migrant flocks are present on the beaches, marshes, tundra, and other open areas from late March to late May (earliest, seven on 29 March 1969 at Cordova; latest, four on 27 May 1971 at Cordova). Flocks are usually uncommon (10 to 50 flocks per season in proper habitat) and small (5 to 50 birds); after early May, flocks are usually of fewer than 20 birds, and occasionally only single birds are seen.

Rausch (1958:235) has provided the only indication that Lapland Longspurs breed in the region, reporting that in 1956 "a few pairs of longspurs were observed on the highest terrace [of Middleton Island], where they were nesting." Rausch collected two males in breeding condition on 9 June and an adult female on 26 June. Middleton Island is the southeasternmost location along the coast of Alaska where this longspur has been reported as a breeder, and there are no other coastal islands with similar habitats within the region. Possibly this longspur breeds locally in alpine areas in the coastal mountains, although there are no summer reports from these areas.

Grinnell (1910a) reported alpine observations of longspurs between 25 August and 4 September 1908 at Knight and Disk islands in Prince William Sound and at Thompson Pass. These observations are undoubtedly of fall migrants, as fall migrants are fairly common on the marshes of the Copper River Delta between late August and late September (latest, three on 26 October 1968 at Hartney Bay, Orca Inlet). Fall migrants are locally more numerous in the Copper River Delta than are spring migrants and occur in large flocks (50 to 200+ birds).

Although Mary A. Miller of Soldotna (pers. comm.) reported a small wintering flock of longspurs on 24 January 1966 at Cohoe on the Cook Inlet side of the Kenai Peninsula, there are no known winter records along the North Gulf Coast.

Estimates of populations utilizing the North Gulf Coast and Prince William Sound: migration-spring, a few 1,000's; migration-fall, several 1,000's; summer, a few pairs locally on Middleton Island.

Plectrophenax nivalis – Snow Bunting

The Snow Bunting is probably a resident of the North Gulf Coast-Prince William Sound region, occurring seasonally as an uncommon spring migrant, a probably rare and local breeder, a rare fall migrant, and a rare winter visitant.

Spring migrants appear as scattered, small flocks along the coast from mid-March until early May (earliest, two on 20 March 1968 at Cordova; latest, one on 4 May 1972 at Cordova).

There are no reports indicating breeding within the region, but Snow Buntings undoubtedly nest, at least locally, in the mainland alpine areas. Isleib has seen pairs, apparently breeding, at several locations only a few miles from the North Gulf Coast drainages, in the Kenai Mountains at approximately 2,500-4,000 ft (750-1200 m) elevations in shale scree; and they are fairly common breeders in the adjacent upper Glacier Bay region (Wik and Streveler, 1968).

A few small flocks appear in coastal areas from late October through November; it is not known whether these birds are transients or winter visitants.

Snow Buntings are rare winter visitants. Although they probably occur annually in small numbers, only two instances of wintering are known, probably because of the relative inaccessibility of their preferred mid-winter habitat – the outer coastal beaches. Figgins (1904) reported several at Valdez in the latter part of December 1901, and O'Farrell and Sheets (1962) observed a Snow Bunting on Middleton Island on 25 February 1961 and collected what was probably a different bird on 26 February 1961.

Estimates of populations utilizing the North Gulf Coast and Prince William Sound: migration-spring, several 100's, probably a few 1,000's; migration-fall, 10's, probably a few 100's; summer, a few, probably several 100's; winter, a few individuals or 10's, possibly 100's.

Hypothetical List

In one way or another, the occurrence of the following species has not been adequately substantiated for inclusion in the list of birds known to occur within the North Gulf Coast-Prince William Sound region. On the basis of descriptive details provided by the observer, however, and, in some instances, aided by the plausibility of its occurrence in the region, they are listed here as "hypothetical."

Aechmophorus occidentalis — Western Grebe

On several occasions, outdoorsmen and fishermen have reported Western Grebes in the eastern areas of Prince William Sound, describing them as "striking black and white loon-sized birds with exceptionally long, straight necks." Confirmation of these observations has failed, but occurrence in the region is plausible, based on regular sightings in southeastern Alaska at Juneau (Univ. Alaska unpubl. records) and records at closely adjacent Glacier Bay (Wik and Streveler, 1968).

Fregata magnificens — Magnificent Frigatebird

Two separate descriptions have been received that seem to describe the Magnificent Frigatebird, in spite of the fact that this species has been recorded previously only as far north as Oregon on the Pacific coast (American Ornithologists' Union, 1957). Solf has relayed a report from Upton Henderson and John Walker, U. S. Fish and Wildlife Service, that they closely observed a frigatebird in Montague Strait during July 1957: "an exceptionally large, dark, swallow-tailed bird," apparently much larger than a jaeger. A more detailed description has been provided by Humberg (pers. comm.) of two birds that were present for nearly an hour, soaring over his vessel and a nearby fishing trawler that had attracted a large group of pelagic birds on the Fairweather Bank on 16 September 1969. Humberg was unfamiliar with the species and did not identify the birds, but he described male frigatebirds: "dark, large, swallow-tailed birds, resembling Black-footed Albatross in size but having a long tail that forked occasionally." He reported that these birds soared almost continually at higher altitudes than the other pelagics and even appeared to hang for periods of time at 200-300 ft (60-90 m) above the vessels.

Botaurus lentiginosus — American Bittern

In the marshes of the upper Copper River Delta, below Mile 39 Copper River Highway, Cordova trapper/fisherman James Webber, (pers. comm.) in early September 1969, flushed with his airboat a "long-legged, crane-like bird that was similar in size and coloration to, but somewhat darker and larger than, the brown marsh owl [Short-eared Owl]." Although Webber had had no previous experience with bitterns, the accuracy of his description, the habitat, and the location lead us to believe that he saw an American Bittern, which breeds in British Columbia (Godfrey, 1966) and has been reported in southeastern Alaska (Gabrielson and Lincoln, 1959).

Anas cyanoptera — Cinnamon Teal

A male Cinnamon Teal was observed in early May 1954 by Cordova resident Robert Ingebo (pers. comm.) on the marshes near the outlet of the Eyak River. Ingebo, who was quite familiar with the waterfowl of western North America, described the coloration of the teal he observed as "burnt red." The nearest known breeding locality for the Cinnamon Teal is southern British Columbia (Godfrey, 1966), although it has been recorded north to Quesnel, B.C. (ibid.) and is casual in southeastern Alaska (four observations since 1969 [Univ. Alaska unpubl. records]).

Hydroprogne caspia – Caspian Tern

On 28 August 1965, Isleib saw a large, large-billed tern, which he identified as a Caspian Tern, that closely overflew his boat in Egg Island Channel of the Copper River Delta. This bird did not call, and attempts to follow it to obtain additional views were unsuccessful, the bird losing itself in a mist that obscured visibility beyond half a mile.

Sphyrapicus varius – Yellow-bellied Sapsucker

Evidence for the presence of the Yellow-bellied Sapsucker in the region is circumstantial. In the Dan Bay and Fish Bay areas of Hinchinbrook Island, in November of both 1964 and 1970, Isleib found extensive series of punctures on trees, such as are typical of the sap-feeding holes made by the Yellow-bellied Sapsucker. Solf has seen similar "sap holes" in trees in Prince William Sound at Port Etches and on Montague Island. To date, however, the birds themselves have not been seen, although they are widespread throughout most of southeastern Alaska.

Vermivora ruficapilla – Nashville Warbler

While sitting at a window in Cordova on 12 September 1971, Isleib got a brief but close look at a Nashville Warbler. He watched it at less than 10 ft (3 m) for less than a minute as it searched for food in shrubbery. He noted its prominent eye-ring, yellow throat, gray-blue head, and lack of wing bars. Its dingy overall shading suggested a female or young bird. Attempts to find the bird again failed.

Anticipated Birds

Following is a list of birds that have not yet been observed in the North Gulf Coast-Prince William Sound region, but, with more comprehensive coverage in the future, they are likely to be recorded:

Pterodroma cookii – Cook's Petrel
Lampronetta fischeri – Spectacled Eider
Bartramia longicauda – Upland Plover
Larus delawarensis – Ring-billed Gull
Pagophila eburnea – Ivory Gull
Nucifraga columbiana – Clark's Nutcracker
Molothrus ater – Brown-headed Cowbird

New Records

The following species have been seen within the region since this paper went to press:

Dendragapus obscurus – Blue Grouse, 8 May 1973, 15 km northeast of mouth of Alsek River
Calidris fuscicollis – White-rumped Sandpiper, 8 September 1973, Cottonwood Point
Tyrannus verticalis – Western Kingbird, 16 August 1973, Alaganik Slough
Myadestes townsendi – Townsend's Solitaire, 6 September 1973, Cordova
Spizella passerina – Chipping Sparrow, 14 August 1973, Cordova

ADDENDUM
1989 Reprinting

NEW RECORDS

The following species have been recorded in the North Gulf Coast-Prince William Sound region since this work was published in 1973:

Podilymbus podiceps—Pied-billed Grebe. In 1978 a bird overwintered (18 November 1977 through mid-March 1978) at Eyak River; then, one, 5 May, Alaganik Slough; three adults, early and mid-summer, at separate ponds on Copper River Delta; and adult with flightless young, July and August on ponds near Alaganik Slough. Subsequently, one immature, twice in mid-August 1983, Mile 10 Copper River Highway.

Aechmophorus occidentalis—Western Grebe. A very rare fall and winter visitant since 1975: one, 29-30 September 1975, and two, 2 January to mid-February 1977, Orca Inlet; one, 30 December 1977, and three, last week December 1978, Cordova; one, 3 November 1983, Port Valdez; and one, 27 December 1984, and one, 27 November 1987, Cordova.

Puffinus bulleri—Buller's Shearwater. May be rare summer visitant to outer shelf waters of the North Gulf Coast: total of nine on five occasions, 16-29 September 1974, off Cape Yakataga, and single birds on eight occasions, April-October 1975-1978, North Gulf Coast shelf waters; one, 26 April 1985, Gulf of Alaska at 58° 40'N, 139° 00'W; singles, 26 and 27 September 1987, Middleton Island.

Casmerodius albus—Great Egret. One, 14 May 1984, Cordova; subsequently, an "egret" present during third week of May 1984, Pete Dahl Slough.

Bubulcus ibis—Cattle Egret. One, 10 November 1984, Whittier, on barge from Seattle that came across the Gulf of Alaska; timing of occurrence identical to three other widely separated sightings in Southeast Alaska.

Cygnus cygnus—Whooper Swan. Two, 23 October 1977, Orca Inlet.

Aix sponsa—Wood Duck. Male in late eclipse plumage, 11 September 1988, Eyak River.

Anas rubripes—American Black Duck. Male, 17 May 1975, Mile 11 Copper River Highway; male, 18 October 1977, Copper River Delta; one, 27 December 1982, Cordova.

Anas querquedula—Garganey. Immature male, 29 September 1982, Middleton Island.

Anas cyanoptera—Cinnamon Teal. Adult male, 2 May 1975, eastern Copper River Delta, and adult male, 10-22 May 1981, Middleton Island.

Aythya fuligula—Tufted Duck. Female, 18-22 January and 22-25 February 1976, female, 2 October 1977, pair, 29 December 1979-26 April 1980, and up to three, mid-October 1981-late February 1982, all Eyak River; pair, 20 May 1983, Alaganik Slough; two, 2 January 1984, three males, April 1985, and female, 2 February 1989, all Cordova.

Mergellus albellus—Smew. Subadult male, 1-2 January 1982, Mile 14 Copper River Highway.

Oxyura jamaicensis—Ruddy Duck. Pair, 15 May 1984, eastern Copper River Delta.

Buteo swainsoni—Swainson's Hawk. Light morph, 2 May 1975, Mile 8 Copper River Highway; dark morph, 16 May 1976, Mile 16 Copper River Highway; light morph, 21 August 1987, Valdez.

Porzana carolina—Sora. One, 22 September 1984, Pete Dahl Slough.

Charadrius mongolus—Mongolian Plover. Adult, 9 July 1983, Port Valdez.

Charadrius morinellus—Eurasian Dotterel. One, 27 August 1981, Cordova.

Recurvirostra americana—American Avocet. One, 12-18 May 1981, Port Valdez.

Heteroscelus brevipes—Gray-tailed Tattler. Juvenile, 24 September 1982, Middleton Island.

Bartramia longicauda—Upland Sandpiper. One, 8-14 May 1977, Sheridan Glacier near Cordova; one, early September 1978, eastern Copper River Delta; one, 23 September 1982, Middleton Island.

Limosa fedoa—Marbled Godwit. Apparently a rare spring and casual fall migrant in region, especially at the deltas of the Bering and Copper rivers: two, 9 May 1969, north of Cape Fairweather; one, 30 April 1975, Boswell Bay, Hinchinbrook Island; one, 6 May 1975, Orca Inlet; one 30 April 1976, eastern Copper River Delta; three, 3 May, six, 8 May, and five, 9 May 1977, Controller Bay; two, 30 April and one 8 May 1978, eastern Copper River Delta; seven, 1 May 1978, Bering River; one, 3 May 1978, Egg Island; and, in fall, one, for week during mid-October 1977, Green Island, and one, 26 August 1979, eastern Copper River Delta.

Calidris ruficollis—Rufous-necked Stint. One, 18-19 August 1976, Valdez Narrows.

Calidris ferruginea—Curlew Sandpiper. Breeding-plumaged bird, 3 May 1978, Egg Island.

Calidris himantopus—Stilt Sandpiper. Very rare fall migrant: one, 13 September 1975, Cottonwood Point; one, 15 September 1979, eastern Copper River Delta; four, 4 September, and one, 9-12 September 1982, Middleton Island; two, 4 September 1988, Seward.

Tryngites subruficollis—Buff-breasted Sandpiper. Very rare fall migrant, especially on Middleton Island: two, 6 September 1974, Copper River Delta; and, on Middleton Island, one, 16 September, and two, 17

September 1981, singles on five occasions, 1-28 September 1982, one to three, 28-30 September 1987, and one, 15-17 September 1988.

Philomachus pugnax—Ruff. One, 15 August 1977, Cordova; immature, 23 September 1982, Middleton Island.

Phalaropus tricolor—Wilson's Phalarope. Pair, 6 June 1984, Valdez.

Larus ridibundus—Common Black-headed Gull. Subadult, 14 August-12 September 1977, Orca Inlet and Cordova.

Larus delawarensis—Ring-billed Gull. Very rare visitant: one, 4 August 1973, Seward; one, 27 June 1974, Cordova; one, mid-July to 28 September 1975, Cordova, and one 24 September 1975, Port Valdez; one, 24 April 1977, Cordova; one, August-October 1987, Cordova, and one, 28 September 1987, Middleton Island.

Larus schistisagus—Slaty-backed Gull. One, 30 January 1977, over shelf break south of Kenai Peninsula (58° N, 150° W); one, 17 May 1981, Gulf of Alaska off Ressurrection Bay; adult, 27 December 1983, and adult 11-12, August 1987, Cordova; second-year bird, 20 April 1984, on shelf off Yakutat; second-year bird, 15 September 1988, Middleton Island.

Rissa brevirostris—Red-legged Kittiwake. Shelf break at western end of North Gulf Coast, one, 26 January (57° 57′N, 148° 47′W), and four, 27 January 1977 (58° 08′N, 150° 58′W); one, 29 June (58° 07′N, 145° 00′W), and one, 6 July 1980 (57° 10′N, 150° 29′W); one to five daily, 4 October-15 November 1983 (58° N, 148° W). Also, immature, 13 September 1981, Middleton Island.

Pagophila eburnea—Ivory Gull. One, 21 August 1981, Cordova.

Sterna caspia—Caspian Tern. Since first confirmed in summer 1983 (but see p. 139) has become rare summer visitant and probable breeder: In 1983, two, 24 June, Port Nellie Juan; one, late June, Seward; two, 12 July, Yakutat Bay; two, 14 August, Orca Inlet; then, two, 9 June 1984, Robe Lake, Valdez. Recorded annually thereafter, especially on the western Copper River Delta and in Orca Inlet, where highest numbers were a single and a flock of 33, all adults, 6 August 1987, and where the earliest was a pair on 12 May 1987 and the latest an adult on 8 October 1988. In 1988 in Orca Inlet, a flock of about 20 birds on 12 August included two flying juveniles, and on 2 September four juveniles were being fed salmon smolt by adults.

Columba fasciata—Band-tailed Pigeon. One, 13 September 1981, Middleton Island.

Cypseloides niger—Black Swift. One, 22 August 1977, Wooded Islands.

Chaetura vauxi—Vaux's Swift. Two, 6 and 9 September, and one, 19 September 1977, Cordova.

Sphyrapicus varius—Yellow-bellied Sapsucker. One, 9 June 1977, Wooded Island.

Sphyrapicus ruber—Red-breasted Sapsucker. One, 29 October 1978, Cordova; and in 1981, one, 2 May, Eyak River, one to three males, 19-21 September, Middleton Island, and one, 28 September eastern Copper River Delta. Drumming males, probably territorial, late April-June 1983, 1984, and 1985, Mile 6 Copper River Highway.

Empidonax minimus—Least Flycatcher. One, 23 September 1988, Middleton Island.

Tyrannus tyrannus—Eastern Kingbird. Two, 20 August 1981, Cordova; one, 19 September 1981, Middleton Island.

Stelgidopteryx serripennis—Northern Rough-winged Swallow. Pair, 30 May 1976, Storey Island; one, 30 June 1976, Port Gravina; two, 31 May 1978, Mile 27 Copper River Highway.

Sialia currucoides—Mountain Bluebird. One, 20-21 May 1984, and one, 1 October 1987, Middleton Island.

Mimus polyglottos—Northern Mockingbird. One, 8-16 September 1982, Middleton Island.

Motacilla flava—Yellow Wagtail. One, 18 August 1976, Orca Inlet; one, 28 September 1979, eastern Copper River Delta; one, 9 September 1982, Middleton Island.

Anthus cervinus—Red-throated Pipit. One to three, 12-21 September 1981, singles on four occasions 13-27 September 1982, and two, 25 September and one, 26 September 1987, all Middleton Island.

Bombycilla cedrorum—Cedar Waxwing. One, probably two, immatures, 19-20 September 1981, Middleton Island; flock of six, 25 September 1981, Cordova; two immatures, 24 September 1987, and one bird, 17 and 24 September 1988, Middleton Island.

Vireo gilvus—Warbling Vireo. One, 17 September 1981, Middleton Island.

Vireo philadelphicus—Philadelphia Vireo. One, 14 September 1982, and one, 29 September 1987, Middleton Island.

Vermivora peregrina—Tennessee Warbler. One, possibly three, 20 September, and one, 21 September 1981; one, 29 September and one 1 October 1987; and one, 23 September 1988; all Middleton Island.

Parula americana—Northern Parula. One, 23-24 September 1987, Middleton Island.

Dendroica magnolia—Magnolia Warbler. One, 26-27 September and one 29 September 1987, and one, 23 September 1988, Middleton Island.

Oporornis philadelphia—Mourning Warbler. Immature female, 29 September 1987, Middleton Island.

Oporornis tolmiei—MacGillivray's Warbler. One, mid-May 1981, Situk River; one, 22 August 1984, Mile 16 Copper River Highway.

Melospiza georgiana—Swamp Sparrow. One, 27 September 1987, Middleton Island.

Zonotrichia querula—Harris' Sparrow. Adult, 3 June 1977, Wooded Islands; adult, 5 October and immature, 6 October 1987, Middleton Island.

Plectrophenax hyperboreus—McKay's Bunting. One, 17 December 1983, Valdez.

Xanthocephalus xanthocephalus—Yellow-headed Blackbird. Immature male, 18 August 1974, Mile 7 Copper River Highway.

Molothrus ater—Brown-headed Cowbird. Very rare late summer and fall visitant: female, 19 September 1976, Mile 14 Copper River Highway; one, 6 August, and another, 10 August 1979, Port Fidalgo; three, 28 August, and singles on three occasions, 1-12 September 1979, eastern Copper River Delta; one, 1 September 1980, eastern Copper River Delta; one, 1 October, and adult, 17 November 1981, Cordova.

Fringilla montifringilla—Brambling. At Cordova, male, 6 November 1977, one bird, 2 January-late February 1978, female, 26 January-2 February 1979, and male, 15 December-late January 1981; at Seward, female, 20 November-4 December 1985.

Carpodacus purpureus—Purple Finch. Immature, 4 October 1982, Middleton Island.

Appendix

Gazetteer of geographic localities of the North Gulf Coast-Prince William Sound Region

Key to Area Designations:

ENGC	Eastern North Gulf Coast
WNGC	Western North Gulf Coast
CRD	Copper River Delta
NGC-PWS	Outer Coast Prince William Sound
NEPWS	Northeast Prince William Sound
SEPWS	Southeast Prince William Sound
SWPWS	Southwest Prince William Sound
NWPWS	Northwest Prince William Sound

(The quadrats of Prince William Sound are divided along the lines of 60°35'N. Lat. and 146°55'W. Long.)

Locality	*Area Designation*	*Latitude*	*Longitude*
Alaganik Slough	CRD	60°26'N,	145°17'W
Alsek River	ENGC	59°11'N,	138°30'W
Ahrnklin River	ENGC	59°24'N,	139°22'W
Barry Arm, Port Wells	NWPWS	61°02'N	148°08'W
Barwell Island, Blying Sound	WNGC	59°51'N,	149°17'W
Bear Lake, Seward Highway	WNGC	60°11'N,	149°22'W
Bering Lake	ENGC	60°17'N,	144°18'W
Bering River	ENGC	60°13'N,	144°12'W
Bering River Delta	ENGC	60°09'N,	144°20'W
Big Glacier Slough	CRD	60°27'N,	145°33'W
Black Glacier, Disenchantment Bay	ENGC	59°58'N,	139°40'W
Blackstone Bay, Port Wells	NWPWS	60°45'N,	148°34'W
Boswell Bay, Hinchinbrook Island	SEPWS	60°24'N,	146°07'W
Caines Head, Resurrection Bay	WNGC	59°59'N,	149°23'W
Canoe Pass, Hawkins Island	SEPWS	60°31'N,	146°05'W
Cannery Creek, Unakwik Inlet	NWPWS	61°01'N,	147°31'W
Cape Cleare, Montague Island	SWPWS	59°47'N,	147°54'W
Cape Fairweather	ENGC	58°48'N,	137°57'W
Cape Hinchinbrook	SEPWS	60°14'N,	146°38'W
Cape Junken, Blying Sound	WNGC	59°55'N,	148°38'W
Cape Resurrection, Blying Sound	WNGC	59°52'N,	149°17'W
Cape St. Elias, Kayak Is.	ENGC	59°48'N,	144°37'W

Locality	*Area Designation*	*Latitude*	*Longitude*
Cape Suckling	ENGC	60°00'N,	143°50'W
Castle Island Slough	CRD	60°20'N,	145°15'W
Channel Island, Orca Bay	SEPWS	60°37'N,	145°48'W
Channel Isle, Montague Strait	SWPWS	60°15'N,	147°22'W
Chenega Island	SWPWS	60°20'N,	148°05'W
Chiswell Islands, Blying Sound	WNGC	59°36'N,	149°34'W
Chugach Islands	WNGC	59°08'N,	151°30'W
Coghill Lake, College Fiord	NWPWS	61°06'N,	147°50'W
Coghill River, College Fiord	NWPWS	61°05'N,	147°52'W
Coghill River Flats	NWPWS	61°04'N,	147°56'W
College Fiord, Port Wells	NWPWS	61°10'N,	147°51'W
Constantine Harbor, Hinchinbrook Is.	SEPWS	60°21'N,	146°39'W
Controller Bay, mouth Bering River	ENGC	60°05'N,	144°18'W
Copper River Highway (Cordova to Mile 50)	CRD		
Copper Sands (barrier islands)	CRD	60°23'N,	145°38'W
Copper Slough	CRD	60°25'N,	145°30'W
Cordova	SEPWS	60°33'N,	145°45'W
Cordova Airport (Mile 13 CR Hwy)	CRD	60°29'N,	145°28'W
Cordova Glacier	NEPWS	60°50'N,	145°30'W
Cottonwood Point	CRD	60°17'N,	144°56'W
Culross Passage	NWPWS	60°40'N,	148°13'W
Dan Bay, Hinchinbrook Is.	SEPWS	60°25'N,	146°21'W
Disenchantment Bay, Yakutat Bay	ENGC	60°00'N,	139°32'W
Disk Island	SWPWS	60°30'N,	147°39'W
Double Bay, Hinchinbrook Is.	SEPWS	60°28'N,	146°29'W
Dry Bay	ENGC	59°08'N,	138°37'W
Egg Island (barrier islands)	CRD	60°22'N,	145°45'W
Egg Island Channel	CRD	60°23'N,	145°44'W
Eldorado Narrows, Resurrection Bay	WNGC	59°56'N,	149°18'W
Eshamy Bay	SWPWS	60°28'N,	148°00'W
Eshamy Lake	SWPWS	60°28'N,	148°06'W
Esther Island	NWPWS	60°50'N,	148°05'W
Esther Passage	NWPWS	60°52'N,	147°56'W
Evans Island	SWPWS	60°06'N,	147°57'W
Eyak Lake, Cordova	SEPWS	60°33'N,	145°41'W
Eyak River	CRD	60°29'N,	145°40'W
Fairweather Bank	ENGC	58°20'N,	138°40'W
Fish Bay, Hinchinbrook Is.	SEPWS	60°27'N,	146°23'W

Locality	Area Designation	Latitude	Longitude
Flag Point	CRD	60°27'N,	145°06'W
Fool Island	NWPWS	60°46'N,	147°55'W
Fourth of July Creek, Resurrection Bay	WNGC	60°06'N,	149°20'W
Fox Island, Resurrection Bay	WNGC	59°57'N,	149°18'W
Galena Bay, Valdez Arm	NEPWS	60°57'N,	146°42'W
Gore Point	WNGC	59°12'N,	150°58'W
Grass Island Bar (barrier islands)	CRD	60°14'N,	145°15'W
Grass Island Slough	CRD	60°18'N,	145°12'W
Gravina River, Port Gravina	NEPWS	60°48'N,	146°03'W
Green Island	SWPWS	60°15'N,	147°25'W
Hanning Bay, Montague Island	SWPWS	59°58'N,	147°43'W
Harriman Fiord, Port Wells	NWPWS	61°03'N,	148°18'W
Harrison Lagoon, Port Wells	NWPWS	60°59'N,	148°12'W
Hartney Bay, Orca Inlet	SEPWS	60°30'N,	145°52'W
Hawkins Island Cutoff	SEPWS	60°27'N,	146°20'W
Hawkins Island	SEPWS	60°32'N,	146°00'W
Hinchinbrook Entrance	SEPWS	60°20'N,	146°50'W
Hinchinbrook Island	SEPWS	60°25'N,	146°25'W
Humpback Creek, Yakutat Bay	ENGC	59°39'N,	139°34'W
Humpy Cove, Resurrection Bay	WNGC	59°58'N,	149°18'W
Icy Bay	SWPWS	60°16'N,	148°15'W
Icy Bay	ENGC	59°55'N,	141°30'W
Indian Creek, Galena Bay	NEPWS	60°57'N,	146°38'W
Jonah Bay, Unakwik Inlet	NWPWS	61°01'N,	147°39'W
Katalla	ENGC	60°12'N,	144°32'W
Kayak Island	ENGC	59°56'N,	144°23'W
Keystone Canyon, Lowe River	NEPWS	61°04'N,	145°53'W
Khantaak Island, Yakutat Bay	ENGC	59°35'N,	139°48'W
Knight Island	SWPWS	60°20'N,	147°45'W
Kokinhenik Bar (barrier islands)	CRD	60°13'N,	145°07'W
Latouche Island	SWPWS	60°00'N,	147°55'W
Little Glacier Slough	CRD	60°26'N,	145°31'W
Little Smith Island	SWPWS	60°31'N,	147°26'W
Lone Island	NWPWS	60°41'N,	147°45'W
Long Island	CRD	60°27'N,	145°00'W
Lost Lake, Resurrection Valley	WNGC	60°16'N,	149°26'W
Lost Lake Trail	WNGC	60°13'N,	149°25'W
Lost River	ENGC	59°28'N,	139°36'W

Locality	*Area Designation*	*Latitude*	*Longitude*
Lowe River, Port Valdez	NEPWS	61°05'N,	146°13'W
MacLeod Harbor, Montague Island	SWPWS	59°53'N,	147°48'W
Malaspina Glacier	ENGC	60°00'N,	140°30'W
Martin Islands	ENGC	60°10'N,	144°36'W
Martin Lake	CRD	60°22'N,	144°33'W
Martin River	CRD	60°25'N,	144°38'W
Martin River Slough	CRD	60°17'N,	144°40'W
Middle Ground Shoal, Orca Bay	SEPWS	60°32'N,	146°22'W
Middleton Island	NGC	59°26'N,	146°20'W
Miles Glacier, Miles Lake	CRD	60°39'N,	144°35'W
Mirror Slough	CRD	60°16'N,	144°40'W
Montague Island	SWPWS	60°00'N,	147°30'W
Montague Point, Montague Is.	SWPWS	60°23'N,	147°06'W
Montague Strait	SWPWS	59°55'N,	147°50'W
Mosquito Creek, Barry Arm	NWPWS	61°02'N,	148°06'W
Mt. Marathon, Seward	WNGC	60°07'N,	149°29'W
Mt. Tebenkof, Yakutat Bay	ENGC	59°43'N,	139°26'W
Naked Island	NWPWS	60°40'N,	147°25'W
Nash Road, Seward	WNGC	60°08'N,	149°22'W
Nassau Fiord	SWPWS	60°16'N,	148°22'W
Nellie Juan River	SWPWS	60°20'N,	149°01'W
Nuka Bay	WNGC	59°22'N,	150°31'W
Nunatak Fiord, Russell Fiord	ENGC	59°51'N,	139°15'W
Ocean Cape, Yakutat Bay	ENGC	59°32'N,	139°51'W
Orca Bay	SEPWS	60°34'N,	146°15'W
Orca Inlet	SEPWS	60°30'N,	145°55'W
Paradise Lakes, Kenai Mts.	WNGC	60°21'N,	149°00'W
Passage Canal, Port Wells	NWPWS	60°48'N,	148°24'W
Pete Dahl Bar	CRD	60°17'N,	145°27'W
Pete Dahl Cutoff	CRD	60°24'N,	145°23'W
Pete Dahl Slough	CRD	60°23'N,	145°25'W
Pigot Bay, Port Wells	NWPWS	60°50'N,	148°20'W
Pinnacle Rocks, Orca Inlet	SEPWS	60°27'N,	146°02'W
Point Elrington, Elrington Is.	SWPWS	59°56'N,	148°15'W
Point Martin	ENGC	60°11'N,	144°37'W
Point Whitshed	CRD	60°27'N,	145°54'W
Porpoise Rocks, Port Etches	SEPWS	60°19'N,	146°41'W
Port Ashton, Evans Island	SWPWS	60°04'N,	148°03'W

Locality	*Area Designation*	*Latitude*	*Longitude*
Port Chalmers, Montague Is.	SWPWS	60°15'N,	147°13'W
Port Dick	WNGC	59°15'N,	151°03'W
Port Dick Creek, Port Dick	WNGC	59°18'N,	151°20'W
Port Etches, Hinchinbrook Is.	SEPWS	60°20'N,	146°36'W
Port Fidalgo	NEPWS	60°47'N,	146°40'W
Port Gravina	NEPWS	60°40'N,	146°20'W
Port Nellie Juan	NWPWS	60°36'N,	148°07'W
Port Wells	NWPWS	60°50'N,	148°12'W
Portage Pass, Whittier	NWPWS	60°46'N,	148°47'W
Portlock Bank	WNGC	58°30'N,	151°30'W
Resurrection Bay	WNGC	60°05'N,	149°23'W
Resurrection River, Resurrection Bay	WNGC	60°10'N,	149°29'W
Richardson Highway (Valdez to Thompson Pass)	NEPWS		
Rugged Island, Resurrection Bay	WNGC	59°51'N,	149°23'W
Russell Fiord, Disenchantment Bay	ENGC	60°00'N,	139°27'W
Seal Island	SWPWS	60°26'N,	147°24'W
Seal River	ENGC	60°03'N,	143°32'W
Seal Rocks, Hinchinbrook Entrance	NGC-PWS	60°10'N,	146°50'W
Seward	WNGC	60°06'N,	149°26'W
Seward Highway (Seward to Mile 12)	WNGC		
Shag Rock, Orca Inlet	SEPWS	60°28'N,	145°58'W
Sheep Bay, Orca Bay	NEPWS	60°38'N,	146°03'W
Shipyard Bay, Orca Inlet	SEPWS	60°34'N,	145°48'W
Simpson Bay, Orca Inlet	NEPWS	60°39'N,	145°56'W
Situk Lake	ENGC	59°38'N,	139°24'W
Situk River	ENGC	59°27'N,	139°34'W
Smith Island	SWPWS	60°32'N,	147°20'W
Softuk Bar (barrier islands)	CRD	60°12'N,	144°53'W
Southeast Breakers	ENGC	59°58'N,	144°00'W
Spike Island, Orca Inlet	SEPWS	60°33'N,	145°46'W
Stockdale Harbor, Montague Island	SWPWS	60°19'N,	147°11'W
Storey Island	NWPWS	60°44'N,	147°24'W
Strawberry Bar	CRD	60°23'N,	146°03'W
Tatitlek Narrows	NEPWS	60°52'N,	146°43'W
Tawah Creek	ENGC	59°29'N,	139°40'W
Thompson Pass, Chugach Mts.	NEPWS	61°09'N,	145°37'W
Thumb Cove, Resurrection Bay	WNGC	60°00'N,	149°19'W
Turner Glacier, Disenchantment Bay	ENGC	60°01'N,	139°35'W

Locality	*Area Designation*	*Latitude*	*Longitude*
27-Mile Bridge, CR Hwy.	CRD	60°26'N,	145°05'W
Unakwik Inlet	NWPWS	61°00'N,	147°33'W
Unakwik Reef, Unakwik Inlet	NWPWS	61°01'N,	147°32'W
Valdez	NEPWS	61°08'N,	146°20'W
Valdez Arm	NEPWS	60°55'N,	146°50'W
Valdez Narrows	NEPWS	61°04'N,	146°00'W
Walhalla Slough	CRD	60°21'N,	145°19'W
Whittier	NWPWS	60°47'N,	148°43'W
Whiskey Pete Slough	CRD	60°20'N,	145°20'W
Wooded Islands	NGC-PWS	59°52'N,	147°25'W
Yakataga	ENGC	60°06'N,	142°28'W
Yakutat	ENGC	59°33'N,	139°44'W
Yakutat Bay	ENGC	59°40'N,	140°00'W
Zaikof Bay, Montague Island	SWPWS	60°19'N,	147°00'W

Literature Cited

American Ornithologists' Union. 1957. Check-list of North American Birds. 5th ed. American Ornithologists' Union, Baltimore, Md. 691 p.

Case, J. E., D. F. Barnes, G. Plafker and S. L. Robbins. 1966. Gravity survey and regional geology of the Prince William Sound epicentral region, Alaska. U. S. Geol. Surv. Prof. Pap. 543-C. 12 p.

Chapman, J. A., C. J. Henny and H. M. Wight. 1969. The status, population dynamics, and harvest of the dusky Canada Goose. Wildl. Monogr. No. 18. 48 p.

Committee on the Alaska Earthquake. 1971. The great Alaska earthquake of 1964: Biology. NAS Publ. 1604. Nat. Acad. Sci., Washington, D. C. 287 p.

Cooper, W. S. 1942. Vegetation of the Prince William Sound region, Alaska; with a brief excursion into post-Pleistocene climatic history. Ecol. Monogr. 12:3-22.

Crow, J. H. 1968. Plant ecology of the Copper River Delta, Alaska. Ph.D. thesis, Washington State Univ., Pullman. 120 p.

———. 1971. Earthquake-initiated changes in the nesting habitat of the dusky Canada Goose, p. 130-136. *In*: Committee on the Alaska Earthquake, the great Alaska earthquake of 1964: Biology. NAS Publ. 1604. Nat. Acad. Sci., Washington, D. C.

Delacour, J. 1951. Preliminary note on the taxonomy of Canada Geese, *Branta canadensis*. Amer. Mus. Novitates, No. 1537. 10 p.

Einarsen, A. S. 1965. Black Brant, sea goose of the Pacific coast. Univ. Washington Press, Seattle. 142 p.

Ellsworth, C. E., and R. W. Davenport. 1915. A water-power reconnaissance in south-central Alaska. U. S. Geol. Surv. Water-Supply Paper 372. 173 p.

Figgins, J. D. 1904. Field notes on the birds and mammals of the Cook's Inlet region of Alaska. Abst. Proc. Linn. Soc. N.Y. 15-16:15-39.

Friedmann, H. 1935. The birds of Kodiak Island, Alaska. Bull. Chicago Acad. Sci. 5:13-54.

Gabrielson, I. N. 1944. Some Alaskan notes. Auk 61:105-130, 270-287.

———, and F. C. Lincoln. 1959. The birds of Alaska. Wildl. Mgt. Inst., Washington, D. C. 922 p.

Gibson, D. D. 1970. Recent observations at the base of the Alaska Peninsula. Condor 72:242-243.

Godfrey, W. E. 1966. The birds of Canada. Bull. Nat. Mus. Canada, 203 (Biol. Series No. 73). 428 p.

Gray, J. A., Jr. 1945. Land birds at sea. Condor 47:215-216.

Grinnell, J. 1910a. Birds of the 1908 Alexander Alaska Expedition with a note on the avifauna relationships of the Prince William Sound district. Univ. Calif. Publ. Zool. 3:361-428.

———. 1910b. Miscellaneous records for Alaska. Condor 12:41-53.

Gruchy, C. G., A. A. R. Dykes and R. H. Bowen. 1972. The Short-tailed Albatross recorded at Ocean Station Papa, North Pacific Ocean, with notes on other birds. Canad. Field-Nat. 86:285-287.

Hansen, H. A. 1962. Canada Geese of coastal Alaska. Trans. N. Amer. Wildl. Conf. 27:301-320.

———, P. E. K. Shepherd, J. G. King and W. A. Troyer. 1971. The Trumpeter Swan in Alaska. Wildl. Monogr. No. 26. 83 p.

Harris, R. D. 1971. Further evidence of tree nesting in the Marbled Murrelet. Canad. Field-Nat. 85:67-68.

Hemming, J. E. 1966. Notes on the status of some birds in south-central Alaska. Condor 68:163-166.

Hudson, G. E. 1956. Breeding of the Short-billed Dowitcher on the Copper River flats, Alaska. Condor 58:238.

Hultén, E. 1968. Flora of Alaska and neighboring territories. Stanford Univ. Press, Stanford, Calif. 1008 p.

Johnson, L. J. 1968. Common Grackle at Yakutat, Alaska. Bull. Alaska Ornith. Soc. 6(1966):10.

Kenyon, D. W. 1950. Distribution of albatrosses in the North Pacific and adjacent waters. Condor 52:97-103.

Kuziakin, A. P. 1963. K biologii dlinnokliuvogo nyzhika. [A contribution to the biology of the Marbled Murrelet]. Ornitologiia 6:315-320.

Laing, H. M. 1925. Birds collected and observed during the cruise of the Thiepval in the North Pacific, 1924. Canad. Dept. Mines, Bull. 40. 46 p.

Miller, D. J. 1953. Late Cenozoic marine glacial sediments and marine terraces of Middleton Island, Alaska. J. Geol. 61:17-40.

———. 1958. Gulf of Alaska area, p. 19-29. *In*: H. Williams, ed. Landscapes of Alaska, their geologic evolution. Univ. Calif. Press, Berkeley.

Moffit, F. H. 1954. Geology of the Prince William Sound region, Alaska. U. S. Geol. Surv., Bull. 989-E:225-310.

Monson, M. A. 1956. Nesting of Trumpeter Swan in the lower Copper River basin, Alaska. Condor 58:444-445.

Murie, O. J. 1959. Fauna of the Aleutian Islands and Alaska Peninsula. North American Fauna 61:1-364.

Nelson, U. C., and H. A. Hansen. 1959. The Cackling Goose — its migration and management. Trans. N. Amer. Wildl. Conf. 24:174-187.

O'Farrell, T. P., and A. M. Sheets. 1962. Birds observed wintering on Middleton Island, Alaska. Condor 64:440-441.

Olson, S. T. 1953. Copper River Delta banding operations, p. 34-42. *In*: U. C. Nelson, Federal Aid in Wildlife Restoration — Alaska, 8 (1), 30 September 1953. U. S. Fish Wildl. Serv., Juneau (Processed).

Plafker, G. 1967. Geologic map of the Gulf of Alaska Tertiary Province, Alaska. Misc. Geol. Invest. Map I-484.

———. 1969. Tectonics of the March 27, 1964, Alaska earthquake. U. S. Geol. Surv. Prof. Pap. 543-I. 174 p.

Rausch, R. L. 1958. The occurrence and distribution of birds on Middleton Island, Alaska. Condor 60:227-242.

Sanger, G. A. 1964. A possible sight record of a Short-tailed Albatross. Murrelet 45:47.

———. 1972. The recent pelagic status of the Short-tailed Albatross (*Diomedea albatrus*). Biol. Conserv. 4:189-193.

Savile, D. B. O. 1972. Evidence of tree nesting by Marbled Murrelet in the Queen Charlotte Islands. Canad. Field-Nat. 86:389-390.

Shepherd, P. E. K. 1959. Summary of 1959 duck nesting and brood production studies, Copper River Delta, Alaska. 3 p. *In*: H. A. Hansen,, Annual Waterfowl Report — 1959. U. S. Fish Wildl. Serv., Juneau. (Processed).

———. 1962. A breeding record of the Red-winged Blackbird in Alaska. Condor 64:440.

Shortt, T. M. 1939. The summer birds of Yakutat Bay, Alaska. Contr. Royal Ontario Mus. Zool. No. 17. 30 p.

Stejneger, L. 1936. Georg Wilhelm Steller — The pioneer of Alaskan natural history. Harvard Univ. Press, Cambridge. 623 p.

Stresemann, E. 1949. Birds collected in the North Pacific area during Capt. James Cook's last voyage (1778 and 1779). Ibis 91:224-255.

Thomas, J. H. 1957. The vascular flora of Middleton Island, Alaska. Contrib. Dudley Herbarium 5:39-56.

Trainer, C. E. 1959. The 1959 western Canada Goose (*Branta canadensis occidentalis*) study on the Copper River Delta, Alaska. 11 p. *In*: H. A. Hansen, Annual Waterfowl Report — 1959. U. S. Fish Wildl. Serv., Juneau. (Processed).

U. S. Coast and Geodetic Survey. 1964. United States Coast Pilot 9, Pacific and Arctic coasts: Alaska, Cape Spencer to Beaufort Sea. 7th ed. U. S. Government Printing Office, Washington, D. C. 348 p.

U. S. Environmental Science Services Administration. 1971. Climatological summaries. National Weather Service, Anchorage. Unpublished.

U. S. National Ocean Survey. 1970. Surface water temperatures and density. Pacific Coast, North and South America and Pacific Ocean Islands. 3rd ed. National Ocean Survey Publ. 31-3. U. S. Government Printing Office, Washington, D. C. 88 p.

———. 1972. Tide tables, high and low water predictions, 1973. West coast of North and South America, including the Hawaiian Islands. National Ocean Survey, Washington, D. C. 222 p.

VanKammen, I. I. 1916. "Whale birds." Oologist 33:171-172.

Wahl, T. 1970. A Short-tailed Albatross record for Washington State. Calif. Birds 1:113-115.

Walker, E. P. 1920. Probable breeding of the Aleutian Tern in southeastern Alaska. Condor 22:111-112.

———. 1923. Definite breeding record for the Aleutian Tern in southern Alaska. Condor 25:113-117.

Webster, J. D. 1941. Notes on the birds of Sitka and vicinity, southeastern Alaska. Condor 43:120-121.

Wik, D., and G. Streveler. 1968. Birds of Glacier Bay National Monument. Updated edition. U. S. National Park Service. 80 p. (Processed).

Willett, G. 1915. Summer birds of Forrester Island, Alaska. Auk 32:295-305.

———. 1923. Comments on two recent numbers of Bent's Life Histories of North American Birds. Condor 25:25-27.

———. 1928. Notes on some birds of southeastern Alaska. Auk 45:445-449.

Williamson, F. S. L., and L. J. Peyton. 1963. Interbreeding of Glaucous-winged and Herring Gulls in the Cook Inlet region, Alaska. Condor 65:24-28.

———, ———, and M. E. Isleib. 1965. New distributional and overwintering records of birds from south-central Alaska. Condor 67:73-80.

Wood, F. J., ed. 1966. The Prince William sound, Alaska, earthquake of 1964 and aftershocks, Vol I. Operational phases of the Coast and Geodetic Survey program in Alaska for the period March 27 to December 31, 1964. U. S. Coast and Geodetic Survey, Washington, D. C. 263 p.

Yocom, C. F. 1963. July bird life in the Copper River Delta country. Murrelet 44:28-34.